PERCEPTION IN ARISTOTLE'S ETHICS

SERIES EDITOR

John Russon

REREADING ANCIENT PHILOSOPHY

PERCEPTION IN ARISTOTLE'S ETHICS

EVE RABINOFF

NORTHWESTERN UNIVERSITY PRESS • EVANSTON, ILLINOIS

Northwestern University Press
www.nupress.northwestern.edu

Printed in the United States of America

10 9 8 7 6 5 4 3 2 1

Library of Congress Cataloging-in-Publication Data

Names: Rabinoff, Eve, author.
Title: Perception in Aristotle's ethics / Eve Rabinoff.
Other titles: Rereading ancient philosophy.
Description: Evanston, Illinois : Northwestern University Press, 2018. | Series: Rereading ancient philosophy
Identifiers: LCCN 2017039337 | ISBN 9780810136434 (cloth : alk. paper) | ISBN 9780810136427 (pbk. : alk. paper) | ISBN 9780810136441 (ebook)
Subjects: LCSH: Aristotle—Ethics. | Aristotle. Nicomachean ethics. | Aristotle. De anima. | Perception (Philosophy)—Moral and ethical aspects.
Classification: LCC B491.E7 R323 2018 | DDC 171.3—dc23 LC record available at https://lccn.loc.gov/2017039337

For Eric

CONTENTS

ACKNOWLEDGMENTS

My first thanks are to John Russon, my teacher and friend, for encouraging and directing my personal and philosophical growth. I would not be where I am today were it not for him and the world he introduced me to. I also owe a great debt of thanks to Marina McCoy, who supervised the first version of this project and helped me shape it, and whose support and generosity has been unflagging. Some of the seeds for this project were sown in the context of Bill Wians's Aristotle seminars at Boston College, and I am grateful for the guidance of such an insightful teacher and reader of Aristotle. Thanks also to Bill and to Arthur Madigan for their feedback on this project in its earlier forms, and to Drew Hyland for his generous feedback on the manuscript. I owe thanks to Mitchell Miller, who illuminated Plato, and philosophy in general, for me. I would like to thank my many other teachers at Boston College, St. John's College, the University of Guelph, and elsewhere for sharing their wisdom, time, and insight. Thank you to my philosophical friends, from whom I've learned so much, including Sharon Cohen, Deirdre Rubin, Whitney Howell, Greg Kirk, Ömer Aygün, Eli Diamond, Patricia Fagan, David Ciavatta, Kym Maclaren, Greg Recco, Ryan Quintana, the participants in the Toronto Seminar, and many others. Thanks also to my colleagues in the philosophy department at the University of Minnesota, Duluth, who maintain an ideally supportive philosophical and work environment, and to Paula Derdiger and Kelly MacPhail for their tireless support and friendship. Most especially, to Eric Sanday, whose wisdom and courage sustains me.

I am grateful also for the hard work of the editors and staff at Northwestern University Press: Nathan MacBrien, Henry Carrigan, Marianne Jankowski, and Trevor Perri; and for that of Steven Moore for compiling the index.

PERCEPTION IN ARISTOTLE'S ETHICS

INTRODUCTION

The project I have undertaken is to account for ethical perception (*aisthēsis*) in Aristotle's ethics—to give perception a place of importance in ethical reasoning, choice, and action—and to offer an account of the faculty of perception that is expansive enough to include reception of the ethical significance of particulars. This project is motivated philosophically both by particular features of Aristotle's thought and more generally by an increasing philosophical awareness that the ethical agent is an embodied, situated individual, rather than primarily a disembodied, abstract rational will. Traditionally, the human soul (*psuchē*) or human nature has been understood to have a nonrational part characterized by desires and perceptions and a rational part characterized by thinking, knowledge, and argument (*Nic. Eth.* 1102a26–28). Depending on how the relationship between these two sides is conceived, the nonrational side is either a bane to be controlled (or ignored) by the rational side, or it plays an irreducible role in contributing to moral choice and action. By establishing and accounting for perception's place in ethics, I seek to show the importance for ethical life of integrating both elements of human nature, the rational and nonrational, the human and the animal.

Aristotelian Motivations: Perception and Intellect

Aristotle is famous for offering what might be called a situational ethics: discerning what one ought to do is not derivable from universal laws, but must be assessed with respect to the very particulars that make up the situation in which one must act. Famously, Aristotle argues that what virtue calls for is acting and feeling in an appropriate manner; that is, at the right time, to the right degree, in the right manner, with respect to the right people, and so on (*Nic. Eth.* 1106b21–24). Moreover, because of the situational specificity of right action, one must also have the right *character* in order to discern what virtue calls for—only the virtuous person sees what is truly good. If one has a faulty character, the particulars will appear in a distorted manner, just as the wine tastes bitter to those who are ill (1113a25–29).

It appears that a consequence of the situational specificity of virtuous action is that in order to be virtuous one must *see* rightly, in a literal sense.

Aristotle is consistent in designating perception (*aisthēsis*) as the faculty that apprehends the particular (*De anima* 417b21–29; *Nic. Eth.* 1109b23, 1113a1–2, 1126b4, 1142a27, 1143b6, 1147a27, 1147b18). Moreover, if those who are not virtuous cannot discern instances of virtuous action as virtuous (as a person who is ill cannot taste wine as sweet), this means that there is a limit to what the powers of intellect can accomplish with regard to virtuous action, for if virtue were simply a matter of understanding, whether one does or does not have the right character should not matter. Discerning virtuous action, then, seems to be a matter of *perception*.

This consequence, however, carries some difficulties with it. In the first place, it appears to contradict the very definition of virtue as the excellent activity of the rational part of the soul (*Nic. Eth.* 1098a11–18). This definition suggests that it is not *perception*, a faculty of the nonrational part of the soul shared with animals (1098a1–3), that determines what is virtuous, but intellect and reason. In the second place, Aristotle conceives of perception as a bodily power in an important way: it is a power that operates with sense organs that are impacted (physically) by the objects of sense (via a medium). But it would be strange to consider *goodness* (or justice, or temperance, etc.) as a physical object capable of impacting the sense organs and producing perception. Aristotle seems to be in a theoretical bind: perception is the faculty that discerns the particulars, yet it is not equipped to discern *ethical* particulars. There are two ways one might get Aristotle out of this bind. One way is to give perception a merely instrumental role in the discernment of ethical particulars, where it is by the judgment of intellect upon the data provided by perception that one apprehends ethical particulars. If one adopts this strategy, one maintains that it is indeed the rational part of the soul that discerns virtuous action. Another way out of the bind is to offer an account of perception such that it *is* receptive to ethical particulars. Adopting this strategy straightforwardly resolves the second difficulty, but is left with the first. Despite this, I adopt this latter strategy. I will first offer reasons why the first strategy fails, and then I will offer a way out of the bind of seeming to make virtue a nonrational excellence.

Say that perception offers only what it can, objects of sense such as color, sound, shape, number, and so on (*De anima* 418a7–20), which intellect interprets using its own categories and thereby discerns the ethical relevance of particulars. This strategy fails on two accounts. First, if it were the case that perception is merely instrumental, providing the data to be interpreted by intellect, there would be no reason that virtuous action would not be subject to universal formulae. The discernment of the particular, ethical or not, would just be subsuming that particular under a certain category (for example, colorful shape is an instance of "person"), and if the discernment of the *particular* is an application of a category, why would the discernment of the virtuous action not also be the application of a category? If, in other words, all ethical information were in the province of intellect—if there were nothing ethical to be supplied by another faculty—the discernment of the virtuous act would be a matter of subsuming particulars under general ethical categories, that is, rules. But Aristotle insists that this is not the case, and this implies that there is something *ethical* that is out of the reach of intellect by itself. To render perception instrumental does not do justice to Aristotle's insistence on the situatedness of ethical discernment.

Second, and more generally, if all perception apprehended were colors, shapes, and so on, it seems that it would provide too little information to be the basis for intellectual judgment. Intellect would indeed be a powerful faculty if it could sort out what would be the "blooming, buzzing confusion" offered by the perception of shapes, sounds, colors, and so on. How would intellect single out objects such as tables and chairs among such perceptual data, let alone people, friends, and enemies? To render perception merely instrumental does not do justice to the complexity of perceptual experience.

The instrumentalist may respond by pointing out that, in addition to sounds and shapes, Aristotle lists incidental perceptibles such as the son of Diares among the objects of perception (*De anima* 418a20–24). So, the instrumentalist might say, perception offers such sophisticated information as that this colorful shape is the particular person, the son of Diares, but nonetheless intellect is required to judge that the son of Diares is or is not the appropriate target for generosity (for example). But even allowing that perceptual data is complex does not avoid the problem of explaining why general ethical rules cannot be formulated. Presumably one would *judge* that the son of Diares is not the appropriate target for generosity on the basis of some rule, such as "one ought not to be generous to one who has an abundance of wealth" (and the son of Diares is such a person).

Aristotle resists the formulation of ethical rules for the reason that ethical action concerns the particular, and there is much variability in particulars (*Nic. Eth.* 1094b16–18, 1104a3–5, 1141b16, 1140b1–3). The idea seems to be that one must be prepared to act *contrary* to a general rule or to one's prior deliberation, should the situation call for it (1104a5–10). This means that the virtuous action is *always* a matter of situational discernment, of being able to tell whether this particular situation is one in which one should abide by one's deliberation (as, for example, Neoptolemus seems to do [1151b17–21]). In so doing, Aristotle maintains the possibility that the particular situation be *surprising*, be unpredictable, unavailable to the kind of foreknowledge that intellect may provide. I don't see how one can maintain this and still maintain that perception is merely instrumental to intellect's reasoning.

Let me offer some examples of the sort of thing I think Aristotle is protecting by maintaining that virtuous action is not articulable in rules. It is a common experience: stage fright. One may *know* exactly what one must do—recite the Gettysburg Address, say—and one may be fully prepared to do it. But it is still possible that one finds oneself speechless at the very moment one is to perform one's task. Or, to offer a positive example, one may be fully prepared for an interview, having had the questions in advance, and one need only to recite one's answers in a lively manner when the time comes. When the time does come, one is struck by inspiration and offers a new answer. Similarly, a dancer may practice her performance to perfection and will perform it perfectly on stage, yet these two performances, the practice and the recital, are quite significantly different acts for the dancer. What these examples show is that a present reality has a force that cannot be known intellectually in advance; the particulars one actually faces in action have an irreducible impact on one that can only be experienced. This, I suggest, is the sort of thing that Aristotle is protecting by resisting the formulability of ethical rules and maintaining that perception discerns the particular. Being fully prepared to act virtuously by having all the principles and being able to enact them just is not the same as actually acting virtuously; knowing what to do is not the same as doing it, and what makes the difference must come from the perception of particular, present circumstances.

For these reasons, I opt to get Aristotle out of his bind by offering an account of human perception such that it is receptive of ethical particulars, by which I mean that human perception is able to apprehend particulars in their significance to virtuous action. For example, when one sees a person in distress one perceives this as an occasion for courage. This is a *perception*, not a judgment that courage is necessary here.

But this strategy saddles me with the first difficulty in maintaining that perception apprehends ethical particulars, namely, that this appears to make virtue not excellent rational activity but excellent nonrational, perceptual activity. To avoid this, I propose a shift in perspective and in the meanings of "rational" and "nonrational." Rather than consider perception abstractly, outside of the context of a human soul and a human life, I consider perception as an integrated part of the intellectual soul. This holistic perspective enables me to offer an account of intellectual perception: a way of perceiving that is informed by intellectual accomplishments. For example, reading or hearing speech in one's native language is a kind of intellectual perception. The words on the page are perceptually intelligible—even when drunk or asleep, when intellect is dormant, one comprehends words. Yet one must *learn* the language in order for such perceptual comprehension to occur. I suggest that human perception generally and ethical perception specifically is a similarly intellectually informed perception.

This avoids the problem of virtue being discerned by a nonrational capacity because intellectual perception *is* rational—it is infused, so to speak, with intellect. The nonrational perceptual part of the soul is fully integrated with the intellectual part. Given this integration, I suggest that it is better that we say that the virtuous *soul* is rational, and virtue is the activity of the whole soul in cooperation. This way of understanding virtue aligns with Aristotle's claims that the soul of the virtuous person is in harmony with itself (*Nic. Eth.* 1102b26–28), and that the virtues are inseparable from one another (1144b32–1145a2).

Scholarly Motivations: Perception and Moral Psychology

Aristotle's account of perception has been the subject of much scholarly work focusing on *De anima*, and much scholarly work has been done on Aristotle's moral psychology, focusing on the ethical writings. My hope is that this project will contribute to this impressive body of scholarly work by offering a new perspective from which to view issues of moral psychology, one rooted in the account of the soul given in *De anima*.

One fundamental question in Aristotle's moral psychology concerns the relationship between reason and desire in determining the goals of action (and more generally the relationship between the virtues of character and the intellectual virtues). Near the end of book VI of the *Nicomachean Ethics*, Aristotle remarks, "virtue makes the target right, *phronēsis* the things toward the target" (1144 a7–9), and "It is clear that there will be no correct choice in the absence of *phronēsis*, nor in the absence of virtue; for the latter makes one do the end, the former the things toward it" (1145a7–9).[1] As Jessica Moss points out in an illuminating paper, the straightforward interpretation of this as saying that the virtue of the nonrational part of the soul (virtue of character) makes the aim right, and the virtue of the rational part of the soul responsible for practical thinking, *phronēsis*, merely contributes toward that aim, unsettles many commentators.[2] The worry is that if intellect does not set the aims, it then falls to desire to do so, and then Aristotle would be claiming that we act for the sake of something not because it is *good* but because we *desire* it.

Moss aims to avoid such worries and still maintain the straightforward interpretation of these passages. She identifies a mistake that lies at the base of this Humean idea: the identification of nonrational with noncognitive. She blocks this identification by arguing that virtue of character involves a nonrational *cognition* of something as good, and this is what sets the end, and that practical intellect reasons only about things toward the end. By blocking the move from nonrational to desire, she saves Aristotle from being a Humean about motivation and maintains the straightforward reading of the passages.

I am sympathetic to Moss's argument, but I think there is more to the worry about nonrational elements setting the goal than is addressed by her solution. Such a claim would seem to turn upside-down Aristotle's notion of the hierarchy of the capacities of soul. For Aristotle, thinking and intellect are better and nobler than the nonrational elements of soul (*Nic. Eth.* 1177a12–17), and to say that intellect is instrumental or subordinate to nonrational cognition would seem to contradict this basic Aristotelian principle. Aristotle brings up this kind of worry in the very discussion in which the passage appears: he notices that "it would seem strange if *phronēsis*, though inferior to wisdom [*sophia*], will exercise greater authority than it, for what makes or produces each thing rules over and arranges that thing" (1143b33–35). It would be equally strange for nonrational cognition to exercise greater authority over rational cognition in deciding the aims of action.

My hope is to contribute to this kind of disagreement about Aristotle's moral psychology by introducing a third option, a different way of conceiving of the soul. Worries about whether what sets the goal is rational or nonrational may be resolved if we take seriously the merely heuristic nature of this division of the soul in the *Nicomachean Ethics* (1102a26–28). If, instead, one keeps in mind the unity of the soul that Aristotle argues for in *De anima*, on my interpretation, then we may see virtue as the good state of the whole soul, rather than separate virtues for separate parts. If, say, the nonrational cognition that sets the goals is informed by intellect, the sort of thing I argue perception is, then we are in a position to say that it *is* intellect that decides the ends, but it does so *as* mediated by perception. The sharp distinction between rational and nonrational falls away, and with it the worry about the nonrational part of the soul setting the ends.

Philosophical Motivations and Promise: Modern and Contemporary Ethics

The project of giving an account of ethical perception in Aristotle is motivated not only by Aristotle and Aristotelian scholarship, but also more generally by a phenomenon that is receiving considerable philosophical attention right now. This is the phenomenon of unintentionally behaving in ways that betray one's actively and explicitly held beliefs. Freud was influential in bringing this kind of phenomenon to light—we even call slips of the tongue "Freudian slips"—but it was something Augustine struggled with long before, famously characterizing his youthful prayers as: "grant me chastity, but not yet." Currently, the phenomenon is gaining prominence in studies of implicit bias. Implicit bias is a bias manifest in behaviors but not in explicit awareness; similarly, alief "is a mental state with associatively linked content that is representational, affective and behavioral, and that is activated—consciously or nonconsciously—by features of the subject's internal or ambient environment."[2] To act on the basis of implicit bias or alief is to act in a way that is responsive to features of one's environment that one is not cognizing in an explicit way; one's way of being in the world runs contrary to one's thoughts about how one is in the world. This is an issue that Aristotle saw and addressed in his analysis of *akrasia*, "lack of restraint," which he characterizes as acting contrary to what one knows to be good out of a kind of ignorance (*Nic. Eth.* VII.3). I will argue in a later chapter that to behave akratically is to behave on the basis of a faulty way of perceiving things. One may perceive in a way that contradicts what one thinks, and although one may not even be aware of the discrepancy, one's way of perceiving influences one's way of acting.

In a similar vein, moral philosophies inspired by Iris Murdoch and defended and elaborated more recently by Lawrence Blum (1994) oppose rule-based ethical theories by emphasizing the necessity to first *perceive* a situation as a moral one if one is to make any kind of moral judgment at all. One's moral behavior does not issue simply from one's rational reflection upon it, but importantly from one's sensitivity and way of responding perceptually and emotionally to one's particular circumstances. Being in possession of a principle is not sufficient for moral judgment or action; one must first be attuned to the particulars such that one may discern the moral action that is appropriate. Otherwise, one may fail to act at all or may act contrary to one's principle, unintentionally.

It would be fruitful to study Aristotle with these issues in mind because Aristotle addresses these issues with a unique orientation toward the phenomenon of life as a natural phenomenon. Blum and Murdoch explicitly respond to and oppose typically modern moral theories (such as Kantian deontology) that identify the moral perspective as a third-person, impersonal perspective.[3] This impersonal perspective reflects a Cartesian notion of the self as the cogito, the disembodied rational mind. For the Cartesian self, the body is a nonessential appendage, and its associated emotions and perceptions are to be controlled by the rational will. It follows naturally from this that self-restraint becomes a mark of virtue.[4]

Aristotle takes a decidedly different view of what the ethical subject is, rejecting the idea that self-restraint (*enkrateia*) is virtue. Instead, the virtuous person is one whose soul is in harmony with itself and for whom acting virtuously is not a struggle with the passions but is instead effortless, a second nature. The development of virtue does not occur naturally, but once developed it resembles a natural phenomenon insofar as virtue harnesses and organizes the powers of the soul. In the same way that a mature deer is fully capable of scavenging for food, jumping, running, and so on, so too is the virtuous person able to perform well all the activities that constitute a good human life. Since the activities that constitute a good human life include such nonrational activities as perceiving, emoting, eating and drinking, in addition to the rational ones of thinking, deliberating, contemplating, and so on, there is no reason for Aristotle to privilege the rational at the *expense* of the bodily and the emotions associated with it. A body in a good condition is, for Aristotle, an element of a virtuous life, as is perceiving and emoting well. Because of Aristotle's orientation to natural life, his ethical account may take in all the phenomena of human life. Moral philosophies that reject the restriction of moral phenomena to the explicitly rational and embrace the nonrational and particular elements of moral reasoning and action would do well to consider Aristotle's approach to ethics on the model of natural life.

In Alasdair MacIntyre's recent work, *Dependent Rational Animals*, he develops and defends a notion of animal rationality and develops an ethics emphasizing human dependency that integrates animality into human flourishing. Although this work is not focused on Aristotle's texts, it is an Aristotelian account of virtue and human life, and it is an account that I see my project supporting. MacIntyre develops an account of nonlinguistic rationality that animals employ in pursuing their own goods, which serves as the basis for the development, in humans, of linguistic and reflective rationality. My account of intellectual perception highlights a similar congruence between humans and animals—human rationality *encompasses* animal rationality; it is not different in kind. MacIntyre focuses on the ethical *development* of practical rationality, arguing that such development is possible only on the basis of a primary dependency on others. Similarly, if I am right to give perception an important role in ethical life, moral development will include developing one's ways of perceiving, which, as the phenomenon of implicit bias attests, is not as simple as deciding to see otherwise.

◆ ◆ ◆

Ultimately, the thesis of this book is that developing one's perceptual capacity such that it comes to be intellectually informed is an important and necessary component of being virtuous and acting virtuously. To establish this, I will first discuss the perceptual capacity, both in itself (chapter 1), as Aristotle analyzes it in his psychological works, and as a part of the human soul (chapter 2). Second, I will discuss the role that perception plays in our ethical lives, both in a poorly habituated soul (chapter 3) and in a virtuous soul (chapter 4). I will conclude with some comments on the nature of ethical development.

Chapter 1 lays the groundwork for the account of ethical perception that is developed in the later chapters by discussing Aristotle's account of the perceptual part of the soul and the powers that he attributes to it. Perception must have two features if it is to be capable of apprehending ethical particulars: first, it must be able to apprehend more than the material qualities of particular objects, such as shape and color. It must be able to apprehend concrete individuals, such as Socrates. Second, it must be able to apprehend present particulars in light of futural concerns. In this chapter, I argue that both of these features are to be found in Aristotle's account of perception. I argue that concrete particulars such as Socrates are genuine objects of perception and that the secondary perceptual power of *phantasia* expands the temporal horizons of presently perceived objects.

The first chapter addresses the perceptual part of the soul, and the second chapter situates that part into a human soul, an intellectual soul, and argues that the nature of perception changes by virtue of being an integrated part of an intellectual soul. I first address the structure of the soul, and especially Aristotle's claim that the parts of the soul are in the soul *potentially*. I argue that this means that the parts are functionally incomplete in the sense that their activity is dependent upon the activity of higher parts of the soul. In light of this structure, I argue that human perception—in a well-developed soul—is informed by intellect. I offer an interpretation of incidental perception that supports this notion, while maintaining that incidental perception in humans is of a kind with that of nonrational animals.

The second chapter develops an account of the structure of the soul as an integrated whole of parts. This third chapter addresses a difficulty for this interpretation with respect to the human soul: Aristotle sustains the possibility that intellect is separable from the rest of the soul in a way that the other parts of soul are not. I address this difficulty, arguing that this separability is the basis for the ethical task of developing virtue—it is because the human soul is not a natural whole that human beings must develop the harmony of soul in which virtue consists. Ultimately, this means that the development of virtue requires the integration of the perceptual and the intellectual parts of the soul. I confirm this interpretation with an analysis of the phenomenon of *akrasia*, wherein a person suffers from a divided soul.

The fourth and final chapter further confirms the analysis of virtue and the task of ethical development given in the previous chapter and fleshes out the nature of ethical perception by offering an account of the intellectual virtue of *phronēsis*, "practical wisdom." This is a virtue that bridges the intellectual virtues and the virtues of character, and provides us with a window onto the harmonious, virtuous soul. In this chapter, I address the question of how virtuous action is accomplished in a particular situation of action. I argue that a condition for acting well, and for reasoning well about how to act, is perceiving the particulars of one's situation as occasions for acting. This, I argue, is one aspect of the virtue of practical wisdom—it is to have one's perceptual soul well aligned with the intellect.

CHAPTER 1

The Perceptual Part of the Soul

My project is to show that perception plays an essential role in ethical life, for Aristotle: that perceiving well is a condition that makes possible the reasoning necessary to produce good choices that make an act virtuous. The aim in this chapter is to lay the groundwork for such an argument by discussing Aristotle's account of the perceptual part of the soul given *De anima* and other psychological works. Ultimately, I will argue that the virtuous person, the *phronimos*, is she who is able to act virtuously because she perceives the present situation in which she must act correctly as bearing possibilities for virtuous acts. Insofar as perception is of the present, it conditions the thinking and acting through which one's character is manifest.[1] This chapter begins to establish that perception is a capacity that is robust enough to suit the task of apprehending the present, concrete reality in a way that is ethically relevant. Specifically, it will establish, first, that the power of perception is a part of the soul, in the sense that it is a first principle of animal life (section 1), and is fundamentally a power of awareness (section 3). Second, it will establish that incidental perceptibles are genuinely perceived, and therefore belong among the basic powers of perception (section 2). Third, it will establish that the secondary power of the perceptual part of the soul, the power of *phantasia*, expands the temporal horizons of current perceptions (section 4).

1. The Parts of the Soul

Before addressing the faculty of perception and its powers, it is necessary to address the parts of the soul. The soul, according to Aristotle, has two essential features that require that its configuration be a complex unity: on the one hand, the soul is responsible for the unity of the body (*De anima* 411a24–b14, 416a6–9), and, on the other hand, the soul is responsible for life (413a20–21). As even the most casual observation will show, life includes a variety of activities—walking, eating, sleeping, brushing teeth, talking, swimming, breathing, jumping, running, dancing, blinking, heart-beating, and so on—of which soul is the source. Aristotle must provide an account of the structure of soul such that soul is responsible for this multiplicity of activities without rending the soul into many souls, one for each activity, which would then require something to unify *it*. A whole of parts is a complex unity of the sort that can sustain multiplicity without being divided, and it is this structure that Aristotle ought to, and seems to, attribute to the soul.

Although Aristotle is committed to the unity of the soul, questions about the nature of the parts and how to distinguish them are sustained throughout *De anima*, wherein Aristotle raises such questions as early as I.1 402b1–2 and as late as III.9 432a22–23. Identifying the nature of parts is a delicate business: it is necessary to maintain the unity of the whole while also maintaining meaningful distinctions between the parts. If, on the one hand, one divides too deeply, by positing parts that are simply independent of one another, one runs the risk of positing several souls rather than one single soul responsible for the life of a creature. This is an outcome Aristotle rejects in the discussion with which *De anima* I concludes: the soul must be one if the body is to be one, because the soul is that which holds together the body (411a24–b14). If, on the other hand, one divides too superficially, by identifying parts with the various powers of the soul, one runs the risk of coming up with an unending and arbitrary multitude of parts, which Aristotle rejects as absurd in the discussion at the opening of the account of locomotion (432a22–b7). The question of what a part is and how to distinguish parts of the soul is important if one wants to chart a middle path between this Charybdis and Scylla (which Aristotle surely does): one wants to understand the soul in a way that maintains the unity of the soul as a principle of life and at the same time provides an explanation for the multiplicity of life activities.

Several insightful and influential studies concerning the question of how Aristotle distinguishes the parts of the soul[2] put forward an interpretation of the important point that the parts of the soul are separable (*chōristos*) in *logos*, account, or definition, and not separable unqualifiedly. Although these studies differ in some important respects,[3] they all agree that separability in *logos* means being independent in definition.[4] Independence in definition means that the definition of the capacity in question does not include implicit or explicit reference to any other capacity. Thus, for example, the nutritive capacity is separable in *logos* because its definition is simply "a power [*dunamis*] such as to maintain its possessor as such, while food prepares it for activity" (*De anima* 416b17–19).[5] Understanding what the nutritive capacity is does not require understanding what any other capacity is. By contrast, the capacity for memory is "a state induced by an image [*phantasma*], related as a likeness to that of which it is an image [*phantasma*]; and . . . it pertains to the primary sense faculty [*prōton aisthētikon*]" (*De mem.* 451a14–17).[6] The definition of memory includes explicit reference both to perception and to *phantasia*, and therefore it is not separable in *logos* from either of them. In what follows, I will briefly rehearse the general argument that Aristotle adopts the separability criterion for distinguishing parts of the soul.

Aristotle argues that the parts of the soul are not unqualifiedly separable from each other in *De anima* II.2. Here Aristotle raises the question "whether each of these [nutritive capacity, perceptive capacity, rational capacity, and motion] is a soul or a part of a soul, and if a part, whether it is such as to be separable in definition only or also in place" (413b13–15). The evidence he brings forward here is empirical: some plants and some insects continue to live and exhibit the full range of their capacities when severed in two. This means that the soul is "one in actuality in each plant, although potentially many" (413b18–19), and that the parts of the soul "are not separable as some people say; although that they are different [*hetera*] in definition [*logos*] is clear" (413b28–29).

This conclusion alone is not enough to secure the separability criterion—after all, Aristotle concludes merely that the parts of the soul are *different* in definition. As Whiting, Corcilius and Gregoric, and Johansen all point out, difference in definition does not imply separability; difference is a weaker condition than separability and covers a much wider range of cases. All that difference requires is that the definitions are not the same, but separability requires that the definitions be independent of one another. To illustrate difference in account, Corcilius and Gregoric offer the example of a doctor healing herself.[7] The individual is both doctor and patient. "Doctor" and "patient" have different accounts, but to be a doctor is to produce health in a patient—the accounts are not separable.

Does Aristotle indeed adopt the stronger separability criterion for distinguishing parts of the soul? Corcilius and Gregoric argue that he does.[8] They read the passage concerning the divided plant to stem from a disjunction—either the parts of the soul are separable in account or they are separable in place (*De anima* 413b13–15)—and the evidence of the divided plant rules out the latter. Although Aristotle does not explicitly affirm the first disjunct, they argue that the criterion is affirmed when Aristotle returns to the question of the separability of parts in III.9. In this chapter, he raises the question in terms identical to II.2, this time with regard to locomotion: "we must now inquire what it is in the soul that produces movement, whether it is one part of it separable either in place or in definition" (432a18–20), and he refutes the weak criterion of dividing the soul into parts merely according to its different powers (432a22–b7). By rejecting the difference criterion for parts of the soul—the soul's powers will all have differences in their accounts—Corcilius and Gregoric take Aristotle to affirm the first disjunct and thereby the separability criterion.

Johansen affirms the same conclusion, but his argument takes a different tack.[9] After the "difference" conclusion, Aristotle continues to say that some creatures have all the capacities of soul mentioned (nutritive, perceptive, rational, locomotive), while others only have one (*De anima* 413b32–414a3). Johansen argues that if a capacity can exist separately from another in another kind of living being, as the nutritive can exist independently of the perceptive, it must *also* be separable in account. On this view, ontological separability implies definitional separability—if something can exist independently, its definition, that is, the statement of what it is, must also be independent. On this view, the capacities that serve to differentiate the kinds of soul are also its parts.

These two lines of argument are complementary, and they quite persuasively show that Aristotle adopts the criterion of separability in *logos* to distinguish parts of the soul. The result of both Corcilius and Gregoric's position and of Johansen's position is the same: the parts of the soul, according to Aristotle, are three: namely, the nutritive, perceptual, and intellectual parts. On Corcilius and Gregoric's accounts, these are the powers that are defined without reference to anything but their objects, and are therefore independent. On Johansen's account, these are the parts that differentiate plants from animals, and animals from human beings.[10]

The criterion of separability in *logos* cuts just deep enough in dividing the soul's parts, answering to Aristotle's commitment to the unity of soul and to the multiplicity of activities of which the soul is the source. It is easy to see how separability in account does not threaten the unity of the soul, if we are considering the unity of the soul of an individual organism. Individuals are subject to many descriptions and fulfill many different roles while always being the selfsame individual. Whiting offers the example of the sweetness and whiteness of a sugar cube.[11] Sweet and white have separable accounts, but a sugar cube is both sweet and white throughout—the separability in account does not rend the sugar cube in two. In a similar vein, Johansen notes that although mathematical entities are separable in account from their material, they are not separable in reality.[12] So too the soul has parts which are separable in account, but in an individual soul these parts are unified. Nonetheless, the things that are separable in account are meaningfully different aspects of the whole of which they are parts. Separability in account is just the sort of criterion Aristotle needs to distinguish meaningfully between parts of the soul while still maintaining the unity of the soul.

If Aristotle wants to chart the middle course between the Charybdis of dividing the soul too deeply and the Scylla of dividing the soul too superficially, he ought to take separability in account as the criterion by which to distinguish the parts of soul. Separability in account will limit the number of parts of the soul so that we don't have an indefinite proliferation of parts—many capacities will depend upon the basic powers that define the parts of the soul—and it is a kind of separability that will not rupture the soul because it is an abstract distinction in the sense that all the accounts describe one and the same subject, an individual soul. It is not *simply* abstract, though, because the individual *really is* a nutritive, perceptual, and intellectual individual (if the individual is a human being), and it is all of these all at once.

The result of taking separability into account as the criterion for distinguishing the parts of the soul is, first, that the parts of the soul turn out to be the canonical three: the nutritive, perceptual, and intellectual. The nutritive part is defined as "a power [*dunamis*] such as to maintain its possessor as such, while food prepares it for activity" (*De anima* 416b17–19); the perceptual part is defined as that which "receives perceptible forms without the matter" (424a17–19); and the intellectual part of the soul is defined as that which receives the intelligible forms (429a15–18). These three powers are basic powers that make different modes of living possible and define different kinds of life. Second, because the parts do not include reference to other capacities or powers of the soul but only to their objects, these parts will be the basic elements of soul, the fundamental capacities, in the sense that they are the ultimate explanatory principles of their activities.

Furthermore, this criterion of separability provides structure to the soul in the form of an ordered hierarchy: those capacities whose definitions include reference to a part of the soul will be the activities *of* that part of the soul. We might think of the relationship between parts of the soul and derivative capacities (capacities that refer to the parts in their definitions) by analogy with language: knowing a language gives one a basic power to speak, communicate, and express oneself. But it also makes possible the acquisition of more sophisticated abilities, such as writing poetry. It is by virtue of having language that one can be a poet, but poetry is not basic to the power of language. Similarly, the perceptual part of the soul will have some basic powers that make possible further, derivative powers. The parts, then, will be responsible for not only the soul's primary activities but also some range of activities associated with those.

Identifying separability in account as the criterion for being a part of the soul is a criterion by which to identify which life activities are basic first principles. The soul is the first principle of life, as Aristotle establishes in

II.1, but life is only ever lived in the exercise of particular capacities. Not all the capacities of soul, though, are basic sources of activity (no one would consider the ability to snap one's fingers as basic), and the criterion of separability in account provides a measure by which to distinguish the capacities in which the first principle of life consists, and which capacities are derivative of those capacities. The nutritive capacity, the perceptual capacity, and the intellectual capacities are all parts of the soul, which means that they are basic powers, first principles of certain modes of living, and definitive of certain kinds of life.

2. Perceptual Powers

Perception, then, is a part of soul in the sense of being a fundamental capacity, a basic mode of life. Perception is one of the powers invoked to explain other powers, but it itself is not explained by anything prior to it. But what exactly *is* perception? The perceptual part of the soul houses a number of powers, including the five senses receptive of the special perceptibles (color, sound, odor, the tangibles, flavor), a central sense power that unites the five senses (*De anima* 425a30–b2),[13] and perception is receptive of incidental perceptibles (such as the son of Diares) (II.6) and of the common perceptibles (shape, number, motion, rest, magnitude) (425a27). The special and common perceptibles are perceived in themselves (*kath' hauta*), whereas the incidental perceptibles are perceived, of course, incidentally (*kata sumbebēkos*). Moreover, perception also discerns (*krinein*) differences between the proper perceptibles (426b12–15) and is apperceptive—we perceive *that* we see and hear (425b12–17). Finally, *phantasia* is a movement that results from perception (429a1–2) and is an affection of common sense power (*De mem.* 450a13), memory belongs to the primary perceptive power (*prōton aisthētikon*) (*De mem.* 450a14), sleeping and waking are affections of the primary perceptive power (*prōton aisthētikon*) (*De somno* 454a22–24), and dreaming is an activity of the perceptive power (*aisthētikon*) but belongs to it *as* imaginative (*De insom.* 459a21–22).

What is the configuration of the perceptual *part* of the soul? Which of these activities are properly called *perception*, rather than, say, quasiperception? The capacity for *phantasia*, memory, and dreaming can be designated quasiperception: *phantasia* depends upon perception (*De anima* 429a1–2), and so is a derivative power; and memory and dreaming both require *phantasmata*—these are quasiperceptual phenomena in the sense that they are activities of the perceptual part of the soul but depend upon more basic perceptual activities. Genuine perception, by contrast, is to be understood as a fundamental, nonderivative operation of the perceptual part of the soul. Which activities qualify?

Understanding the perceptual part of the soul as a first principle of a certain kind of life bears on this question by providing an orientation to the phenomenon under consideration. The kind of life and activity that the perceptual part of the soul provides and explains is animal life, and the essential characteristic of animal life is that it is sensate. Just as soul in general is a first principle that explains the difference between living and nonliving things, so the perceptual part of the soul is a first principle that differentiates sensate living things from nonsensate living things. And what makes the animal's perceptual sensitivity different from, say, the sunflower's sensitivity to the sun is that the animal is made aware of the objects to which it is sensitive. An animal *feels* the heat of the sun, rather than simply reacting to it (*De anima* II.12 424a32–b2). That is, the animal is perceptually *aware* of the heat. This perceptual awareness, I take it, is broadly speaking the phenomenon under discussion in *De anima* II.5–III.2. The question, then, is: *of what* are animals perceptually aware? To what are animals perceptually sensitive?

Aristotle identifies three types of perceptual object in *De anima* II.6: special, common, and incidental perceptibles. That he introduces all three types as *aisthēta* suggests, at least superficially, that all three are genuinely perceived. However, his characterizations of these perceptual objects, and in particular their relation to the senses, differ in such a way that doubt has been cast on the incidental perceptibles. In the first place, Aristotle affords a sort of primacy to the special perceptibles, calling the perception of these objects *kuriōs* perception, articulating an essential relationship between these special objects and their respective senses whereby the sense is affected by its object so as to become like it, and devoting the bulk of his discussion of perception to a detailed analysis of the mechanisms of each sense and sensory object. This contrasts sharply with Aristotle's minimal discussion of the incidental perceptibles, and with his claim that the incidental object of perception does not affect the perceiver as such (*De anima* 418a20–24). The common objects occupy a middle ground between these: like the special objects they are perceived in themselves, but, unlike the special objects, they do not have a dedicated sense.

What are we to make of this? On the one hand, it would be unnecessarily misleading on Aristotle's part to say that the incidentals are perceptual objects if he didn't mean that they are genuinely perceived; on the other hand, they are perceived *incidentally*, and if they are genuinely perceived, it is by a different (and unnamed) mechanism than the perception of the special objects. What does it mean to be perceived incidentally?

In *De anima* III.1, Aristotle uses the notion of being perceived incidentally to address two perceptual phenomena: the perception of the common perceptibles by the senses, and the perception of one special object (say, sweet) by another sense (say, sight). Although we perceive the common perceptibles incidentally by each sense, Aristotle reasons that there cannot be a dedicated sense for the common perceptibles because, if there were, then the common perceptibles would be perceived in the same manner that sweet is perceived by sight, "and this we do because we in fact have a perception of both, as a result of which we recognize [*anagnōrizomen*] them at the same time when they fall together" (425a22–24). Neither, however, do we perceive the commons in the manner that we perceive the son of Cleon, which we perceive "not because/that [*hoti*] he is the son of Cleon but because/that [*hoti*] he is white, and the white object happens to be the son of Cleon" (425a25–27). Instead, there is a common sense for the common objects of perception, by which they are perceived in themselves. The terrain that Aristotle is marking out here shows four kinds of relationship a sense may bear to various objects. (1) The relationship of sense to its proper object, as sight is related to color: color is perceived in itself by the sense of sight. (2) The relationship of a sense to the proper object of a different sense, as sight is related to sweet: sweetness is recognized by sight, and perceived incidentally by sight, on the basis of having both seen and tasted a sweet white thing. (3) The relationship of a sense to an incidental object of perception, as sight is related to the son of Cleon: the colored thing that we see happens to be Cleon's son. (4) The relationship of a sense to the common objects: relative to any particular sense, the common objects are perceived incidentally, but relative to a common sense, they are perceived in themselves. So what does it mean to be perceived incidentally?

Three things strike me as noteworthy about this passage. First, what is said to be perceived incidentally is perceived in this manner by a particular sense: sweetness is perceived incidentally by sight (but not by taste), the common objects are perceived incidentally by any one of the senses taken by itself (but not by the common sense), and the incidental perceptibles are incidental to sight. Second, in the case of the common objects, shifting the referent also shifts the status of the perception: although perceived incidentally by a sense, common objects are perceived in themselves by a common sense. Third, at least in the cases of the common objects and the special objects perceived by a different sense, there is no doubt that these objects enter into the perceptual experience of the perceiver, despite being perceived incidentally by the sense in question.[14] These observations suggest that incidental perception refers to a mode of perceptual awareness that cannot be explained by appeal to the senses alone—we certainly perceive squares by sight, even if such perception is incidental to sight.

However, in the case of incidental perceptibles such as Cleon's son, the case is different: unlike the special and common perceptibles, which are perceived incidentally in one respect but perceived in themselves in another, Cleon's son is not perceived in itself at all. In other words, the reason that we incidentally see sweetness is because we have *tasted* sweetness on prior occasions, and the reason that we incidentally see shape is because the common sense properly perceives shapes. But there is no sense or sense power that properly perceives the son of Cleon. Indeed, although Aristotle introduces incidental perception in *De anima* II.6, alongside the special and common perceptibles, he denies that the incidentals affect the perceiver: "An object of perception is spoken of as incidental, e.g., if the white thing were the son of Diares; for you perceive this incidentally, since this which you perceive is incidental to the white thing. Hence too you are not affected [*ouden paschein*] by the object of perception as such" (*De anima* 418a20–24). This description of incidental perceptibles is puzzling, for in the previous chapter, Aristotle declares, "perception consists in being moved [*kineisthai*] and affected [*paschein*] . . . for it is thought to be a kind of alteration" (416b33–34). Here in II.6 Aristotle seems to be saying at once that the son of Diares *is* an object of perception and that the son of Diares does *not* directly affect the perceiver. For this reason, one might deny that incidentals are genuinely perceived.

There are reasons to resist this line of interpretation. Most generally, Aristotle does not call incidental perceptibles anything *but* objects of perception (*aisthēta*). They cannot be objects of the nutritive faculty, obviously, and there is no textual basis for assigning them to the intellect.[15] Moreover, there *is* a textual reason for thinking that the incidental perceptibles have an effect over and above that of the special and common perceptibles. In his discussion of *phantasia* in III.3, Aristotle remarks: "The movement which comes about as a result of the activity of perception will differ insofar as it comes from these three kinds of perception [proper, common, and incidental]" (*De anima* 428b25–27 with 428b17–25). Aristotle here identifies *three* kinds of movements originating in perception, not two. This suggests that incidental perceptibles cause a similar sort of effect that the in-itself perceptibles do, and that it should therefore be included among the basic powers of perception.

What are we to conclude from this? The problem raised by the initial description of incidental perceptibles still stands and is perhaps aggravated by the comment about *phantasia*: perception is a potential to be affected, and the son of Diares *qua* son of Diares does not produce an affection in the sense power. Said otherwise, Aristotle seems to be saying that we perceive

Diares's son despite having no sensation of *him* (we only have a sensation of his colors and shapes, for example). One way of explaining this oddity is by appeal to the distinction between perceiving *x* and perceiving *that x*: to say that the son of Diares is incidentally perceived is to say that it in fact is the son of Diares that produces the sensations of colors and shapes, so that when we perceive tall and pale we are perceiving Diares's son, but we are not thereby perceiving *that* tall and pale is Diares's son.[16] On this interpretation, one perceives the son of Diares but the son of Diares does not enter into the content of the perception. In other words, insofar as the son of Diares is the incidental object of perception, the perceiver is not made aware of *the son of Diares*; instead, the perceiver is made aware of a pale, tall, moving shape that, as a matter of fact, is Diares's son.

This account is appealing in part because of how easily and often perceiving something and recognizing what it is come apart: without being acquainted with Diares's son (or with Diares), one will perceive him without recognizing *who* he is. However, it is a phenomenologically odd claim, for within experience the special and common perceptibles are always perceived as belonging to *something*; in other words, it is only through artificially induced conditions that one's perception consists only of colors and shapes.[17] So, while it is common to see something and not recognize the *particular* thing it is, it is always a *something* that one sees. Of course, Aristotle was not a phenomenologist. Nevertheless, given that the part of the soul he is explaining is the source of perceptual awareness, it strikes me as odd in such a context to speak of perceptual objects that do not enter into the content of perception. Just as the sweetness one incidentally sees enters into the content of the perception, so too, it seems, some incidental perceptible or other enters into the content—I may not see the son of Diares, but I do see a man; my cat may not see human being, but she certainly seems to see caregiver.[18] Aristotle suggests as much early in *De insomniis* in the course of distinguishing dreaming from opinion: "For we do not merely say that the thing approaching is a man or a horse but also that it is white or handsome; but on these points opinion could not pronounce, either truly or falsely, without perception. Yet the soul actually does this in sleep; for we seem to see that the approaching object is white no less than that it is a man" (458b10–14).[19] That is, in sleep just as in waking perception, we see that what approaches is a man and that it is white, equally.

It may be urged that the incidental perceptibles still cannot be genuinely perceived, for the incidental perceptibles are not material objects—the incidental perceptibles do not produce an affect in the sense power. The difficulty with this inference is that Aristotle does not seem to restrict *even* the special perceptibles to the material change in the sense organ. In his discussion of sound and hearing, Aristotle includes some comments on voice. Voice (*phōnē*) is a species of a special perceptible—it is "a particular sound made by something with a soul" (*De anima* 420b5–6). Voice will, of course, be a certain quality on the continuum of sound, having a certain pitch and tone (see 420a26–b4), but what is perceived in hearing a voice is *more* than the tone or the pitch. Voice is an expression (*hermēneia*) for the sake of well-being (420b19–20), and it is a "particular sound that has meaning [*sēmantikos*]" (420b32–33). If the special perceptibles are perceived in themselves because they produce a direct effect on the sense *organ*, voice could not be a special perceptible: the *meaning* of a sound, the *expression* that voice conveys, is not simply a quality on a continuum of high and low pitch that can be taken on by the material structure of the sense organ. If what is perceived in itself is so perceived by virtue of its effect on the sense organ, this effect already includes more than taking on the material quality of, say, B-flat, and if it already includes more than B-flat, the principle by which what is perceived incidentally is excluded from perception strictly speaking would also rule out a special perceptible. Put simply, the distinction between being receptive of the material quality of a perceptible and its nonmaterial aspect (or between perceiving and perceiving-that)—that is, meaning—does not seem to be a distinction Aristotle is policing to demarcate proper and incidental perception. Deborah Modrak notes, with regard to incidental perceptibles such as the son of Diares, that "the sensory basis for the perception of an incidental object does not fully determine the content of perception";[20] the same point holds for the perception of voice.

In II.12 Aristotle distinguishes the sense organ from the sense power in just these terms: "that which perceives must be a particular extended magnitude, while what it is to be able to perceive and the sense are surely not magnitudes, but rather a certain *logos* and potentiality of that thing" (424a26–28). The effect on the magnitudinal organ, while a necessary condition for perception, is actually perception by virtue of the nonmagnitudinal power to perceive. This suggests that the power of perception, while employing material organs, is not restricted to the materiality of the sense object. Ultimately, the perceptual faculty is receptive of more than the sense organs, strictly speaking, transmit.

Is there any reason, then, *not* to include the incidental perceptibles among the basic powers of the perceptual part of the soul? It may be objected that perceiving the son of Diares *qua* son of Diares cannot be a basic perceptual power because, at the very least, perceiving him requires that one be acquainted with him, and it may also require (as Kahn [1992] argues) universal categories such as "son" and "man" which are intellectual, not perceptual, categories. On this account, what would distinguish what is perceived strictly speaking, that is, perceived in itself, from what is perceived incidentally is the nonperceptual input required. This is the problem raised if incidental perception takes the form of perceiving *that* the white is the son of Diares, rather than perceiving the son of Diares: the "*that*" indicates that the son of Diares is not perceived but inferred, based on memories and categories.

There is indeed a distinction that may be drawn between the immediate and natural ability to perceive the common and proper perceptibles and the learning or experience that may be required to perceive incidental perceptibles. Aristotle makes clear that perception is an already developed power, not in need of being learned (*De anima* 417b16–19). However, this need not imply that incidental perception is the *application* of intellectual categories to the data provided by perception. A baby deer, for example, will learn how to walk, and this may require developing the ability to discern which rocks are too high to step over. This is to educate the perception of what is an in-itself perceptible—the perception of the common perceptible, magnitude—which does not involve the application of any category. Even in-itself perception may be developed and refined, without the input of intellect. Moreover, as Cashdollar points out, there is spontaneity *even in* the perception of learned incidental perceptibles that precludes the process of inference from a category (be it an intellectual category or not) to the content of perception.[21] That the white thing is the son of Diares is *perceived*, not inferred.

Aristotle does not preclude incidental perceptibles from the content of perception in his discussions of it, and there seems not to be a satisfactory principle to employ to preclude it on his behalf—neither the immediate effect on the sense organs, nor the unmediated (unlearned) operation of the in-itself perceptibles.[22] We ought to conclude, then, that the basic powers of perception—those included in the definition of the perceptual part of the soul—are the powers to perceive special, common, and incidental perceptibles.

3. The Primary Perceptual Faculty

There is one other factor to consider in determining the structure of the perceptual part of the soul, namely, Aristotle's claim that perceptual power is ultimately unified in one central primary power.[23] In general, the primary perceptual faculty is invoked to explain the possibility of perceiving different sense objects at once (*De anima* 425a30–b3, 426b17–23; *De sensu* 449a6–20;

De somno 455a17–22) and to explain how we perceive that we see, hear, and so on (*De somno* 455a15–17). There are two general ways of interpreting this primary perceptual faculty: as the joint activity of the five senses, or as a general power distinct from the power of the five senses.[24] What is at stake in the question of the nature of the primary perceptual faculty, with respect to the issue of the configuration of the perceptual *part* of the soul, is whether the powers to differentiate between special perceptibles and to perceive that we perceive are derived from the basic powers to perceive the special, common, and incidental perceptibles, or whether they are distinct powers that are to be included as basic perceptual powers. In fact, as we will see, the relationship between the reception of the perceptible objects, on the one hand, and the awareness of them (perceiving that we see and hear [*De anima* III.2 425b12–25]) and the ability to differentiate between them, on the other, are powers that are so intimately related that the relationship between the two can be described *neither* as the joint activity of the senses *nor* as a distinct power. It is more properly conceived as a relationship of part to whole.[25]

To begin with, we may note that the question of perceiving that we perceive and the question of differentiating the special perceptibles are related questions. They are both questions of awareness, the former being a question of awareness of single objects, the latter being a question of comparative awareness, the awareness of the individual objects as different from one another or that the individual objects differ.[26] That these two questions are related is indicated by the parallel ways that Aristotle formulates the questions. For Aristotle, the question of awareness is a question of how it is that we *perceive* that we perceive (*De anima* 425b12–13), and the question of *comparative* awareness is a question of how we *perceive* that the perceptual objects differ (426b14). The first question can be glossed as "how is it that we are *aware* of our perceptions?" The second question, too, can be glossed in these terms: "how is it that we are *aware* that perceptual objects differ?" In both cases, the kind of perceiving in question is a way of being aware of the objects of perception. That these questions are related gains support from a passage in *De somno* (455a12–22), wherein Aristotle explicitly links these two notions (discussed below).

If it is true that both of these questions are questions of awareness, how we answer the first question will have implications for the second. The question of awareness may be put this way: is the awareness of the object of perception accomplished by the sense itself? That is to say, is sight itself aware of red? Or does awareness require something over and above the sight itself? The question of how one distinguishes the special perceptibles will be affected by the answer. If it is the former, that sight by itself is aware of color, then the question about distinguishing the special perceptibles will be "how are these modes of awareness united?" In other words, the awareness of red will *already* be distinct from the awareness of B-flat, so the question of discerning their distinctness is a question of how the distinct awarenesses come to be unified. If, on the other hand, the awareness of an object of sight involves a general power of awareness, the question concerning the distinction between the special perceptibles will be "how does a single power of awareness distinguish difference?" In other words, if the power of awareness is one, how does it accommodate multiplicity?

De anima III.2, the chapter wherein Aristotle addresses the questions of awareness and discernment of differences, proceeds roughly as one would expect, given the connection between the two questions. He begins with a consideration of the question of awareness and proceeds from there, after an interval in which he discusses the unity of the special perceptible object and the perception itself in the act of perceiving (425b26–426b8), to discuss the question of comparative awareness. The chapter opens: "Since we perceive that we see and hear, it must either be by sight that one perceives that one sees or by another [sense]" (425b12–13). Difficulties follow each of these two possibilities. If it is by another sense that one sees that one sees, (1) one and the same sense would perceive both color and the vision,[27] and (2) there will be an infinite regress of senses that see that one sees that one sees, and so on. This regress, I take it, rests on the assumption that awareness takes the same form as perceiving objects: perception is *of* an object (say, red), and if awareness is also a perception, it will also be *of* an object, the seeing of red. But if the initial perception *of* an object does not include *awareness* of the object, neither will the second-order perception *of* the perception.[28] To avoid the regress, Aristotle must reject this assumption. Let us see if he does so when he considers the second possibility, namely that it is by one and the same sense that we both see and are aware that we see.

After dismissing the option that another sense perceives that we perceive because of the regress problem, Aristotle considers the possibility that the sense is aware of itself (*De anima* 425b15–17). If it is by sight that one sees that one sees, and what it is to see is to see *color*, then the sense itself will have to be colored in order to be seen in its action of seeing (425b17–20). Two problems arise from this. The first is that, if sight is aware of itself as seeing, then its function is split into two—receiving the perceptible object, on the one hand, and being aware of that reception, on the other. Second, for that which sees to be colored is a problem because, in order to be receptive of the perceptible object, the sense itself cannot actively *be* any of its objects (424a7–9). However, in the lines that follow, Aristotle removes both of these obstacles and seems to affirm something like the sense being aware of itself. He says:

> It is clear then that to perceive by sight is not a single thing; for even when we do not see, it is by sight that we discern [*krinein*] both darkness and light, though not in the same way. Moreover, even that which sees is in a way colored; for each sense organ [*aisthētērion*] is receptive of the object of perception without its matter. That is why perceptions [*aisthēseis*] and imaginings [*phantasiai*] remain in the sense organ even when the objects of perception are gone. (*De anima* 425b20–25)

Aristotle removes the obstacles to attributing awareness to the sense itself by pointing out that (a) it is not a problem for a single sense to have more than one power, because it *already* has more than one—sight, for example, both sees color and discerns darkness from light. Johansen (2005) nicely explicates the relevance of this point to the problem of explaining awareness:[29] discerning light and darkness is not *seeing*, for seeing is of color and light is the medium, not the object, of seeing (as Aristotle lays out in *De anima* II.7). Darkness, the absence of light, is the condition under which seeing (i.e., seeing color) does not happen. Thus, the distinction between perceiving color by sight and discerning darkness and light by sight "is also a way of showing, via the negative example, how the sense of sight may be involved in registering both its own activity and its own inactivity with respect to first-order perception." Aristotle also points out that (b) in a way the sense *is* colored, because it takes on the perceptible form without the matter. In affirming that the sense has more than one function (a), Aristotle opens the possibility that the sense is self-aware, that is, that it includes awareness in the very reception of the object. In affirming that the sense is in a way colored (b), he allows that somehow the sense can have *itself* as its object; seeing is both *of* red and also *of* the red-being-perceived.

But if the sense is *of* both its object and itself in the same way, then we are thrown back into the problem that underlies the regress problem, which is a problem only on the assumption that awareness has the same structure as the original perception. If the act of perceiving an object does not include awareness in itself, then a second-order act of perceiving an object (in this case, the object is the original act of perception) will not accomplish this either, but will require a third-order perception, ad infinitum. But the same problem holds of the sense itself: if the act of perceiving an object (say, red) does not include awareness in itself, then a second aspect of perceiving an object (the red-being-perceived, or the original act of perception) should not either. If the sense itself perceiving that it sees successfully avoids the problem of the regress problem, the sense must be *of* itself in a manner that differs (in a way that is yet to be determined) from the way it is *of* its special object.[30] Moreover, these must be two aspects of the same act of perception. Aristotle considers the act of perception to be a fully complete one (*Met.* 1048b23; *De sensu* 446b2–3), so that if perception is aware, this perceptual awareness must be included in the same act by which the object is perceived.

It is noteworthy that Aristotle does not here conclude that it is the sense as individual sense that is self-aware; he concludes instead with the puzzling comment about lingering perceptions and *phantasiai*. This suggests that the question of awareness has not yet been fully resolved, although some of the difficulties to resolving it have been addressed. The reference to *phantasia*, moreover, hints that awareness is accomplished by the primary perceptual faculty: at *De memoria* 450a10–12 Aristotle remarks that *phantasmata* are affections of the common sense (*koinē aisthēsis*), which he immediately identifies with the *prōton aisthētikon*.[31] We will have to address later the questions of (a) how the sense is *of* itself, how this is different from being *of* a special object, and (b) how, given this difference, awareness is still *perceiving* that we perceive.

The question about discerning perceptible differences takes the form one would expect if perceptual awareness were accomplished by each sense itself, but the solution offered is the one that would be expected if awareness were accomplished by the central perceptual power. After an interim in which Aristotle argues that in the activity of perception the object of perception and the sense are the same (*De anima* 425b26–426b8), he articulates the question thus:

> Each sense, therefore, is concerned with the subject perceived by it, being present in the sense-organ *qua* sense-organ, and it discerns [*krinein*] the varieties of the subject perceived by it, e.g. sight for white and black, and taste for sweet and bitter; and similarly for the other senses too. Since we discern [*krinein*] both white and sweet and each of the objects of perception by reference to each other, by what do we perceive also that they differ? (*De anima* 426b8–14)

If each sense is aware of its own objects, by what means are the differences between them perceived? It cannot be the senses taken individually—these are concerned only with their own objects: "Nor indeed is it possible to discern by separate means that sweet is different from white, but both must be evident to one thing" (*De anima* 426b17–19). Neither can it be some other faculty that makes these distinctions: "This must indeed be by perception; for they are objects of perception" (426b14–15). Instead, some single perceptual power must make this distinction (426b20–23).

This by itself does not explain *how* individual senses become unified so as to be discerned as distinct, only *that* they do. For the remainder of the chapter, Aristotle considers the problem of how something that is one and undivided can be "moved simultaneously with opposite motions" (*De anima* 426b30), as it would have to be to perceive both sweet and white (426b31–427a1). His solution is familiar. One thing can be single and undivided in place and number, while divisible and divided in being (427a3–5). This single perceptual faculty is like the soul itself, which is single and undivided while also being divisible in *logos* or being (Aristotle uses these phrases interchangeably) according to its parts.

This is the solution we would expect if awareness were accomplished by the central perceptual power, rather than the individual senses—it is a solution that accommodates multiplicity in a single power, not a solution that unites many modes of awareness. If each sense were singularly aware of its object, then the faculty that discerns the differences between the sense objects (in the interim between the awareness question and the difference question, Aristotle argues that the active faculty and the object are the same, although different in being) would have to include a third instance of awareness—awareness *of* these singular awarenesses as compared to one another. But this is not what Aristotle describes here. Rather, he says that the single perceptual faculty is like a point, which is both one and two insofar as it is both the beginning and the end of a discrete line (*De anima* 427a9–16). This solution behaves as if the senses themselves are *not* individually aware, at least not *qua* individual senses.

There is a passage in *De somno* (mentioned earlier) wherein Aristotle directly connects the issue of awareness with the issue of discerning perceptibles, and so it has direct bearing on these issues.

> Now every sense has both something special [*ti idion*] and something common [*ti koina*]. The special function, e.g., of the sight is seeing, that of the auditory, hearing, and similarly with all the rest; but there is also a common faculty [*koinē dunamis*] associated with them all, whereby one perceives that one sees and hears, for it is not by *sight* that one sees that one sees; and one discerns [*krinein*] and is capable of discerning [*dunatai krinein*] that sweet is different from white not by taste nor by sight, nor by a combination of the

> two, but by some part [*morion*] which is common [*koinē*] to all the sense organs; for there is one sense faculty [*mia aisthēsis*], and one paramount sense organ [*to kurion aisthētērion hen*], but the being of its sensitivity varies with each class of sensible object, e.g., sound and color. (*De somno* 455a12–22)[32]

Here Aristotle explicitly connects the issue of perceiving *that* we perceive with the issue of perceiving perceptible differences. He attributes perceptual awareness to a common power, *koinē dunamis*, and explicitly denies that it is the faculty of sight itself that is aware. Instead, there is one perceptual faculty (*mia aisthēsis*), presumably that which is the source of the *koinē dunamis*, that provides *both* the awareness of the perceptual object and the discernment of their differences. Although the way these questions were taken up in *De anima* III.2 is not entirely perspicuous, this is consistent with the account there, if we take the question of awareness to have concluded only that in *some* sense, sight is self-aware. We may now take it to mean that it is self-aware, not *qua* sight, but *qua* part of the central perceptual power. This is further confirmed by a passage in *De sensu*, in which Aristotle considers how it is possible to perceive different perceptual objects simultaneously.

> If then it is true that the soul perceives sweet with one part [*meros*] and white with another part, then either the compound of these is one, or it is not. But it must be one; for the perceptual faculty is one part [*meros*]. What one object, then, does that one faculty perceive? For surely no object can be composed of these. There must then, as has been said before, be one part of the soul with which it perceives everything, although it senses different objects with different [parts]. (*De sensu* 449a5–10)[33]

There is some one part of the soul that perceives all things, although it perceives different objects with different parts of itself. This suggests that the five senses perceive—in the sense of being affected by their objects such that they are *aware* of them—only by virtue of being parts of a perceptual *whole*.

We may now return to the questions put off above, namely, (a) what the difference is between the way that the sense is *of* an object and the way that it is *of* itself perceiving, (b) and how, despite this difference, awareness is nonetheless *perceiving* that we perceive. The distinction between a part and a whole is, in a sense, an artificial one—the parts are not separable in the sense of existing independently from the whole. As Kahn says, "The conception of the individual senses as independent faculties would be just as alien to

Aristotle as the conception of individual organs in abstraction from the body of which they form a part."[34] Any activity of a part of a whole is made possible by, and is ultimately the activity of, the whole. For example, while it is true to say that it is the hand that grasps, it is *also* true to say that the person grasps by means of her hand. So, similarly, it is true to say that sight is aware that it sees, but it is *also* true to say that the perceptual power is aware that it perceives by means of sight. The body as a whole is the source of the power to move, and this power is specified in the hand's power to grasp; so too it is the perceptual power as a whole that is the source of awareness, and this power is specified in vision's power to see. As Kosman put it, "To see then, as Aristotle says in our text (425b18) . . . is to be aware, we might say, sightfully."[35]

So there is a distinction between sight seeing red and sight seeing itself seeing red: sight takes on the perceptible form of red *qua* individual sense, but it takes it on *as* aware of it *qua* part of a perceptual whole. In other words, the *way* that sight sees—in the sense of being aware of—its object is predicated upon the awareness of the whole perceptual system. Just as the hand grasps by drawing on the power of the whole motive body, without the body thereby being directed at the hand, so seeing is awareness of color by drawing on the power of the whole aware perceptual system, without that system being directed at vision. In the *De anima* III.2 passage, Aristotle affirms that sight is in a way colored, because it takes on the perceptible form without the matter, as a way of satisfying the condition for sight being visible to itself. Now we see that sight is in a way colored and is visible to itself, but not as an object for itself. Rather, it is visible to itself in the mode of being colored, that is, in being aware of its color. Sight *qua* vision is of red, and sight *qua* awareness is of the seeing accomplished by sight *qua* vision. This is not a second-order perception—the perceptual whole is not affected by the seeing in the way that sight is affected by red. It is, rather, a *way* that sight is of red, namely, with awareness. But it is a perception that we perceive in the sense that it is perception taken generally that is aware of the activity of any individual sense.[36]

There is one passage in the *Metaphysics* that has been taken as evidence against the sort of interpretation I have been giving of the relationship between perceiving an object and being aware of that perception. I have been arguing that awareness is a primary perceptual capacity, as primary as the reception of perceptual objects. It may be objected that in *Metaphysics* XII.9, we find Aristotle saying, "evidently knowledge and perception and opinion and understanding have always something else as their object, and themselves only by the way" (1074b35–36).[37] This seems to distinguish between the act of perceiving (and knowing, and so on) and the awareness of such acts, and to relegate the awareness to a secondary position—these processes have themselves as objects only "by the way."[38] However, I have argued that, strictly speaking, it is not *sight* that is of itself, but the perceptual faculty as a whole that is of the activity of seeing (in the sense of providing the awareness to the activity of seeing). The *Metaphysics* passage fits this distinction quite well: sight *qua* sight is, first of all, of its object, but sight *qua* part of perception as a whole is of itself. The latter may be described as "only by the way" because it is not sight strictly speaking that is of itself, but perception as a whole that is of sight.

To sum up: in the *De anima* passage, Aristotle affirmed that a sense has more than one function and that it is in a way colored, which suggested that in some sense sight is self-aware, but not in the sense of being a perceptual object for itself (which would set us back in the regress problem). The passages from *De somno* and *De sensu* suggest that the way that sight is self-aware and has more than one function is by virtue of being a part of a unified perceptual system. What does this mean? How does this solve the problem of awareness? The introduction of the unified perceptual system provides a new orientation for the question of awareness by situating the individual senses in an integrated whole. If the individual senses are parts of a whole perceptual system, rather than independent entities, then what it is for them to be the senses that they are is conditioned by the whole of which they are a part—the whole is prior to the parts. If this is the case, then the question of awareness is better asked, not of the senses taken individually, but of the perceptual whole. However, one cannot strictly distinguish the parts from the whole—what is true of the whole will *also* be true of the parts. If awareness is achieved by the whole perceptual system, it will also be achieved by the individual senses *qua* parts of the whole. Thus it is in a way true to say that we see that we see, but it is better to say that we *perceive* that we see, where perception names the general faculty of awareness and sight names its particular use.

If the senses are parts of a unified perceptual power, this means that they are what they are in virtue of the whole. Given that the senses were, at first, seen to be the primary candidates for the powers of the perceptual part of the soul, the introduction of a central, unified sense power changes the picture of the perceptual part of the soul significantly. Now, it seems, the perceptual part of the soul is *first of all* the general power for perceptual awareness, and this power is actualized through the reception of the special, common, and incidental perceptibles.[39]

It may still be asked *how* exactly this unified central perceptual power *has* the power of perceptual awareness. But, as Kosman concludes, this is just the nature of perception: "Just as form, though not nothing, is not something in addition to the elements of an entity, and just as soul, though not nothing, is not something in addition to the alive body, so awareness, though not nothing, is not something in addition to the active, embodied perceptual faculty at work in a unified sensitive organism."[40] In other words, the power of perception *just is* a power of awareness, and this power is a first principle of animal life; this is just what it means to be a part of the soul.

4. The Derivative Powers: *Phantasia*

The primary perceptual capacity, in addition to being the source of perceptual awareness, is also the seat of other perceptual powers—*phantasia* and memory, in particular. Aristotle summarizes his arguments concerning memory in *De memoria* 1 thus: "Now, it has been said what memory and remembering are, namely the having of an image [*phantasma*] regarded as a likeness of that of which it is an image, and to which part in us memory belongs, namely the primary perceptive part [*prōton aisthētikon*] and that with which we perceive time" (451a14–17). In this section, I will discuss what *phantasia* is and how it relates to the basic perceptual powers. I will argue first that *phantasia* is derived from and dependent upon the perception of the special, common, and incidental perceptibles, and second that its role in the perceptual life of an animal is to expand the temporal horizons of perceptual experience. It thus enriches perceptual experience, but is nonetheless conditioned by the original perceptions. This is important for the basic argument of this book, which is that virtue requires that one *perceive* well, not merely that one have the right *phantasmata*.[41] I also argue that to perceive well requires that one bring the perceptual part of one's soul into harmony with the intellectual part, and insofar as *phantasia* is a power of the perceptual *part* of the soul (albeit a derivative one), we may still take Aristotle's claims about *phantasia* to be informative concerning the perceptual *part* of the soul.

In *De anima* III.3, Aristotle introduces *phantasia* as "that in virtue of which we say an image [*phantasma*] occurs to us" (428a1–2), and, after distinguishing it from a number of other capacities (including perception), he concludes that *phantasia* is "a movement [*kinēsis*] produced by [*gignesthai*] perception according to its activity [*kat' energeian*]" (429a1–2). This alone is enough to establish that *phantasia* depends upon the basic perceptual powers, and as such is to be included as a secondary power of the perceptual part of the soul: the definition of *phantasia* includes *aisthēsis*, and as a result the *phantastikon* is not a separable part of the soul. Moreover, Aristotle does not list *phantasia* among powers that he holds as candidates for being parts of the soul (413b11–13). That the *phantastikon* is not a distinct part of the soul is confirmed by a passage in *De insomniis*:

> But since we have discussed *phantasia* in the treatise *On the Soul*, and the imaginative faculty [*to phantastikon*] is the same as the perceptual faculty [*to aisthētikon*], although the imaginative faculty and the perceptual faculty are different [*heteron*] in being; and since *phantasia* is the movement produced by perception according to its activity, and a dream appears to be some sort of image (for an image which appears in sleep, whether simply or in a special sense, we call a dream); it is clear that dreaming belongs to the perceptual faculty, but belongs to it *qua* imaginative. (*De insom.* 459a14–23)

Here Aristotle explicitly addresses the faculty of *phantasia* with respect to the faculty of perception, and asserts that they are the same (*to auto*) but *different* (*heteron*) in being. If the faculty of *phantasia* were *separable* in being, it would be a candidate for a distinct part of the soul. But, as it is, this faculty is only different in being, as we would expect by its explicit reference to perception in its definition. Insofar as *phantasia* is produced by perceptual activity, it is a power *of* the perceptual part of the soul, and insofar as it is derived from the basic powers of perception, it is a secondary power, one that is made possible by the basic power.[42] Aristotle says explicitly that *phantasia* is produced by the powers to perceive special, common, and incidental perceptibles at 428b17–30.

Phantasia is also a power of the perceptual part of the soul in a second sense: it is an activity of the primary perceptual faculty. Aristotle makes this clear in *De memoria*, where he first argues that memory belongs to the same part of the soul to which *phantasia* belongs (450a22–25), and then identifies this with the primary perceptual faculty (451a15–18). Victor Caston persuasively argues that *phantasia* belongs to the primary perceptual faculty in the following sense: an original perception is received via the peripheral senses by the primary sense organ (the seat of the primary perceptual power [*De somno* 455a12–22]), causing a perceptual experience of that object. At the same time, the perception of the object causes a "side-effect" motion in the organ, and this is the *phantasia*.[43] This *phantasia* resides in the perceptual system, and may, through a variety of causes including choice (*De anima* 427b16–18) or another occurrent perception, cause a change in the primary sense organ, creating an experience that is like the original perceptual experience (although it may be distorted by, for example, being drunk or asleep [*De insomn.* 461a8–24]).[44]

Some scholars have found that the account of *phantasia* given in *De anima* III.3 is inconsistent,[45] although current favor seems to tend in the direction of finding ways to overcome apparent inconsistencies.[46] *Phantasia* has been variously taken to perform quite discrete functions, such as being responsible for nonparadigmatic and doubtful perceptual experience,[47] or to supply a global function necessary to all cognition, such as representing objects such that one becomes aware of them,[48] or interpreting perceptions.[49] To give an exhaustive account of *phantasia* that addresses each of these positions in detail is a work too lengthy to take up here. However, the causal account of *phantasia* that Caston offers, and incarnations of which are given by Everson and Moss, provides a strong framework within which to consider such questions.[50] Although Caston takes the argument in III.3 to be aimed at explaining the possibility of error, his account of what *phantasia* is and how it works enables it to serve other functions as well. For example, Moss (2012) argues for a similar conception of the mechanism of *phantasia* to the one Caston defends, but she emphasizes the role that *phantasia* plays in animal motion by virtue of presenting the animal with an apparent good.[51] All I intend to show is that *one* of the effects of *phantasia* is the temporal expansion of perceptual experience.[52]

The causal account of *phantasia* that Caston offers is persuasive, and one of its strengths is that it makes sense both of the basic definition of *phantasia* as "a movement [*kinēsis*] produced by perception according to its activity [*kat' energeian*]" (*De anima* 429a1–2) and of the variety of features Aristotle attributes to *phantasia* in III.3. In III.3 a number of features of *phantasia* emerge from the distinctions Aristotle draws between it and other capacities (427b16–428b9), and from his own account of what *phantasia* is (428b10–429a9). I organize these features into three groups:

(1) *Phantasia* is derived from the activity of perception:
   a. *Phantasia* is a kind of motion that is produced by perception, that is, the perception of special, common, and incidental perceptibles (*De anima* 428b11–12, 428b25–27, 429a1–2)
   b. It is similar to perception (428b14)
   c. It is of the objects of perception (428b12–13)

(2) The activity of *phantasia* is independent of perception:
   a. *Phantasia* is up to us, in the sense that it is within our power to form an image (427b17–20)
   b. The way that it presents things is at one remove from reality, so that *phantasia* affects us the way that looking at a picture of, say, a

lion affects us as opposed to the way believing that we see a lion affects us (427b21–24)
   c. *Phantasia* can occur when perception is not occurring, as for example in dreams one has visual images although one's eyes are closed (428a5–8)

(3) *Phantasia* can be either true or false:
   a. It is not tied to truth and falsity the way that opinion is (427b20–21)
   b. *Phantasia* can be false (428a11–12, 428a16–17, 428b17–30)
   c. It does not include conviction (*pistis*) or *logos* (428a19–23, 428a23–24)

Caston's account makes perspicuous how *phantasia* can be both derived from perception and independent in its own activity. If the primary perceptual power in the primary sense organ stores the effects of perception with their causal power to produce an experience like the perceptual experience, it will not depend upon the *presence* of the object of sense, but will have been begotten by an original perception. It is, then, (1b) similar to perception and (1c) of the objects of perception in the sense that it has a similar power to cause an experience like the one caused by the original object of perception. It is nonetheless independent of perceptual activity because, once established, the *phantasia* has its own causal power; it can therefore (2a) be brought before one's mind at will (or as the conclusion of a process of recollection), and (2c) occur without a present perception.

Caston's aim is to show that *phantasia* is exactly that power that accounts for error insofar as its effect is divorced from any external cause to which it must correspond.[53] The matter is complex: Aristotle seems to have two different senses of falsity in mind in the three passages in which he makes that claim. The contrasts that generate this feature are informative here. First, supposition (*hupolēpsis*), as Aristotle tells us, includes belief, understanding, and knowledge; all of these are discursive forms of knowledge in the sense that all include *logos* (*De anima* 428a19–24). *Phantasia*, by contrast, presents an image, which is subject to different criteria of truth or falsity. In this context, it is appropriate to say that (3a, 3c) *phantasia* is neither true nor false (427b16–21). Similarly, a painting is neither true nor false by the standards of argument or scientific demonstration. Second, the contrast drawn with perception is between perception of special perceptibles and *phantasia*. The perception of the special perceptibles is always true because the activity of perceiving is one and the same with the activity of the object of perception, and so there is no room for error—the object of sight and the seeing correspond exactly. *Phantasia*, then, is (3b) "mostly false" by contrast to this because, as Aristotle has just told us, it need not correspond to any currently present object (428a11–12; see also 428b17–18, 418a11–16).[54] Caston focuses on the second sense of falsity, but his account is suitable to both.

In addition to these three basic features of *phantasia*, Aristotle mentions two others. *Phantasia* can:

(A) Fill out indistinct perceptions such that something indistinct "appears to us to be a man" (428a12–15), and
(B) Make its possessor able to do and be affected by many things (428b15–17, 429a2–8).

These two features bring out the role of *phantasia* that I would like to emphasize: that it extends the temporal horizons of perceptual experience. I will begin with the general account I want to give, and then I will turn to the textual evidence for such a story. The primary perceptual power, on Caston's account of *phantasia*, is a repository of images of previously perceived objects—special, common, and incidental perceptibles—that have causal power to produce new experiences of these former perceptions. In many cases, these *phantasiai* will produce experiences in the absence of perception, as they do in sleep. In other cases, these *phantasiai* will be evoked by a present perception of some other object of perception. For example, perceiving heat may trigger a *phantasia* of water, which serves as the basis for a desire for water. In yet other cases, a perceptual object will trigger a *phantasia* of a previous encounter with that object. For example, Thrasymachus has a conversation with Socrates one day, and he becomes embarrassed in the course of that conversation. The next day he sees Socrates in the marketplace and the *phantasia* of the previous day's experience comes to his mind, causing him to see Socrates with embarrassment and anger. In these latter two cases, we see that an object is perceived *in relation to* either some not-yet-present object—the water—or some prior experience—the conversation with Socrates. Strictly speaking, perception is of the present—it depends for its activity on a present perceptible object (*De anima* 417b16–29; *De mem.* 449b10–15)—but the perception of it may ignite *phantasiai* of past and future (expected) perceptions. This will, in turn, alter the character of what is perceived: perception is no longer of the present in the sense of an isolated moment, it is now of the present as integrated in a continuous life.

Now let us see how Aristotle's text supports this role that I am attributing to *phantasia*. Some of the elements required for such an account are already in place. *Phantasia* is of the objects of perception; Aristotle makes it clear that what he means by this is that *phantasia* is a movement caused by the perception of special, common, and incidental perceptibles. He says: "The movement which comes about as a result of the activity of perception will differ insofar as it comes from these three kinds of perception [the perception of common, special, and incidental perceptibles]" (*De anima* 428b25–27, with 428b17–25 for the reference to common, special, and incidental perception). So it is reasonable to say that Thrasymachus's perception of Socrates (an incidental perceptible) may be accompanied by a *phantasia* of Socrates.

That *phantasiai* may be concurrent with perception is evident by the feature, noted above, that *phantasiai* may supply details to imprecise perceptions. The comment comes when Aristotle is distinguishing *phantasia* from perception: "Further, it is not when we are exercising [our senses] accurately with regard to objects of perception that we say that this appears [*phainesthai*] to us to be a man, but rather when we do not perceive it distinctly" (*De anima* 428a12–15). The idea seems to be this: when one sees a figure from a distance, one does not *perceive* that it is the son of Diares, but it *appears* to one that it is. A *phantasia* is called in to help the perceiver make sense of his perception by filling in the gaps.[55] (That the point being made here is that *phantasiai* may be either true or false does not alter the fact that it shows that *phantasia* and perception may be concurrent.)[56]

Furthermore, in *De memoria*, Aristotle draws a close connection between the faculty of *phantasia* and the perception of time. Aristotle first argues that memory is "not a perception or a supposition [*hupolēpsis*], but a state [*hexis*] or affection [*pathos*] of one of these, when time has elapsed . . . and this is why all memory involves time. So only animals which perceive time remember, and they do so by means of that with which they perceive time" (449b24–30). Memory involves time, Aristotle argues, and animals remember by means of that by which they perceive time. Immediately after this argument, Aristotle discusses *phantasia* and concludes that "it is apparent, then, to which part of the soul memory belongs, namely, the same part as that to which *phantasia* belongs. And it is the objects of *phantasia* that are remembered in their own right" (*De mem.* 450a22–24). Thus, Aristotle identifies that which perceives time with the part of the soul to which *phantasia* belongs. He concludes his consideration of memory saying, "Now, it has been said what memory and remembering are, namely the having of a *phantasma* regarded as a likeness of that of which it is a *phantasma*, and to which part in us memory belongs, namely the primary perceptual part and that with which we perceive time" (451a15–18). Not all animals have a perception of time (450a15–19), which implies that the perception of time belongs to the primary perceptual part *qua phantastikon* (a locution Aristotle uses at *De insomniis* 459a22–23). Not all animals have a perception of time, but those that do have it, have it by virtue of having this secondary perceptual power, the power of *phantasia*. This supports the notion that *phantasia* extends the temporal horizons of the presently perceived objects by situating them within a temporally extended life, at least with respect to the past. The *phantastikon* houses images that are memories, and these images may be brought to bear on the current perception.

The second feature that did not fall neatly into the basic features of *phantasia* supports the notion that *phantasia* also enables a futural temporal horizon of the perceptual object. *Phantasia* makes "it possible for its possessor to do and be affected by many things" (*De anima* 428b15–17). Aristotle reiterates this sentiment at the conclusion of his account of *phantasia*, saying, "And since sight is perception par excellence, the name for *phantasia* is taken from light [*phaos*], because without light it is not possible to see. And because *phantasiai* persist and are similar to perceptions, animals do many things in accordance with them" (429a2–6). As Moss (2012) argues, one sense in which it is possible to act in accordance with *phantasia* is insofar as *phantasia* can make one aware of objects of desire, which are not currently present, as goals.[57] So, for example, the heat of the day evokes a *phantasia* of cool water as refreshing and pleasant, and this serves as motivation for the perceiver to seek such water. And in seeking water, the animal acts in accordance with *phantasia*.

In sum, *phantasia* is a secondary perceptual capacity, a power of the perceptual part of the soul, insofar as it is an effect of an actual perception. But it is also a power independent of perception, residing in the primary perceptual organ, and this enables it to feed back into and alter the nature of current perceptions. The *phantastikon* is that whereby animals perceive time, and insofar as they perceive time, the present to which *aisthēsis* is beholden is a moment in a temporally extended life. By contrast, those animals without the perception of time, without *phantasia*, will perceive only in isolated bits—each time the grub perceives its food, it is as if it were the first time it perceived food.

Conclusion

This chapter has established the following points: (1) that perception is a part of the soul, and that this means that it is a foundational power that makes possible animal life; (2) that the perceptual part of the soul is a general power of awareness with three objects of awareness—the special, common, and incidental perceptibles; (3) that *phantasia* is a secondary or derivative power belonging to this part of the soul; and (4) that it is a power that expands the temporal horizons of perceptual experience.

A consequence of the complexity of the perceptual part of the soul is that the term *aisthēsis* gains many meanings. As with many words, *aisthēsis* may be used metaphorically or literally. The metaphorical use is one that refers not (or not only) to any perceptual activity of power at all, such as when we say "I see your point" and mean "I understand." The literal use will refer to some perceptual power or activity. It may refer (i) narrowly to perception of the special perceptibles (mere sensation), or (ii) more broadly to the perception of special, common, and incidental perceptible objects. *Aisthēsis* may also refer (iii) to the activity or power of the perceptual part of the soul without picking out any specific power. The basic meaning of *aisthēsis*, it seems to me, (iv) refers to awareness in general. Awareness is the defining mark of perception—it is what differentiates the perceptual effects of physical objects from the nonperceptual effects. When heat affects a perceiving creature, this means that the creature becomes *aware* of heat, not merely that it becomes hot. These four meanings are asymmetrically nested within one another: the unspecified activity of the perceptual part of the soul includes sensation, perception of the common and incidental perceptibles, and awareness. Awareness in general includes awareness of special, common, and incidental perceptibles, and perception of the common and incidental perceptibles includes the perception of special perceptibles.

That *aisthēsis* has a broad sense does not render my thesis that perception plays an essential role in ethical reasoning moot: even though it is not mere sensation at work in the sophisticated apprehension of particulars as objects of certain kinds, it is still the activity of the perceptual, not intellectual, powers. Of the narrow and broad meanings, only the first is infallible—perception in the broad sense may be erroneous (*De anima* 418a11–16, 425b3, 428a11–15, 428b22–25). One cannot be deceived about yellow, but one may be deceived that the yellow has this certain magnitude, or that the yellow is a sunflower. In other words, the simple perception of seeing yellow cannot be wrong, but the various complex perceptions such as seeing that the yellow is a sunflower (425b3) or that the yellow is over there (418a16) may contain error. Furthermore, in the *Nicomachean Ethics*, Aristotle points out that one's attention will be swayed by the pleasure one takes in one's activities: "when we take intense delight in anything whatever, we hardly do anything else; and when the satisfaction we receive from some things is mild, we turn to other things—for example, those who eat sweets in the theaters do so especially when the actors are poor" (1175b10–13). Feeling pleasure and pain are perceptual activities (*De anima* 431a11–12), to which Aristotle here links attention (*prosecheia*) (*Nic. Eth.* 1175b4), which suggests that not only may one be in error about where or what a thing is, but also one may simply not be aware of something in the first place. The possibility of perceptual error makes it important that the perceptual part of the soul be in a good condition if one is to act well.

In the chapters that follow, I will argue that bringing the perceptual part of the soul into harmony with the intellectual part is a condition of living a virtuous life. What this means, I will argue, is that the perceptual part of the soul must become subordinate to the intellectual part, such that one perceives in accordance with what one thinks and knows. Concretely, this means that one must come to be able to perceive the present particulars of one's circumstances as calling for action, and as calling for action in light of one's conception of the good life. It will become clear how the points established here are important for this argument in the course of it. Generally speaking, however, the account I will go on to give concerning the role of perception in ethical life requires that perception be a robust and complex faculty, a faculty not limited to the reception of shapes and colors (etc.), but one that is able to perceive particulars with respect to ethical concerns. For example, for Neoptolemus to act virtuously with respect to Philoctetes, he must perceive Philoctetes as one suffering injustice, and that this injustice ought to be remedied to whatever degree possible. The points established here help establish that perception is just such a robust capacity. Including the perception of incidental perceptibles as genuine objects of perception already goes a long way to establishing that this sort of ethical perception is possible—Neoptolemus can certainly perceive Philoctetes. Moreover, that *phantasia* extends the temporal horizons of perception makes it possible to say that Neoptolemus perceives Philoctetes as a particular calling for action. Just as the heat may invoke the *phantasia* of refreshing water that serves as the aim of action, so too, seeing Philoctetes in distress may invoke a *phantasia* of a happy person that serves as the aim of action. As I will show in what follows, this will not be a perception divorced from intellect, but one that is informed by it, making human perception properly developed an intellectually informed perception.

CHAPTER 2

Human Perception

In Aristotle's ethics, the good is always realized in the present, particular circumstances; being good and doing good deeds is not a matter of applying universal ethical laws to particular circumstances well, but rather discerning and acting according to the good as it emerges in one's particular circumstance. In some circumstances, for example, it is good to use fatal violence, in some circumstances it is bad to help a friend—and it is up to the person of virtuous character to discern this.

Insofar as perception is the means whereby a person has access to the particular, Aristotle's ethics ought to give perception a central role both in ethical reasoning and in virtuous character.[1] Yet Aristotle does not fully account for or explain the role of perception in his ethical works, nor does his primary account of perception in *De anima* neatly fit into an account of ethics. In *De anima*, perception is of special objects—sight perceives color, hearing sound, and so on—and of common perceptibles—motion, rest, number, magnitude, shape; but the perception that the virtuous character must employ is of a unique and meaningful situation in which she must enact the good. We saw in the last chapter that incidental perceptibles are indeed genuine objects of perception, which greatly enlarges the contents of perception.[2] However, incidental perceptibles are common to both human and nonhuman animals, whereas ethics is a uniquely human sphere. The challenge that we are presented with, then, is one of accounting for ethical perception, that is, answering the question of what makes it possible to *perceive* a situation as a site in which to realize the good and moreover to *discern* the good in it.[3] Insofar as humans are the only ethical creatures, this is tantamount to asking, "What is human perception?"

That there is particularly human perception distinct from the perception of nonrational animals, and that this kind of perception is not adequately explained in the *De anima* account of perception, is suggested by an ambiguity in the way that Aristotle treats of perception elsewhere in his corpus. In *De anima* Aristotle treats *nous* and *aisthēsis* as distinct parts of the soul with distinct objects and distinct powers, yet elsewhere he undermines or blurs this distinction. Explicitly, Aristotle takes perception to be a nonrational faculty whose object is the particular, whereas intellect or thought is that which grasps the universal;[4] these powers are treated as different functions that are the operations of different parts of the soul.[5] Yet, (perhaps most notoriously) in *Posterior Analytics* II.19 Aristotle remarks, "although you perceive [*aisthanesthai*] the particular, perception [*aisthēsis*] is of the universal" (100b1).[6] In the *Nicomachean Ethics* there is a similar confluence of perception and intellect:

> Moreover, intellect is concerned with the ultimate things in both directions, for [what grasps] both the first defining boundaries and the ultimate particulars is intellect and not reason. That is, on the one hand, intellect pertaining to demonstrations grasps the unchanging first defining boundaries; on the other hand, intellect in matters of action grasps also the ultimate particular thing that admits of being otherwise, that is, the minor premise. For these ultimate particulars are principles [*archai*] of that for the sake of which one acts: the universals arise from the particulars. Of these, then, one must have a perception [*aisthēsis*], and this perception is intellect. (*Nic. Eth.* 1143a36–b6)[7]

Similarly, *Metaphysics* VII.10 1036a5 reads: "of these [concrete individuals] there is no definition, but they are known by the aid of *noēsis* or *aisthēsis*."[8] Even within *De anima* itself Aristotle admits ambiguity with regard to the rationality of perception: in III.9, in the context of raising the question of what constitutes a part of the soul, he notes that the perceptive capacity (*to aisthētikon*) "could not easily be set down as either irrational or rational" (432a31).

There is a related ambiguity in the general way in which Aristotle uses *aisthēsis* throughout the *Nicomachean Ethics*, where he appears to operate with an assumed distinction between animal perception and human perception.[9] On the one hand, Aristotle uses the term *aisthēsis* (and its variations) to describe the faculty that defines animals and that humans share only in virtue of their animal nature, that is, as a strictly nonrational faculty.[10] Indeed, perception first appears on the scene as definitive of the life of a nonhuman animal in *contrast* to the life of the human (1098a1–5).[11] On the other hand, Aristotle often treats perception as a cognitive activity that human beings employ in uniquely human ways; for example, twice Aristotle remarks that the discernment (*krisis*) of what is blameworthy is in the perception (*aisthēsis*)[12] (*Nic. Eth.* 1109b24, 1126b4).[13]

These surprising passages seem to indicate that, rather than operating independently of intellect and being unaffected by it, the operation of perception is nearly aligned with the operation of *nous*. This suggests that an account of human perception should take into account its relationship to the other parts of the soul of which it too is a part (and especially its relation to intellect), that is, in the context of the whole soul. Indeed, as I will argue, that the parts of the soul are mutually informing and mutually operational follows from Aristotle's account of the unity of the soul (*Metaphysics* 1023b26–34, 1040b6–15; *De anima* 411a24–b14, 416a6–9) and the separability of its parts (*De anima* 413b11–414a1). The strategy for discovering an account of human perception would therefore be to begin by treating the whole human soul.

The course of my argument will be as follows: in the first section, I will address the composition of the soul in general, showing the soul to be a whole that is prior to its parts in the sense that the parts would cease to be what they are outside of the context of the whole. I will argue that this is consistent with Aristotle's view that the parts of the soul are separable only in *logos*, as opposed to separable in place or magnitude, and further that it is confirmed in Aristotle's designation of the lower parts of the soul as being in the higher one in potentiality. I will interpret this to mean that the lower faculties of soul depend for their operation on the presence and operationality of the higher, defining, part of the soul. In the second section, I will address the relationship of perception and intellect in the human soul. Here I will argue that the dependency of perception on intellect takes the form of perception being always already informed by intellect, that it is a noetic perception.[14]

Specifically, I will argue that the character of human perceptual experience is oriented by the nonperspectival nature of intellect such that human perception always maintains a horizon of indeterminate possibility. In some ways, this position is similar to the one that Modrak espouses, when she addresses the question of the relationship between perceptual and intellectual faculties. She argues, "There is a single continuum of cognitive activity, and the line between perception and intellection is difficult to fix,"[15] and concludes that the noetic faculty and the perceptual faculty, while having distinct objects, are integrated insofar as both faculties represent the same object, and the noetic faculty comes to realize its object by abstracting particularities from the perceptible particulars. Insofar as the perceptual object is the substratum for the intellectual object, the perceptual faculty is the material cause of the noetic faculty. "Thinking is the actualization of a *noēton*, the material substratum of which is a *phantasma* . . . the relation between faculties [mirrors] the relation between their objects. While formally distinct from the perceptual faculty, the noetic faculty is the perceptual faculty differently disposed in the sense that the latter is its material cause."[16] Without disagreeing with this conclusion, I will take a stronger position on the relationship between the faculties. I will argue that not only does the noetic faculty *employ* the perceptual, but also the perceptual faculty is informed in its very operation by the presence of the noetic capacity. This difference emerges as a result of distinct ways of approaching the problem—where I begin by considering the soul as a whole, Modrak begins by considering the parts of the soul. In the next chapter, I will address how the relationship between intellect and perception constitutes the ground for ethical development.

1. The Unity of the Soul

Aristotle's *De anima* is an analytic treatise: in it, Aristotle singles out and treats of the parts of the soul as abstracted from the whole soul and in isolation from the other parts of soul. Yet the role of perception in ethical life requires that the parts of the human soul be examined in their connectedness and interaction. This is somewhat of a departure from the usual way of approaching *De anima*, which more frequently examines particular functions or particular features of Aristotle's account.[17] However, Aristotle himself treats of the connection between faculties of intellect and of perception at important junctures of his corpus, and such a unity is implied by the structure of the soul that Aristotle himself lays out in *De anima*. I will therefore begin by investigating the structure and unity of the soul. Setting forth Aristotle's position on the structure and unity of the soul will set the stage for the discussion of the relations of the parts of the human soul. In this section, I will argue first, drawing on passages from the *Metaphysics*, that the soul is a natural, continuous unity, and further, that this is reflected in Aristotle's conclusion in *De anima* that the parts of the soul are separable only in *logos*, not in place or in magnitude. Finally, I will argue that this particular structure implies that the operations of the parts of the soul are not independent; rather, the whole soul is implicated in the operation of each part, or in other words the operation of each part requires the presence and operationality of the others.[18]

The Whole Is Not the Sum of Its Parts

To begin with, it is clear that, methodologically speaking, Aristotle does not think that the whole soul is equivalent merely to the sum of its parts. He first raises the question of the composition of the soul in *De anima* I.1, asking whether the soul is divisible or without parts (402b1). If the answer to this is the former, as Aristotle decides it in a certain respect is, a related methodological question follows: "And further, if there are not several souls but rather parts of soul, there is a question whether it is necessary to seek the whole soul or the parts *first*" (402b9, my emphasis).[19] With this question, Aristotle may be suggesting that there is a distinction between the account of the whole soul and the account of its parts. At the very least, the question acknowledges that there is a question of the distinction between accounts of the parts and an account of the unified whole.[20]

Although Aristotle explicitly decides the compositional question in *De anima* II.2 (deciding that the soul has parts divisible in *logos*), and he implicitly answers the methodological question by proceeding to give an account of the parts of the soul in what follows, he leaves unsaid whether this account of the parts suffices as an account of the whole. However, that the soul is a complex whole that is not reducible to its parts, and that therefore their accounts would not be the same, is evident from Aristotle's discussion of parts and wholes in *Metaphysics* V.25–26 and VII (especially 10–12, 16–17) and *De anima* II.1–3.

Metaphysics V.26 distinguishes three ways a thing is said to be a whole (*holon*), the second of which secures a strong unity that applies to the soul. Aristotle first identifies the two minimal conditions that a thing must attain in order to be a whole: first, that it not be missing any of its natural parts (1023b26), and second, that the whole contain the things it contains in such a manner that they form a unity (*hen*) (1023b27). Both conditions are necessary for a thing to be a whole: if only the second applied, the whole would be incomplete and therefore not a whole. If only the first applied, we would have a mere heap or pile, and we would not want to claim that a heap of working car parts (for example) would be just as much a whole as a working car. Rather, a whole must have all its components and those components must be brought together in a particular way, a way that is not determined by the parts but by the whole. The car parts do not determine their relationship to one another; on the contrary, they are brought together in a certain relationship because they must be in that relationship if the car as a whole is to function. The whole is the organizing principle of the relationship of parts.

Aristotle further identifies two senses in which the components can be brought together such that they form a whole, either as a collection of items sharing something essential in common or as a unity in the stronger sense of one single thing:

> For (a) that which is true of a whole class and is said to hold good as a whole (which implies that it is a kind of whole) is true of a

> whole in the sense that it contains many things by being predicated of each, and by all of them, e.g., man, horse, god, being severally one single thing, because all are living things. But (b) the continuous and limited is a whole, when it is a unity consisting of several parts, especially if they are present only potentially, but failing this, even if they are present actually. (*Met.* 1023b28–34)

The difference between the first and the second sense of unity here rests on whether or not the parts of the whole are separable and independent wholes themselves, or whether they are parts in the stronger sense of being dependent upon the whole of which they are parts. In the first case, what instantiates the whole "living things"—concrete individual gods, horses, and people—are themselves wholes composed of body parts and soul parts, and they are separable and independent in the sense that the whole "living things" would remain a complete whole regardless of whether or not a particular individual is present in it. In the second case, however, the parts are not independent and separable in this manner. If anything were to be removed from the continuous and limited unity, the unity would either be destroyed or rendered incomplete, and the thing removed would not be able to stand on its own. For example, a hand is a part of the body in this second sense: if it is separated from the body, it is no longer a hand, except equivocally (*Met.* 1035b25), and the body without a hand is said to be missing something.[21]

It is this second, stronger sense of the whole as a unity that applies to the soul, as indicated in the *Metaphysics* and confirmed in *De anima*. In *Metaphysics* VII.16 Aristotle remarks:

> Evidently, even of the things that are thought to be substances, most are only potencies [*dunameis*]—both the parts of animals (for none of them exists separately; and when they *are* separated, then too they exist, all of them, merely as matter) and earth and fire and air; for none of them is a unity, but as it were a mere heap, till they are worked up and some unity is made out of them. One might most readily suppose the parts of living things *and the parts of the soul* nearly related to them to turn out to be both, i.e., existent in complete reality [*entelecheia*] as well as in potency [*dunamis*], because they have sources of movement in something in their joints; for which reason some animals live when divided. *Yet all parts must exist only potentially* [dunamis], *when they are one and continuous by nature.* (*Met.* 1040b6–15, my emphasis)

This passage clearly suggests that the soul is a strong unity and that its parts are inseparable from the whole. The parts of the soul are not independent pieces that happen to be joined together into one soul; they are rather like the parts of the body that need to be organized into a whole in order to truly be the parts that they are.[22] Parts of a natural, continuous unity are dependent upon the whole in the sense that they receive their character and definition from the whole of which they are parts; the parts receive their form, so to speak, from the whole. If separated from the whole, the parts cease to be what they are, just as a hand is not a hand (except equivocally) when separated from the body. The same is perhaps more obviously the case with the parts of the soul: there *is* no perception apart from a perceptual or intellectual soul—perception is nothing outside of a soul. The parts of the soul are not separable from the whole, in the way, say, a Scrabble tile is separable from its Scrabble game. Moreover, both this passage and the previous one describe the parts as in *dunamis*, existing potentially within the whole, which is how Aristotle describes the parts of the soul at *De anima* II.3 414b30. (I will address this claim in a later section.)

The Incompleteness of the Parts

This inseparability of the parts from the whole is confirmed and specified in *De anima* II.2, where Aristotle argues that the capacities of soul are not many souls within one living creature, but rather parts of a single soul (413b11–414a1), and that these parts are separable only in *logos*, as opposed to separable in place or magnitude. After laying out the powers of soul and their order of necessity (the nutritive power is necessary for all living things, some living things have perception in addition, and few have also intellect [413a35–b13]),[23] Aristotle raises the question of whether each of these "is a soul or a part of soul, and if a part, whether it is such as to be separable only in definition [*logos*] or also in place" (413b14–16).[24] Coming as this does on the heels of a discussion about the increasing complexity of kinds of souls—that the plant has nutrition alone, while all animals have perception in addition—one expects Aristotle to mean that the plant is the clear case where a power of soul is a whole soul. But instead Aristotle offers this explanation:

> For, just as in the case of plants, some clearly live when divided and separated from each other, the soul in them being actually one in actuality in each plant, though potentially many, so we see this happening also in other varieties of soul in the case of insects when they are cut in two; for each of the parts has perception and motion

> with respect to place, and if it has perception, also imagination and appetite. (*De anima* 413b17–23)

What this evidence shows is that the soul maintains its complexity even when the living thing of which it *is* the soul is divided—each part of the severed insect has a perceptive soul. The parts of the soul are thus determined by the whole of which the powers *are* parts: it is because the insect has a perceptive soul that it has the capabilities of motion, perception, imagination, and appetite.[25] If this were not the case, the parts should be separable in such a way that one part of the severed critter could just be a nutritive soul, the other part just having the power of perception, for example. But this way of dividing the soul is not possible precisely because the whole is prior to and determinative of the parts.[26]

I take this kind of inseparability of the parts and priority of the whole to imply that the soul *operates* as a whole: separability in *logos* does not imply separability in actual function; it only shows that the parts of the soul are *definitionally* independent.[27] Some examples of kinds of parts will help make this point. A wheel is a necessary part of a bicycle—without the wheel, the bicycle would cease to be a bicycle (at best it would be a unicycle, but more likely it would just be a deficient bicycle, and a bicycle only equivocally). But the wheel does not cease being a wheel when it is separated from the bicycle—it still rolls, embodies its definition, and maintains its capacity as a wheel; it is merely rendered a temporarily inactive wheel, and one that could be made active in a number of different contexts. In this example, the part of the whole is in a real sense *complete* on its own; being a part of a particular whole does not endow it with completeness.

A second way of being a part of a whole is the way a word is a part of a sentence. Here, too, the word is a necessary part of the sentence, but it is not complete on its own in the way that the wheel is. The word garners meaning from the whole sentence of which it is a part: a word takes on a number of senses and nuances and associations depending on the sentence it is in. The ordinary verb "run," for example, has a very different sense when it is found in a sentence about elections than when it is in a sentence about a well-oiled machine than when it is in a sentence about the Olympic games. The incompleteness of the part is perhaps even more evident in living organisms: a part of a living organism, such as a hand, will not be a hand if severed from the body;[28] a blood cell will die if outside the living body.[29] In a very real sense, the word is *incomplete* when it is separated from the particular whole of which it is a part.[30]

In both of these examples (wheels, "run"), the parts are separable in *logos*—each has a definition that does not include reference to the whole or to other parts of the whole. Independence in *logos*, then, does not by itself achieve a completeness or independence of the parts. Further, the definition of "run" by itself does not determine whether it signifies the movement of a machine, a candidate, or an athlete. In a sense, the verb "run" exists only abstractly outside of concrete whole sentences, despite being separable in *logos*. Even more so is this true of the parts of the soul: there are *no* instances of animals living without perception or without the nutritive capacity. Just as the word, on the one hand, can only fully do its work within the context of a working sentence as a whole, and on the other hand, the full work of the sentence requires the intertwined operation of all of its parts, so too the parts of the soul are only fully operational in the context of the life of the organism, and also the parts work together to constitute the life of the organism. Just as the *Metaphysics* passages suggest, then, the parts of the soul are not independent items grouped together within a whole; if they were, we would have to say either that they were many souls or that they were separable in place, but Aristotle refutes both of these characterizations. The nutritive capacity and the intellectual capacity are separable *simpliciter* from other capacities of soul, as is evident by the fact that they *do* exist separately in the plant soul, on the one hand, and in the divine, on the other. But this does not mean that the nutritive or intellectual *parts* are separable *simpliciter*, only that these capacities as *kinds* of soul are separable. A person in a vegetative state, one whose nutritive power has been separated from her perceptive and intellectual powers, cannot survive without artificial support. The nutritive part of her soul is not sufficient when separated to maintain life, which shows that it is not separable *simpliciter*. Similarly, a person could not live by her intellect alone.

In sum, then, the composition of the soul is such that the whole is prior to the parts and the parts are what they are only within the context of the whole; and this means that the parts do not operate independently but as a function of the soul as a whole. A consequence of this conclusion is that the account of the parts of the soul given in *De anima* is not identical to the account of a whole soul, human or otherwise.[31] It is the whole that determines the parts, and the particular whole of which the parts *are* parts will influence the manner in which the parts operate.[32]

The Potentiality of the Parts

That the parts of the soul operate differently according to the kind of whole of which they are a part is confirmed by Aristotle's explanation of the inadequacy of the most common account of soul to account for any actual soul in *De anima* II.3. Here Aristotle seems to commit himself to the position that the account of the parts of the soul is not identical to the account of the whole soul, and further, to commit himself to *giving* accounts of each kind of soul (plant, animal, human) (see *De anima* I.1 402b5–9). After giving the *koinotatos* account of the soul as the first actuality of a natural, organized body in II.1,[33] Aristotle makes a new beginning, where he identifies *living* as the distinguishing mark of ensouled beings (413a21) and continues to articulate the various manifestations of life (intellect, perception, locomotion, nourishment) and their hierarchical sequence (the capacity for nourishment is necessary for all living things, some living things have perception in addition, others have intellect on top of that [II.2]).[34] In II.3, Aristotle infers from the variety of kinds of living beings that it is necessary to advance beyond the general account of soul (the hylomorphic account given in II.1) and to supplement it with accounts of "what is the soul of each thing, what is that of a plant, and what is that of a human or a beast" (414b32–33). Here Aristotle appears to promise accounts of *kinds* of soul (that is, of whole souls) which, as he has just remarked, are constituted by different configurations of parts. We have already established that the account of the parts ought to be supplemented by an account of the whole, and indeed Aristotle goes on to indicate that the relationship between the parts of the soul is not one of indifference to the other parts. To put it otherwise, the parts of the soul are not merely externally joined to one another, as if they were independent and separable parts; rather, they exhibit an intrinsic relation to one another.[35]

In order to explain the inadequacy of the general account of soul to capture the specificity of each kind of soul Aristotle introduces an analogy with geometrical figures, and with this analogy, Aristotle reveals that the structure of the soul is not a mere conjunction of parts. Rather, Aristotle remarks that, with regard to ensouled beings just as with regard to geometrical figures, the soul that is higher in the sequence holds within it the previous soul *potentially* (*dunamis*). Aristotle explains that in the same way that the triangle is in the quadrilateral, so too is the nutritive (*threptikon*) in the perceptive (*aisthētikon*) (*De anima* 414b29–32).[36] This analogy begs for interpretation, but at the very least it indicates that, say, the plant soul will not be identical to the nutritive part of the animal soul: the *threptikon* is in the mode of *potentiality* in the animal soul, and this distinguishes it from the plant soul.[37] Nor, we may infer, are the parts of the soul on equal footing—the soul, it seems, is characterized primarily by the higher capacity, and the lower capacity ought to be understood in light of that primacy. The soul is *not* constituted by a conjunction of independent parts; rather, it seems that the parts are understood with reference to a governing power that serves as an organizing principle, as the nutritive soul is *in potentiality* with regard to the perceptive soul.[38] More importantly, by designating the parts of the soul that are lower in the hierarchy as present *potentially* in the higher kinds of soul, Aristotle provides us with a clue regarding the relationship between the parts. If we can interpret the nature of this potentiality, we will be better able to construct an account of the human soul in its complexity.[39]

As a guiding idea, let us consider the relationship between the triangle and the quadrilateral. The triangle is in the quadrilateral potentially because, although the quadrilateral is logically independent of—its definition makes no reference to—the triangle, it is a feature of the quadrilateral that it can be construed as being made up of two triangles. Said otherwise, the quadrilateral can be divided, in *logos*, in a particular way such that two triangles will emerge. Aristotle often describes the parts of mathematical objects this way. In *Metaphysics* VII.6, for example, he uses such language to illustrate the concept of actuality (*energeia*): Hermes is potentially in the block of wood and the half line is potentially in the whole line because it can be separated out (*aphairesthai*) (1048a34). But the triangles are not essentially constitutive of the quadrilateral; to be a quadrilateral is not primarily to be made up of two triangles, and this means that the triangles are not in the quadrilateral in full actuality.[40] Analogously, a substantial change is required to bring either Hermes or the half line into actuality: a block of wood is no longer a block of wood once it is a statue of Hermes. To bring the triangles (or the half lines, or Hermes) into actuality would be to reverse the order of priority, dissolving the quadrilateral into a composite of two triangles. Aristotle nearly says as much in *Metaphysics* VII.10: "For even if the line when divided passes away into its halves, or the man into bones and muscles and flesh, it does not follow that they are composed of these as parts of their essence [*ousia*], but rather as matter [*hulē*]; and these are parts of the concrete thing [*sunolou*], but not also of the form [*eidos*]" (1035a17–22). I say *nearly* says as much because, insofar as the triangles are forms of the same order as the quadrilaterals—both triangles and quadrilaterals are figures in their own right—it would not be accurate to say that they are in potentiality in the whole in the way that matter is potentially in the composite. When triangles are separated in place or magnitude, the whole in the sense of the form, rather than in the sense of the composite, would no longer be the whole that it is; but nonetheless the triangles can be singled out in *logos*.

From the figure-soul analogy we may infer that the nutritive soul is in the perceptive soul potentially in the same way that the triangle is potentially in the quadrilateral, that is, insofar as it can be logically, definitionally, singled out within the perceptive soul. Indeed, the case is stronger with regard to the structure of the soul because it is impossible to separate out the parts in magnitude or in place, whereas one can separate in place two triangles out of the concrete quadrilateral. As a result, even though the body, which is the matter of which the soul is the form, can be divided in place, the soul nonetheless remains whole (in some cases). The perceptive soul can *in logos* be divided into a perceptive part and a nutritive part, but in actuality and essentially it is primarily a perceptive *whole*.[41]

The analogy suggests that were a nutritive soul to be fully active as a part of the perceptive soul, the perceptive soul would be reduced to its parts. The question of the sense in which the nutritive soul is in the perceptive in potentiality thus turns on the difference between the nutritive *kind* of soul and the nutritive *part* of soul. What is in some cases a kind of soul is in other cases a part. The nutritive capacity is both a plant soul and a part of the animal soul, and the intellectual capacity is both a divine soul and a part of the human soul. Of course, these will be the same insofar as in both cases they accomplish the same activities—the nutritive capacity and the plant soul both accomplish nutrition and growth. However, there must be *some* difference, for otherwise the animal soul would be a plant soul plus an animal soul, and Aristotle recognizes this difference by calling the nutritive *potentially* in the perceptive soul.

What is potential about the nutritive soul that renders it appropriate to be a part of the perceptive soul? It is perhaps tempting to think that the nutritive soul would emerge were the perceptive part, somehow, to be damaged, just as a triangle would emerge were the quadrilateral really to be cut in half along the diagonal. But this is not the case with souls; as Aristotle notes, an animal *must* have the sense of touch if it is to live at all (*De anima* 413b5–7). If the sense of touch is destroyed, so is the animal (435b2–12). Likewise, a person who loses her brain functioning is not able to survive without artificial support. The nutritive soul does not emerge when the whole is severed, in contrast to the way that geometrical figures emerge. Yet this reflection provides a clue for understanding this relation of potentiality. The difference between one kind of soul and that kind as a part of a different kind of soul is in its directive capacity or lack of it: the *kind* of soul is self-sufficient, but when that kind is a part of another soul it is no longer sufficient to supply the life of the animal. The nutritive soul is all that is necessary for plant life to sustain itself, but the nutritive part of the animal soul is not sufficient to sustain the life of the animal. The higher capacity of the soul is the organizing and unifying principle of the soul of the organism, that which first of all explains its life (see 413b1–2).

This suggestion is borne out by Aristotle's analysis of the sense of touch. Touch, he says, is the most necessary sense, that without which the animal would not be an animal, nor would it be able to survive. And touch is the appetitive sense—it is the sense that produces the desire for food and for drink. Aristotle even goes so far as to say in *De sensu* that flavor—a perceptible object—is an affection of the nutritive part of the soul (436b17–18). The nutritive function, when it constitutes the whole plant soul, is indeed sufficient for life—it needs no other capacity in order to do its work. But as soon as perception is introduced, it no longer does its work independently: it requires the desiring animal to provide it with the means to do its work. The nutritive capacity becomes subordinate to the perceptive capacity, depending upon it to do its work.[42] The sense in which the nutritive is in the perceptive only potentially is that it requires the activity of the perceptive being in order to bring *it* into activity. Hunger becomes a precondition of the activity of the nutritive activity, and hunger is, indeed, an activity of the perceptive part of the soul.

My conclusion is that a part of a soul is in potentiality in the sense that it is not self-sufficient, but is instead guided by the higher capacity, just as the nutritive function requires that the animal perceive its hunger and its food before the nutritive function can do its work of digestion. To say it otherwise, the nutritive function is now for the sake of a creature whose life surpasses the minimal life of reproduction, growth, and decay. But this claim must be qualified, because this analysis seems at first glance only to apply to *some* aspects of the nutritive capacity. The animal needs to perceive and desire food in order to provide the material for the nutritive capacity to move into activity, but all the while the animal's heart is beating, its blood is circulating, and so on. There are plenty of automatic processes that are functions of the nutritive soul that seem *not* to depend upon the higher capacities and possibilities of the animal. Further, if the heart were to cease its beating, the animal would perish—the dependency seems to be reversed.

Still, such dependency does not contradict my conclusion about the structure of the soul, although it does complicate it. These independent, automatic nutritive processes function independently at times but still exist for the sake of the life of the organism, which life cannot be reduced to these processes.[43] Their independence is not entire, but rather circumscribed by this grander life that they are in service of: these processes will themselves cease and go awry if the animal fails to eat, for example. Their independence is thus limited: they are independent processes only for the time being. Thus, even though there is a kind of mutual dependency within the structure of the soul—on the one hand, the nutritive functions depend on the perceptive, but on the other hand, without these automatic nutritive functions there is no living animal at all—nonetheless the primary dependency is of the nutritive faculty on the perceptive soul. The higher faculty of soul is the organizing principle of the parts of the soul; the functions of the parts, even if some occur without the input of the higher faculty, are for the sake of a life that exceeds these functions.

2. Noetic Perception

The geometrical analogy *should* extend to include the intellectual soul, that is, the human soul, but as we shall see, the case of the human soul is more complicated. Aristotle notes that "in the former case [of figures] there is no figure over and above the triangle and the others which follow it in order, nor in the latter case [of souls] is there soul over and above these mentioned" (*De anima* 414b21), suggesting that the subsequent comments about the succession of figures/souls applies to all of them. If the analogy could simply extend, we should find that human perception in some way relies on intellect in order to function, just as the nutritive power relies on the animal's perception and desire to provide it with the opportunity to work. The life of the animal would not be possible in the absence of the perceptive power, and so similarly the life of the human should not be possible without the intellectual capacity. However, one aspect of Aristotle's account of *nous* presents a difficulty for this simple extension of the analogy: in general, intellect differs from perception and nutrition insofar as it must be cultivated or developed in order to be used well. Unlike perception, the first actuality of knowledge must be developed through learning (417b17–19, 417a23–b2), which does not occur just of its own accord or by nature (*Nic. Eth.* 1103a1–3). If it were the case that a person *could* live without developing these capacities of intellect, it would not make sense to say that the perceptual soul is importantly incomplete in that particular person's soul—this person is indeed living by means of perception. Aristotle notes at the end of the chapter on *phantasia* (*De anima* III.3) that "because imaginings persist and are similar to perceptions, animals do many things in accord with them, some because they lack intellect, viz. beasts, and others because their intellect is sometimes obscured by passion, disease, or sleep, viz. humans" (429a5–9). Because *phantasia* is a function of the perceptive part,[44] this implies that, contrary to the necessity of perception for the animal to live at all, the human *is* able to live when her intelligence is either temporarily disabled or, perhaps, not developed at all.[45] Moreover, Aristotle tells us more than once that thinking requires and cannot occur without perception and *phantasia* (431a14–18, 432a8–9), which seems to suggest that intellect rather relies on perception for its operation. If this is the case, we need to develop a different account of the way that the perceptive soul is in the intellectual soul in potentiality.

This difficulty is a consequence of the strange dual nature of human beings: humans are *zōon logon echon*, "animals having reason." We are animals, but with a godlike capacity to reason and think. This is precisely what makes us ethical beings: on the one hand, we *can* and often *do* live by perception alone. But on the other hand, we *can* and *should* develop ourselves through habit to become virtuous—to reason well and choose well—or to become a scientist, a legal expert, a philosopher, or a trivia champion; that is, to become the people who know things of various kinds. The question, then, is whether we maintain our animal natures within or underneath the knowers we become.[46] This is just another way of asking whether and how the perceptual faculty is qualitatively altered by virtue of being within the intellectual soul. Let us, then, assume a fully developed intellectual soul and ask: what does the perceptual power look like within this soul? I will argue in what follows that perception is always already informed by *nous*, whether or not *nous* happens to be active at the moment of perception, by situating perception within a nonperspectival context.[47] The result is that human perceptual experience is characterized by an ambiguity or indeterminacy: the object of perception is perceived as a site of multiple possibilities.

Animal Perception

To Aristotle's mind, perception provides the animal's original cognitive access to the material objects around it. As opposed to plants, which are *simply* affected by material things—they *become* warm by the sun or cold in the snow (*De anima* 424a34–b2)—the animal also *encounters* material objects by virtue of perception being a mean or a ratio (424a23–25). Perception is a power that discriminates (*krinein*) (e.g., 424a6, 432a16), that is, that has access to things that are other than it and *as* other than it.[48] Encountering the perceptible object as other is inherent to the mechanism of perceiving. To perceive, Aristotle tells us, is for the sense organ (and the sense power) to be moved from the mean state by the perceptible object.[49] "For this reason," Aristotle says, "we do not perceive what is as hot or cold, or hard or soft, as we are, but what exceeds us, since the sense is a kind of mean between the contrary attributes in the things perceived. In virtue of this it discriminates the things perceived, for the mean has the discriminating power, since it comes to be either of the two extremes in relation to the other" (424a3–7).[50] The perceptive power discriminates perceptible objects by keeping track, so to speak, of its own original condition, that is, the mean, as it is moved toward one or another extreme by receiving the perceptible form of the object. Insofar as it holds onto its own original condition while being altered, the perceptive power is able to *distinguish* between itself and what is other than it, the perceptible, material, object.[51]

Importantly, the animal's encounters with material objects are not neutral; rather, the animal encounters objects as pleasurable or painful, to be pursued or avoided. Aristotle tells us repeatedly that the power of perception is necessarily accompanied by pleasure and pain, and therefore desire (*orexis*), appetite (*epithumia*), and imagination (*phantasia*), and also spiritedness (*thumos*) and wishing (*boulēsis*) (*De anima* 413b23–25, 414b2–3, 414b4–7, 434a2). Aristotle identifies being pleased or pained with desiring (*orexis*) or fleeing, and he defines being pleased or pained as "to be active [*to energein*] with the perceptive mean towards the good or bad as such" (431a11–12). He explains that perceiving things as pleasant or painful is necessary if the animal is to survive: without perceiving the object as pleasant or painful, the animal would not discern what it should flee and what it should pursue, what endangers its life and what supports it.[52] As Aristotle remarks, "since the animal is an ensouled body, and every body is tangible, and it is that which is perceptible by touch which is tangible, the body of an animal must also be capable of touch, if the animal is going to preserve itself . . . anything which touches things will be unable, if it does not have perception, to avoid some of them and take others. If that is so, it will be impossible for the animal to preserve itself" (434b12–17). A contrast with plant life is illuminating here: the plant does not have the power to perceive, and neither does it need to—it is physically constituted to absorb those things that support its life (nutrients, photons, etc.).[53] Animals, however, have perception, and since "nature neither does anything in vain and never fails in anything that is necessary" (432b21–22), they need *not* be physically constituted to accept only what is good for them. Perception takes over that function, as it must if nature does nothing in vain. In other words, if an animal has perception, perception must play an essential and not extraneous role in its life (because nature does nothing in vain), and being (merely) physically constituted in the way that a plant is would render perception superfluous.[54] It is thus necessary that perception perceive things as pleasant or painful, that is, as good or bad for the perceiving animal. It is here, in the perception of an object as pleasurable or painful, as the reason to flee or pursue, that perception opens itself up to the intellect.

The Possibility of Resituating Perception

Implicit in the discussion of pursuit and avoidance made possible by the perception of pleasure and pain is the animal's capacity for locomotion. In his discussion of locomotion, which directly succeeds the discussion of perception and intellect,[55] Aristotle considers and rejects the possibility that the nutritive, perceptive, or intellectual part of the soul is the source of locomotion. The nutritive part is rejected because nonlocomotive creatures like plants would then have the capacity for locomotion; the perceptive part is similarly rejected because there exist nonlocomotive animals; and the reasoning part or intellect is rejected because (a) theoretical intellect does not contemplate anything to do with action, and (b) in the case of unrestrained people, desires produce acts that are contrary to reason (*De anima* 432b15–433a6). On the other hand, Aristotle continues, desire (*orexis*) cannot be the source of locomotion, since the restrained person *will* act according to reason but contrary to desire (433a6–9). Nevertheless, Aristotle concludes that *to orektikon*, the faculty of desire, is the source of locomotion, because it is shared in common by both *nous* and *epithumia* (433a21–23). Aristotle explains further that ultimately it is the *object* of desire (*to orekton*) that, by arousing desire (433b12), causes motion and that "[the object of desire] is either the good or the apparent good [*to phainomenon agathon*], and not every good, but the good as contained in action [*prakton agathon*]" (433a29–30).[56] Aristotle then explains that desires come into conflict with one another

> when reason [*logos*] and appetites [*epithumia*] are opposed and it takes place in creatures that have perception [*aisthēsis*] of time (for the intellect [*nous*] bids us to resist on account of the future, while the appetite bids us to act on account of what is immediate, since what is immediately pleasant appears [*phainetai*] to be both simply pleasant and simply good, on account of not looking to the future). (*De anima* 433b5–10)

The object of desire (the *orekton*) engages *orexis*,[57] *either* in relation to *nous* and *logos or* in relation to *epithumia*, which motivates the animal to move. The present object, say, a piece of chocolate cake, may be desired epithumetically but resisted rationally, depending on whether the object is engaged perceptually or rationally. But even the rational engagement with the chocolate cake is an engagement with *this* chocolate cake; the rational resistance to the chocolate cake is to a perceptible object taken up rationally. The conflict of desires, then, shows that the perceptible object, that is, what one perceives as pleasurable, can *either* engage the rationally desiderative aspect of the noetic part of the soul *or* the appetitive aspect of the perceptive part, and that when it engages the appetitive, it engages it as the merely *apparent* good.[58] Thus it seems that in the discussion of motion Aristotle has opened up the possibility that the faculty of perception come under the provenance of the noetic faculty in the possible perception of what truly *is* good in the realm of action.

Resituating Perception

Aristotle describes an intimate relationship between perception and intellect in the course of his discussion of intellect in *De anima* III.4–8, both on the side of the faculties of soul and on the side of their objects. Indeed, Aristotle ventures forth into the discussion of the intellect with perception as his guide: he bases his understanding of the mechanism of intellect on the mechanism of perception, deciding that both are receptive of the forms of their objects (424a17, 429a15–16), although not in the same way (429a30–32). Unfortunately, the passage wherein Aristotle most directly addresses the relationship between the perceptive and the intellectual power is rather cryptic. Nonetheless, the passage reveals the way in which the intellect informs the perceptive soul. Specifically, it reveals that the intellect situates perception within a nonperspectival framework—intellect enables the perceiver to see beyond the limitations of her private perspective. An animal is restricted to perceiving things as they directly bear on its survival—as pleasant or painful. This is what I mean by perspectival: the animal is bound to perceive relative to its desires and needs. People do this too, of course, but they are not *bound* to do it. People can distinguish between what appears good to them and what *is* good; that is, people can perceive *either* in a way that is relative only to their own desires and needs *or* in a way that involves other factors. Their perceptual framework is nonperspectival. Thus, just as the power of perception expands the horizons of life in comparison with the nutritive life—the animal is able to pursue what it desires—so too the intellect expands the horizons of life in comparison with the perceptive life—the human person need not be irremediably bound to pursue what merely *appears* good *to her*, but is free to pursue what is truly good (see 431a10, 433a29).

The passage in *De anima* III reads in full:

> Since a magnitude and what it is to be a magnitude are different, and water and what it is to be water (and so too for many other things, but not for all; for in some cases they are the same), we discern what it is to be flesh and flesh itself either by means of something different or by the same thing differently disposed. For flesh does not exist apart from matter, but like the snub it is this in that. It is, then, with the power of perception that we discern the hot and the cold and those things of which flesh is a certain proportion [*logos*]. But it is by something else, either something distinct or something that is to the former as a bent line is related to itself when straightened out, that we discern what it is to be flesh. Again, in the case of those things which exist in abstraction,

> the straight corresponds to the snub, for it involves extension; but "what it is for it to be what it was," if what it is to be straight and the straight are different, is something else—let it be duality. We discern it, then, by something different or by the same thing differently disposed. In general, then, as things are distinct from matter, so it is too with what concerns intellect. (*De anima* 429b11–23)[59]

Here Aristotle addresses two kinds of objects, one that is by definition material (flesh), and one that is abstracted from its materiality but is nonetheless composite (straightness). Aristotle tells us that it is perception that grasps flesh (the material composite) and that the faculty that grasps the being-flesh is a different one, *either* separate from perception *or* related to perception as a straight line is to itself when bent. It is clear from the context, embedded as this passage is in the discussion of the nature of the intellectual activity, that Aristotle intends us to understand that it is the intellect that grasps the being of things. (This is further confirmed by Aristotle's later remarks that the intelligible object is in the perceptible objects, *De anima* 430a5, 432a5). But not much else is clear about this opaque passage: first, what *is* the relationship between a line as straight and that same line as bent, and how might this illustrate the relationship between two faculties of soul? Second, how are we to take the disjunction? Does Aristotle mean to leave open both possibilities, to decide later whether the capacity of intellect to grasp the being of flesh is separate from perception or like perception straightened out? Or does he mean the disjunction to be inclusive, indicating that in *some* cases the intellect is separate, and in others it is straightened-out perception? Aristotle seems to consider intellect to be closely related to perception, but he does not clearly spell out this relationship. However, more than this can be concluded from this passage when one considers the remarks that precede this passage and Aristotle's claim that the material object is potentially intelligible.[60]

Immediately prior to this passage, Aristotle draws a distinction between the manner in which the intellect receives its objects, and the manner in which the perceptive power receives its objects. He argues that if the intellect is to be able to think all things it must be unmixed, having no other nature than potency, and therefore cannot be mixed with body, "since it would come to be of a certain kind, either cold or hot" (*De anima* 429a25), which would interfere with it becoming all things in thinking them. Aristotle continues by drawing a contrast between the manner in which excessively perceptible objects yield no perception and that in which excessively intelligible things aid in the thinking of lesser intelligible things (429a30–b6). This contrast refers back to Aristotle's discussion in II.12 of the destruction of the sense by extreme perceptible objects—sight is blinded by the extremely bright, hearing is deafened by the extremely loud, and so on (424a29–b3). The explanation of this relies on his designation of sense as a mean (*mesotēs*) (424al–7) and a ratio (*logos*) (424a32) of perceptible qualities (for example, the sense of touch is a ratio of hot-cold, hard-soft, etc.). The perceptive power *senses*, is aware of, the perceptible qualities by virtue of discriminating the change the sense undergoes from its mean state. For example, the frying pan is perceived to be hot not in itself but relative to the resting temperature of the hand.[61] The sense is destroyed, then, when the perceptible object exceeds the variation that the sense power can distinguish, when the sense can no longer hold on to both the mean state and the variation from it. Regardless of the details of this explanation, with this contrast Aristotle has put the reader in mind of the manner in which perception is always relative to the perceiver: perceiving always implies a perspective, a mean of perception by which it senses the difference. Without this, there would be no perception; instead, one would be just like the plant, which is affected by heat but does not perceive it (424a34–b3).[62]

By contrast, the faculty that distinguishes the being-flesh, the intellect, is not subject to an analogous destruction by an exceedingly intelligible object precisely because it is nonbodily. (Throughout *De anima*, Aristotle keeps open the possibility that the intellect is a special case—related to the body in a special way, separable in a special way.)[63] But this contrast turns out not to be simply between bodily and nonbodily powers. Because it is insofar as perception is bodily that it is perspectival—that is, as a mean that serves as a standard for discriminating, for example, hot (increasing temperature relative to the mean) or cold (decreasing temperature relative to the mean)—the contrast is both between what is bodily and nonbodily *and* between what is perspectival and nonperspectival. For example (one that Aristotle gives in another context), we perceive the sun to be the size of a quarter, but we *know* it to be much larger than the earth: our perception reflects our position with respect to the thing under consideration, while our knowledge is not constrained in the same manner. Distinguishing the being-flesh, or the being-water or the being-straightness, is precisely to surpass the limits of one's own perspective and to get at what the particular thing in front of a perceiving subject *really is*.[64]

This is an intuitive way of understanding the way that intellect stands to perception both as separate and as a bent line that has been straightened. On the one hand, the absence of body explains why we would take the capacity of intellect that grasps the being of something material to be a separate faculty: insofar as intellect is nonbodily, it must be separate from bodily perception. On the other hand, it is nonetheless the being *of* a material thing that is being grasped, and this provides the basis for understanding the intellectual grasp of the being of flesh to be related to the faculty of perception as perception straightened out—it is perception without the constraints of the body.[65] If this is the right way to take the meaning of the separation or straight-bent relation of intellect to perception, then we can easily take the disjunct to be inclusive: the faculty that grasps the being is *both* a separate faculty *and* the same faculty straightened out, depending on which aspect of intellect one is focusing on.

But it should be noted that what the intellect grasps over and above what perception grasps is in a specific sense not a separate *object*. Aristotle considers the material object that is perceived to be potentially intelligible (*De anima* 430a7), and "the intelligible objects [*ta noēta*] are in the perceptible forms" (432a5). Understanding the being-flesh, the intelligible object, gives one a better understanding not only of being-flesh independent of this flesh here, given to a subject in her limited perspective through perception, but *also* of this flesh here that you perceive. So the intellect surpasses what perception provides, but it does so in such a way that it reshapes the perceptible object itself: the perception is swept up in the new noetic understanding, such that the perceiver perceives, from within her perspective, the way the perceptible object exceeds or is independent of that perspective. *Nous* thus guides perception beyond itself while also maintaining it. And so, for example, when one perceives the sun, or better, a house in the distance, perception *strictly speaking* tells one that it is small. But one's *experience* of the house in the distance is not as small—one's perceptual experience takes into account the distance between oneself and the house and one knows it to be large.

This resituation of perception within a nonperspectival context is not something that occurs only sometimes—rather, perception is always already informed by intellect, whether or not intellect happens to be actively contemplating at the moment one perceives. What distinguishes human perception from animal perception, and the form that the impression of the intellect takes on the perceptual faculty, is that human perception is structured by an ambiguity or flexibility in the perceived objects. Animals perceive their objects as objects of desire or repulsion, simply and abidingly—the character that their perception takes is unquestioning; what they perceive could not be otherwise. For example, my cat always runs from the sound of the broom and any similar sound, not because the broom is a threat to her, but because it is the same sound as, for example, a snake in the grass, a predator. Her perceptual scheme is not flexible enough to imagine a different meaning for that sound. By contrast, human perception always has a horizon of possibility, even if one is not thinking of those possibilities at the moment of perception. For example, when I see a tree I see it *as* a tree, but I also see it as a shade giver, or a jungle gym for children, or paper, or a fruit bearer, or an object of inquiry. I may not actively think of any of these possibilities, but my experience of the tree includes its flexibility. Human perceptual experience is informed by the freedom from private concerns that the intellect makes possible; in the tree I see not only *my* possibilities with respect to it, but also the possibilities that other people have with respect to it and the possibilities the object itself shows, independent of any particular perspective on it (as, for example, a photosynthesizing organism or a home for birds).[66]

This characterization of human perception is reflected in Aristotle's distinction between perceptual and deliberative *phantasia*. Aristotle determines that *phantasia* is "that in virtue of which we say that an image occurs to us" (*De anima* 428a1), being "a movement taking place as a result of actual perception" (429a1). It is in general the power of maintaining and producing images derived from perception, and it is a power that both human beings and (some) animals share. In both cases, *phantasia* provides the creature with some distance and freedom from her immediate perceptual environment: rather than being constrained to desire and pursue the things in her immediate environment, the animal is able to conceive a desire for an absent object and seek after it through the image it has of the desired object (in the case of nonrational animals: 429a5–7, 433a10–21;[67] in the case of humans: 431b2–5).[68] Aristotle introduces the distinction between deliberative (or rational)[69] and perceptual *phantasia* at 433b30, at the conclusion of the argument that the object of desire is the origin of motion, and he elaborates on the meaning of deliberative *phantasia* in his following chapter. "Perceptual *phantasia*, as we have said, is found in the other animals also, but that concerned with deliberative *phantasia* in those which are capable of reasoning (for the decision whether to do this or that is already a task for reasoning; and one must measure by a single standard; for one pursues what is superior; hence one has the ability to make one image out of many)" (434a6–10). Here we see the openness in *phantasia*—and therefore in the perceptual faculty of which *phantasia* is a function—by which the question of what is "better" arises. Nonrational animals cannot choose between different courses of action based on what is better because the manner in which they perceive is not open to the flexibility that such a choice requires. If the things perceived have only one meaning—pursuit or flight—then there is no question of whether or how it is best to pursue or flee.

This understanding of perceptual experience answers the problem that the human is seemingly not dependent on intellectual powers for her life, while the animal *is* dependent on the perceptual powers for *its* life. The dependency of the perceptual capacity on the intellectual capacity is not such that human life could not persist without the activity of the intellect, but rather that the form that human perception takes always relies on the possibilities provided by the intellectual capacity. Nonetheless, the perceptual power can still be said to be within the intellectual soul *potentially* because the very nature of the perceptual freedom that characterizes perception is that it is to be realized by thinking about and deciding upon certain possibilities. It is an act of intellect actually to deliberate, and in deliberating the perception of the object's possibilities is brought to completion.

A Note concerning the Relationship between Intellect and Perception

Before concluding this chapter, I would like to clarify precisely what I take the relationship between the faculty of perception and the faculty of intellect to be. It is uncontroversial, I take it, to claim that there *is* a unique relationship between these two faculties: for example, in *De anima* Aristotle remarks that mortal beings with intellect cannot think without employing *phantasia* (431a14–17). But this relationship as I see it has two registers: in a straightforward way, the operations of intellect can be *applied* to perception, as when one brings to bear on a work of art categories like "expressionism," or the objects of perception can inform the work of thinking, as when one looks at a drawing of a triangle when demonstrating the Pythagorean theorem. But this is not the only or even the most significant way that the two faculties are related. There is rather a deeper connection that I have been developing: that perception is qualitatively altered just by virtue of being a part of an intellectual soul. So when I say that human perception is minimally determined and that it is the work of *nous* to decide upon the possibilities of perception, I do not mean to say that intellect applies its categories to the raw data of sense perception. When I see a tree, I *see* a tree: it does not require the application of the concept "tree" by the intellect to the sensory data in order to recognize the tree. Nevertheless, the manner in which a person sees the tree differs from the manner in which a bird sees the tree insofar as the tree is the site of multiple significances for the person. The presence of intellect marks the difference between the way that a nonhuman animal engages with its world and the way a human engages with her world, where the human has more freedom to influence such an engagement through her ways of being than the nonhuman animal does—but it is still a *perceptual* engagement. I see the tree—the tree presents itself to me—*as* a pretty shade giver, primarily, but an entomologist will see the tree *as* a home for ticks. Neither I nor the entomologist apply different categories to the visual presentation of the tree; rather, the tree speaks to us in different ways. In a similar way, a social situation, such as a party, will feel exciting for an extrovert or a source of anxiety for an introvert. Aristotle articulates the general principle that the way that things appear to one is partly determined by one's subjective state in the *Nicomachean Ethics*, where he argues that things appear differently to virtuous and to nonvirtuous people (III.4), and that those with experience *see* rightly (VI.11 1143b13–14).

I have been appealing to the immediacy and variety of the significances of the things we encounter in our experience to support the claim that these significances are made possible by intellect but are nevertheless perceived. This is not uncontroversial, nor is it uncontroversially Aristotle's position. Kahn, for example, writes, "It is only in the case of *human* perception, enriched by the conceptual resources provided by its marriage with *nous*, that Aristotle can speak of us as *perceiving a man*. If we were restricted to the reception of sensible forms, all we could perceive would be colors and shapes."[70] Modrak, on the other hand, argues that such things as men or the son of Diares are indeed objects of perception and that they are apprehended through the common sense faculty.[71] What is at the heart of the disagreement is the question of how to interpret what Aristotle means by perceiving incidentally (*kata sumbebēkos*).[72] I argued in the previous chapter that there is no reason to exclude the incidental perceptibles from the operations of perception, that they are indeed perceived. Here I would like to adduce some additional considerations that will help make clear the relationship between intellect and perception with respect to the incidental perceptibles.

Kahn argues that these incidental perceptibles cannot, strictly speaking, be apprehended through perception because these incidental perceptibles either are or essentially invoke universal categories, and perception can only access the particular.[73] He writes: "What is not always noted by commentators is that the incidental perceptibles represent the overlap or conjoined action of sense and intellect. 'The son of Diares' is already a *noēton*, a complex conception involving notions of human being and fatherhood . . . Sensation *per se* cannot recognize even individual substances as such, since it has no access to any sortal concepts like *man, horse, tree*."[74] However, Kahn's statement that the operations of perception are restricted to the apprehension of the special and common perceptibles is problematic. In the first place, if one takes Kahn's restriction seriously, it becomes difficult to explain why Aristotle insists on introducing such things as sons and trees as incidental *perceptibles*, and why he introduces them alongside the more straightforward objects of perception. In the second place, the perceptual part of the soul is responsible for many operations that are not strictly acts of sensing, namely imagination (*phantasia*), memory, dreams, and reflexive awareness, pleasure and pain, and it is inseparable from such things as appetite, desire, fleeing and pursuing.[75] Given the multitude of powers and the sophistication of those powers that Aristotle attributes to the perceptual capacity, it seems arbitrary to limit perception to its special objects.[76]

Moreover, nonhuman animals must also perceive incidental perceptibles if they are to be able to respond appropriately to predators and to prey—the hawk, for example, must not only perceive a small patch of color moving around below him, but also see it *as* potential food. The as-structure of this perception indicates that it is an instance of an incidental perceptible. Moreover, this information (that the moving patch of color is food) is not inherent to the special or common perceptibles, nor does it act directly on the sensory organs. But Aristotle designates perception as the faculty by which the animal directs its behavior, pursuing some things and avoiding others (III.12); the apprehension of the food must be a perceptual activity. Kahn recognizes this problem, noting that designating the incidental perceptibles *noēta* creates "a major problem for the interpretation of animal perception. Clearly animals need to 'make sense' of their perceptions. Do they have something corresponding to sortal classifications like *man, dog*, or *my master, my sibling*? Aristotle has apparently nothing to say on this question except that, lacking *logos*, animals cannot have *our* way of understanding what they perceive. The 'incidental sensibles' for animals must be interpreted quite differently."[77] While it is true that animal perception must be understood differently than human perception due to their lack of intellect, this difference does not require that the incidental perceptibles, in the case of human perception, not be apprehended by perception at all. This is only necessary if one understands the incidental perceptibles to be *articulated* wholes, that is, concepts. But the incidental perceptibles need not be understood this way. Even a reflection upon human experience reveals that concepts are not necessarily invoked in one's interactions with sensible objects—when one walks through a door while talking with a friend, one does not necessarily perceive the door as "door," but rather as to-be-opened.[78] (On the other hand, if one is itching to get out of an uncomfortable situation, one may be able to think about nothing else than that the thing over there is a door and an escape!)

I propose, then, that incidental perceptibles be understood, primarily, as the externalization of one's own possibilities in the world, as supported by the concrete objects that make up those possibilities. This way of understanding the incidental perceptibles resolves the problem of animal perception while maintaining a real difference between animal and human perception because the possibilities of humans and animals differ precisely due to *nous*.

So my cat perceives my chair as a scratching post (although of course she could not call it that), and I perceive my chair as a seat—site of scratching and site of sitting are the incidental perceptibles (even if she is not actually scratching it and I am not actually sitting). My cat's perception, however, is limited to that possibility (and possibly one or two others). The object of my perception, however, exhibits an indefinite number of possibilities, including being an object of thought and an instance of "chair." And insofar as the rational capacities are the defining feature of human beings, it is the possibility of realizing these that most of all characterizes human perception.

This understanding of the incidental perceptibles allows perceptual objects to be the bearers of significances, and allows that some of those significances be brought to bear upon a perception by the activity of *nous*. The understanding and naming of the common sensible "site of sitting" as a "chair" are operations of *nous* and *logos*. But it also, importantly for our ethical lives, opens up the possibility that our noetic habits congeal in our perceptions and shape them. I need not think about what a chair is in order to immediately recognize and name what I see in front of me a chair; on the other side, if I lack a concept for or experience of, say, guns, I will not see what is in front of me *as* a gun, but as an oddly shaped metal thing that can be used as a paperweight. In this way we can understand the relationship between the operations of perception and the operations of *nous* to be fluid, where *nous* can shape perception in a strong sense of allowing it to apprehend perceptible objects in a sophisticated way.

Conclusion

In summary, I have argued that an account of any kind of soul—plant, animal, or human—must take into account the complexity and dynamic relationship of its parts, because of the manner in which the whole is prior to the parts of the soul. The parts of the soul are intrinsically related to one another, I argued further, due to their incompleteness outside of the context of a particular kind of soul. The operations of any part of the soul depend upon the presence and operationality of the other parts of soul; Aristotle expresses this relation of dependency by saying that the lower parts of the soul are in the higher part potentially. This dependency relation is easily seen in the case of the animal soul: the operations of the nutritive part of the soul primarily depend upon the operations of the perceptive faculty, especially the sense of touch. The dependency of the faculty of perception on the intellectual faculty in the human soul is more complicated because the human can live by the faculty of perception alone, which implies that perception does not depend upon intellect to operate. I answered this difficulty by arguing that, in a soul with a fully developed intellectual capacity, perception is dependent upon intellect in the sense that intellect reshapes and resituates it in a nonperspectival context, allowing the intellect to inform perception through the establishment of sophisticated incidental perceptibles.

This answer to the difficulty of the relationship between perception and intellect within the human soul is only a partial one. This answer assumed a fully formed intellect in a good relationship to perception. The next chapter will remove these assumptions, and address the development of the relationship between intellect and perception within a person's soul. For the most part, this will take us outside of the context of *De anima* and into the *Nicomachean Ethics*. I will argue that by virtue of the unique separability that Aristotle attributes to *nous*, the human soul is, in an important sense, *not* naturally whole, as in general the structure of soul is, but rather dual: the human soul is a perceptive soul with the additional capacity for thinking and intellect, rather than being a fully integrated noetic soul. I will argue, however, that it is this natural duality that provides the condition for ethical life and ethical development. The first section will address the strange case of the human soul, outlining the ways in which the human soul fails to achieve this natural unity. The second section will explain how this natural lack of unity constitutes the condition for ethical life and ethical development, and the third section will confirm that the nonvirtuous person suffers from a nonintegrated soul through a discussion of the phenomenon of *akrasia*. In the fourth chapter I will give an account of *phronēsis* as intellectual perception, showing the integration of intellect and perception in the soul of the virtuous person.

CHAPTER 3

The Duality of the Human Soul

In the preceding chapter we encountered a problem with our interpretation of the structure of the soul as a continuous, unified whole. The perceptual part of the soul seemed not to be potentially (*dunamis*) in the intellectual soul in a way that upheld this structure. As a first step in resolving this problem, I developed an account of human perception that shows its intimate relationship with intellect: meaningful wholes that are incidentally perceived are reflections of the perceiver's active possibilities with respect to that object, and among the possibilities that are native to human beings are the possibilities of contemplating, thinking, and understanding. Human perception, as a result, is open to the determination of intellect: it is possible to perceive in a manner that transcends the idiosyncrasies of one's personal perspective.

But this is only the first part of the solution. It shows that perception is structured by intellect, and that it is therefore *possible* for one's perception to come under the guidance of intellect; but this solution does not show that perceptual experience is *actually* informed by intellect. The phenomenon of *akrasia*, "lack of self-restraint," attests that it is possible for one to act in pursuit of a perceived pleasure (being driven, as an animal is, by appetite) in spite of one's (intellectual) knowledge. The basic relationship between intellect and perception thus upholds the unity of the soul to a certain degree—the whole determines the parts in the sense that human perception is qualitatively altered by virtue of being in an intellectual soul—but it does not yet guarantee the actual harmony of function of the perceptual and the intellectual parts of the soul, as the phenomenon of *akrasia* shows.

In this chapter, I will address the unique structure of the human soul and show how it forms the basis for ethical development. I will revisit the relationship between intellect and perception, this time covering in detail Aristotle's claim that intellect is separable. I will argue that the separability of intellect is the cause of the duality of human nature as the rational animal: human beings are not simply natural, that is, not simply animal, insofar as nature does not fully govern a person's development, yet neither are human beings fully actualized gods. This duality is due to the presence of an intellect that is not naturally integrated with the rest of the soul. Overcoming this duality and achieving a "natural" integration of the parts of the soul, I will argue, is the psychological side to the project of ethical development. The possibility of such integration has been established by my interpretation of human perception as characterized by intellectual possibilities. My aim in this chapter is to show that it is the character of perception as loosely determined in its relation to intellect that provides the psychological ground for ethical development.

My argument will proceed as follows. I will begin by developing the idea that human nature is dual: animal and rational, natural but not simply natural. I will then address the issue of the separability of intellect, and argue that intellect is *in itself* unrelated to any particularities of an individual thinker, and that therefore it does not naturally bear upon the desires and perceptions upon which one acts. (The issue of the separability of intellect requires a lengthy discussion of the vexed passage of *De anima* III.5.) Once this is established, I will turn to the *Nicomachean Ethics* to show that bringing these two elements of one's soul—the perceptual and intellectual—into harmony is the task of ethical development, and I will confirm this with an interpretation of Aristotle's account of *akrasia*.

1. Neither by Nature nor Contrary to Nature

In *Metaphysics* VII.7 Aristotle introduces a distinction between two kinds of form (*eidos*) that will be relevant for understanding the unique structure of the human soul. In the context of distinguishing between things that come to be by nature (*phusis*) and things that come to be by art (*technē*), Aristotle identifies a difference in the mode of transmission of the form of the generated thing. In both natural becomings and artful becomings, that by which the generated thing comes about is the form (*eidos*). But in the case of natural becoming, on the one hand, the form is transmitted by one who embodies the same form, as, for example, a person begets a person or a collie gives birth to a collie. On the other hand, in the case of artful becoming, the form is transmitted by one of another kind, namely, an artisan, a knower, that is, a human being (1023a24–25, 1032b1). In this latter case, "the form [*eidos*] is in the soul of the artist" (1032b1), but the artist herself does not embody the form.[1] This distinction between modes of coming to be highlights two ways of "having" a form: in the natural case, the animal (for example) has the form in the sense of *being* the form,[2] and indeed the very transmission of the form through reproduction is governed *by* that form. As Aristotle notes in *De anima*, "since it is right to call all things after their end, and the end [of the nutritive soul] is to generate something like itself, the first kind of soul will be that which can generate something like itself" (416b23–25)[3] (and the soul is the form of the living thing [412a19–21]). Similarly, in *De generatione animalium* II.3, Aristotle remarks: "For, e.g., an animal does not become at the same time an animal and a man or a horse or any other particular animal. For the end is developed last, and the peculiar character of the species is the end of the generation of each individual" (736b2–4).[4] By contrast, the artist "has" the form of the artifact *not* in the sense of *being* it (except insofar as she *is* an artist—but this, Aristotle would say, is incidental to her in the way that being musical is incidental to Socrates [*Met.* VII.6 1031a19–21]); rather, she has the form in the sense of *knowing* it and being able to bring it about through her thought and activity (*Met.* 1032b15–17). Further, what the artisan gives rise to does not have a life of its own, that is, its form is not self-sustaining.[5] In a certain sense, the form of the artificial product *remains* in the artist insofar as the maintenance of the artifact is a part of that art (or a related art). For example, both the arts of shipbuilding and ship maintenance are required for a ship to be serviceable as a ship, that is, to *be* a ship. The difference in the two modes of transmission of the form identified here thus reflects a difference in the *kind* of form that is being transmitted: a natural form and an artificial form. The natural form differs from the artificial one insofar as the natural form determines not only what the being is at a given moment, but also how the being will develop over time—it is the soul of the natural being that governs its development from a seed to a fully formed adult (*De anima* II.1 412b25–27); while the artificial form, by contrast, requires the continued input by those who have the form in their souls.

The soul is, of course, paradigmatically a natural form. In *De anima* II.1 Aristotle argues that the soul is the form of the natural body that has life potentially (412a19–21).[6] The soul governs the activities of life: thinking, perceiving, moving, nourishing, growing and decaying (413a22–25); moreover, these activities of the soul *constitute* the life and development of the living thing.[7] In the absence of interference, the plant simply *will* ingest from the soil the appropriate amount of water and nutrients and thereby grow, and the animal cannot *help* but perceive color when its eyes are open in the daylight, all by virtue of the soul. Aristotle expresses this idea in *Metaphysics* IX.5, where he argues that nonrational potentialities only produce one effect, and must be brought into activity in the presence of its object. The plant soul, being a nonrational potentiality, is subject to this description. The perceptive part of the soul is not simply nonrational, but in its basic capacities for seeing color, hearing sound, and so on, it is passive and reliant on its object in a similar manner (*De anima* 417b16–23). Living things "have" their form in the sense of *being* their form.

Human souls are already unique insofar as humans are the only living things that have artifice, but more importantly the form of the human being is *not* naturally brought to fruition, insofar as the form of the human is virtue.[8] The oak seed will become a fully formed oak tree by nature, given enough sunlight and rain and fertile soil, but whereas humans are born with the capacity for perception already formed (*De anima* 417b16–18), "we do not by nature become good or bad" (*Nic. Eth.* 1106a9–10). Neither are there external conditions that can guarantee the development of virtuous habits. As Plato has Socrates note in *Meno*, virtuous people do not always or necessarily produce virtuous children. The human being will only become a fully formed adult *animal* by nature, having an adult body and the natural capacities of nutrition and perception; the human does not naturally come to fruition *as* human, because neither the intellectual virtues nor the virtues of character by nature are accomplished by nature (*Nic. Eth.* 1103a14–26). The human soul is therefore uniquely ambiguous: it is natural insofar as a human being is an *animal*, the life of which is defined and governed by the perceptive capacity, but it is not *simply* natural—and indeed it resembles an artificial form—insofar as its virtue is not brought about by nature. The human seemingly "has" her form ambiguously: she both has her form in the sense of *being* it, but she also *has* her form in the sense of being able to produce virtue in herself, analogously, perhaps, to the way a doctor has the form of health in her soul and is able to bring it about in herself and others through art. The human both *is* her form and also needs to generate her form through something like art.[9] The human form is ambiguously natural, and this ambiguity describes a dual nature: the rational (on the one hand) animal (on the other).

2. The Separability of Intellect

This duality that characterizes the human soul is grounded in the particular structure of the human soul and specifically in the strange separability of the intellectual part of the soul. This is already suggested by the fact that the *having* of the form in the soul is made possible by intellect. As Aristotle says, "Those who say, then, that the soul is a place of forms speak well, except that it is not the whole soul but that which can think, and it is not actually [*entelecheia*] but potentially the forms" (*De anima* 429a27–29).[10] More to the point, Aristotle treats intellect in *De anima* both as the part of the soul that is "most divine" (see also *Nic. Eth.* 1177b30–31) and also as an ordinary part of the soul.[11] On the one hand, intellect is merely a capacity that certain mortal, embodied creatures have which, in a certain sense, is not any different in form from the activities of the other parts of soul. Nutrition, perception, and intellection are all (increasingly sophisticated) ways of engaging with the objects in the world. Plants absorb nutrients and sunlight in such a way that they grow, realizing at the same time the possibility of the nutrients and sunlight to be food and their own plantlike possibility to grow (*De anima* 416b10). Animals receive the perceptible form in such a way that they can navigate their environments according to their perceived best interest (431a9–14), all the while realizing both the potentiality of the perceptible objects to be perceived and their own perceptual potentialities (426a8–26).[12] Similarly, humans receive the intelligible form in such a way that they can engage their world through art (*technē*) and contemplation (*theōria*), all the while realizing the potentially intelligible and their intellectual potentialities (429b29–430a9). From this perspective, intellect is not any more mysterious or special than nutrition or perception. Yet, on the other hand, intellect must be a special capacity because its objects are eternal and unchanging, and contemplation is identical with its object. Intellect therefore *is* in some sense eternal.[13]

In a word, the problem is this: Aristotle considers intellect to be somehow *divine*, yet somehow to be still a part of the *mortal* soul. All living things yearn for "the everlasting and divine" (*De anima* 415a29), and while most achieve this only indirectly, through reproduction (415b2–7), those mortals who have intellect have a unique way of partaking in what is always and is divine: they can know it and contemplate it.[14] The problem is to understand how intellect can be *both* an element of an individual human soul *and* capable of partaking in what is eternal; or to put it otherwise, how the human being can be both merely natural and yet exceed the natural limits of finite creatures in its communion with the divine. As Jonathan Lear observes, "It seems part of man's nature to transcend nature: to organize his soul into a shape which would not arise by nature."[15] This problem comes down to a question about the separability of the intellect: as merely a part of a mortal soul, it should be separable only the way the parts are separable from each other, that is, in account but not in place or *simpliciter*. As somehow eternal, intellect should be separable "as the everlasting from the perishable" (413b26).

In what sense, then, is intellect separable? It should be noted at the outset that there are two issues of separability here: separability from the body and separability from the rest of the soul. These two issues are closely related: if intellect is separable from the body, it will also be separable from the other parts of the soul, which are not separable from the body.[16] I will address the issue of separability from the body first and afterward consider the implications of the separability from the rest of the soul.

At the heart of the problem that intellect poses for Aristotle's account of soul is the principle that the nature of the parts of the soul is determined by their objects. Aristotle introduces the features of intellect by means of an analogy with perception: as what perceives is to perceptible objects, so too intellect is to intelligible objects (*De anima* 429a17–18): it is impassive but receptive of form and potentially such as the form is (429a15–16). But this very analogy reveals a disanalogy: unlike perceptible objects, which are specific materially constituted objects, the objects of thought include all things (429a18), and so intellect cannot be under bodily constraints the way perception is (429a20–21); therefore intellect is unmixed with body (429a24–25) and separable (429b5), and its nature is nothing other than potential (429a21–22), which means that it is nothing in actuality before it thinks (429a24).[17]

The limit of the analogy with perception speaks to the heart of the problem of interpreting intellect: what distinguishes *nous* from perception is the nature of its object, and it is the object that determines the nature of the part. But intelligible objects are not *simply* part of the (material) natural world—intellect thinks all things, including the nature of souls, animals, trees, and also the Pythagorean theorem and the unmoved mover. Because of the principle that the capacities of soul are defined by their objects, the variety of objects seems to imply different things about how intellect is related to materiality: in the case of becoming identical in thought with the unmoved mover, it seems that intellect must be separable *simpliciter* from body, but in the case of contemplating the essence of a deer, it cannot be utterly separate from body. Aristotle recognizes something like this ambiguity, when discussing what faculty it is that discerns the being of flesh, water, and the straight (*De anima* 429b10–22). The conclusion he reaches is that "in general, then, as things are separable from matter, so it is too with what concerns intellect" (429b21–22).

In what follows, I will address, first of all, the dependency of human intellect on the body for thinking, and I will argue that this implies that human intellect is separable only in account from the body. I will then address the challenge posed to this interpretation by the discussion of intellect in *De anima* III.5. There is, of course, a great deal of controversy over whether Aristotle is introducing divine intellect in this chapter, or whether he is describing human intellect.[18] This controversy stems from a real ambiguity about the nature of thinking: it is an activity of a particular, embodied person, but by its very nature thinking is an impersonal and nonparticular activity. I do not intend (or attempt) to reinvent the wheel on this difficult subject; instead I will follow those accounts I find most insightful and persuasive. For the most part, I follow Aryeh Kosman's (1992) argument, although I will discuss positions that are in various ways similar to this position (Wedin [1988] and Gerson [2004]). I am persuaded by Kosman (1992) and Victor Caston (1999) that III.5 lays out a necessary condition for human thinking provided by divine intellect. But, as Kosman concludes, it describes divine intellect *as* related to human thinking, and so it is ambiguously describing divine intellect and human intellect.[19] It is not, I will argue, *human* intellect that is eternal and immortal when separate (430a22–23), but that which makes human thinking possible. This analysis will prepare me to conclude that human intellect is separable from the rest of the human soul only in the sense that its activity exceeds the limits posed by the body; that is, that it achieves a nonperspectival activity.[20]

Separability from Body

The question of separability peppers almost the whole of *De anima*:[21] as early as I.1, Aristotle notes that thinking (*to noein*) seems to belong to the soul alone, separable from the body (403a3–15), and as late as III.7 he wonders whether or not it is possible for something to think what is separate from material without itself being separate (from material) (431b18–19). In II.1, Aristotle argues that the soul is the form and actuality (*entelecheia*) of the body, and because it is its *entelecheia*, body and soul are one (412a11–412b9), but he reserves the possibility that this argument only applies to some parts of the soul. Intellect, for instance, cannot simply be said to be inseparable from the body by virtue of being the *entelecheia* of it because it is not the form of any part of the body: intellect has no organ (429a23–27). Aristotle concludes his argument concerning the relation of body and soul by saying:

> But just as the pupil and sight are an eye, so in this case the soul and body make up an animal. That, therefore, the soul or certain parts of it, if it is divisible, cannot be separated from the body is quite clear; for in some cases the actuality is of the parts themselves. Not that anything prevents at any rate *some* parts from being separable, because of their being actualities of no body. (*De anima* 413a2–7)

And indeed, in his discussion of intellect in *De anima* III.4, Aristotle argues that if intellect is to think all things, it must be unmixed with body (429a23–27) and separable (*chōristos*) (429b3–5). On this basis, one might conclude that intellect is separable from the body.

As the long history of scholarship attests, the issue cannot be decided so simply. *De anima* II.1 is not the first time that Aristotle has suggested that a part of the soul is separable from the body, and the reason he suggests it earlier, in I.5, is relevant for the interpretation of the separability of intellect from body. At 411b15–18, Aristotle considers an impasse:

> One may be at a loss concerning the parts of the soul, about what power each has in the body. For if the whole soul holds together the whole body, then it is fitting that each part hold together some part of the body. But this seems impossible: for it is hard even to imagine what sort of part intellect holds together, and in what way.

Despite the aporetic context, here Aristotle denies that what is true of the relation of the soul as a whole to the body as a whole is also true of the relation of parts of the soul to parts of the body. We may take him at his word here because the further argument he offers in support of this claim—that for the soul to unify the body, it need not correspond with it part to part—is one that he reiterates in his positive account of the soul, namely, that severed creatures live when divided (see *De anima* 413b17–23). It is not right, then, to infer from the soul's holding together the body that each part of the soul holds together a corresponding part of the body. This undermines the inference from the immaterial nature of the intellect to its separability, at least *simpliciter*, from the body. The soul as a whole may be inseparable from the body, even if some part of it does not directly inform some part of the body. Insofar as intellect is a part of a *soul* that is inseparable from a body, it, too, may be inseparable.

It may be objected that, in passage 413a2–7 quoted above, Aristotle does not unequivocally conclude that the soul as a whole is inseparable from the body as a whole. Rather, he concludes that *either* the soul is inseparable from the body *or* whatever parts are the actuality of some body part are inseparable, and that if there is a part of the soul that is not the actuality of some part of the body, it might be separable. More precisely, he says that nothing *prevents* such a part from being separable. Yet this is hardly an endorsement of the intellect's separability from the body; at this point, all that can be concluded is that Aristotle is holding open that possibility. This possibility appears to be forestalled later by Aristotle's insistence that mortal thinking requires the use of images (*phantasmata*) and imagination (*phantasia*) (*De anima* 431a16–17, 432a7–10). Imagination is a result of perception (428b30–429a2), and perception is a bodily process; imagination, then, is not without body, and by extension human thinking is not without body.[22] Aristotle himself offers this argument in I.1: thinking *seems* most of all to belong to the soul by itself, but if it is a kind of imagination or not without imagination, it is not able to exist without the body (403a5–10). It would seem, then, that something *does* prevent intellect from being separable from the body: its dependence upon imagination.[23]

Why does human thinking require an image? A person engaged in pure mathematics might object to Aristotle's assertion—surely, abstract mathematical thinking is only *hindered* by images. Moreover, the course of education that Plato prescribes for the philosopher in the *Republic* describes a move *away* from images to pure conceptual thinking.[24] There seem to be two ways that thinking depend upon the perceptual part of the soul, that is, on perception itself, *phantasia*, and memory. First, perception is the faculty that provides the prior "knowledge" from which first principles are learned.[25] In *Posterior Analytics* II.19, Aristotle expresses a familiar difficulty concerning the acquisition of first principles: we must acquire them, but learning seems to require prior knowledge (99b26–28). He famously responds to this difficulty by naming perception (*aisthēsis*) as the innate discriminating faculty (99b35) that offers the prior "knowledge" from which first principles are learned. Perception gives rise to memory (100a3),[26] and from many memories of the same thing a single experience emerges (100a4–6). The emergence of a single experience, insofar as it is the emergence of a one out of many, constitutes a universal "that has come to rest in the soul" (100a6–7).[27] This universal is the prior knowledge necessary for coming to know the first principles.[28] Aristotle expresses a similar thought in *De anima* III.8. In examining how it is that "the soul is in a way all existing things" either as objects of thought or of perception (431b20–24), he argues:

> Since there is no actual thing which has separate existence, apart from, as it seems, magnitudes which are the objects of perception, the objects of thought are included among the forms which are objects of perception, both those that are spoken of in abstraction and those which are dispositions and affections of objects of perception. And for this reason unless one perceived things one would not learn or understand anything. (*De anima* 432a3–8)

Perception is necessary for learning about those things that are not separable from magnitude because the object of thought is in the objects of perception (see also *De anima* 430a6–7).

By itself, the role of perception in acquiring knowledge does not secure intellect's inseparability from the body, for it does not establish that intellect *continues* to depend upon perception once it has acquired knowledge. Indeed, the universals, once learned, "are somehow in the soul itself. For this reason, it is open to us to think when we wish, but perceiving is not similarly up to us; for there must be the object of perception" (*De anima* II.5 417b23–25). But Aristotle goes further than this. The passage above continues: "and when one contemplates [*theōrein*] one must simultaneously contemplate an image; for images are like perceptions, except that they are without matter" (432a8–10). Why is it that, once one acquires the object of thought, one still cannot think it without an image? The reason that practical thinking requires an image is fairly straightforward. One always acts with regard to *specific* objects, not essences or definitions; one drinks water, not the being of water. If one is to decide how to act, that is, what to pursue and what to avoid, in the future or in general when one is not presently perceiving, one must employ images of the things with regard to which one will act. So, Aristotle says, "Perceiving, then, is like mere assertion and thought; when something is pleasant or painful, one pursues or avoids it, as it were asserting or denying . . . and that which can desire and that which can avoid are not different, either from each other or from what can perceive . . . To the thinking soul images serves as perceptions" (431a8–15).[29] The case is similar with empirical science: in the same way that perceiving is not up to us, but instead requires and depends upon the presence of an external, perceptible object, "the situation is similar with the sciences dealing with the objects of perception, and for the same reason, that the objects of perception are particular and external things" (II.5 417b25–27).

The case is less straightforward for theoretical, abstract, thinking. In what respect might contemplating, say, mathematical truths or divine mind depend upon an image? In general, what role might images/*phantasmata* play in the thinking of nonmaterial, nonparticular, theoretical matters? Commentators have offered various explanations aiming to explain how theoretical thinking is dependent upon images. Dorothea Frede argues that the function of *phantasia* with regard to abstract thought is to provide something like a Gestalt, an overall impression, within which the formal understanding of, say, the definition of a circle is situated. Without such a Gestalt, one may know the definition of a circle without being able to recognize any, which would surely be an imperfect understanding of what it is to be a circle.[30] According to Frede, Aristotle's insight is that "our thinking cannot be entirely abstract but always needs a kind of *Gestalt*"[31] and it is this that *phantasia* provides. Even more strongly, Victor Caston argues that *phantasmata* are "representations that underwrite the content of mental states," serving as the vehicle by which our mental states are *about* something.[32] Images are thus necessary quite generally, no matter what sort of thinking (practical/theoretical, discursive/simple) is under consideration. Much less strongly, abstract thinking may incidentally depend on images for the reason that images are necessary for calling to mind an object of contemplation. In *De memoria*, Aristotle argues that even memories of objects of thought are not without images (450a12–14), and furthermore that memory belongs to that to which *phantasia* belongs (450a22–25). This suggests that bringing to mind an object of thought that one has learned requires memory, and therefore an image.[33]

If it can be established that intellect depends upon the body by virtue of its dependence on images in one of the ways mentioned, what are we to make of Aristotle's claim, in *De anima* III.4, that intellect not only lacks an organ, but it is also separable (*chōristos*)? Here we must consider the sense in which intellect is separable from the body. There is already reason to doubt that intellect is separable *simpliciter*, that is, that intellect is capable of existing independently from the human body, at least insofar as intellect is a part of a *human* soul: the dependence on imagination seems to preclude this. And, indeed, at the opening of his discussion of intellect, Aristotle postpones the question of "whether this [part of the soul by which one knows and understands] is separable or not separable in place but only in *logos*" (429a11–12).[34] Aristotle's question with regard to intellect concerns only separability in place or *logos*, not separability *simpliciter*. Neither can Aristotle mean that human intellect is separable in magnitude or place—this kind of separability would require that intellect itself be bodily. Unless Aristotle is using *chōristos* loosely in this instance, he must mean that human intellect is separable from body only in account. Aristotle argues that intellect is nothing actual before it thinks, and when it thinks it is identical with its object. Its object, however, is not bodily. Even though human thinking requires images, the essence of that thinking is not imagistic: when taken in itself, the account of intellect does not involve the body. By contrast, the account of perception must include reference to the bodily organs.[35]

De anima III.5

This sort of argument concerning the separability of intellect is complicated by the endlessly vexing text of *De anima* III.5, wherein Aristotle says of intellect, "in separation it is just what it is, and this alone is immortal and eternal" (430a22–23). As is commonly noted, interpreters of this text do not even agree about what the subject is, some taking it to describe divine intellect,[36] others taking it to describe human intellect.[37] Advantages and difficulties accompany both sides: those who understand the subject to be divine intellect are freed from the need to explain how a divine nonbodily faculty is consistent with Aristotle's hylomorphic account of soul,[38] but are then taxed with the need to explain why Aristotle invokes divine intellect in a treatise concerned with *mortal* natures, seemingly out of nowhere and without calling attention to the shift in topic.[39] Those who argue that the subject of III.5 is human intellect avoid saddling Aristotle with the mysterious introduction of divine intellect, but must explain how human intellect is divine, eternal, and bodiless without undermining the unity of soul.[40] With respect to the issue of separability, if the subject of III.5 is divine intellect, we may be satisfied that human intellect is only separable from the body in *logos* and not *simpliciter*, and it is divine intellect that is separable *simpliciter*. If the subject is human intellect, that interpretation is fatally threatened.

It seems to me that III.5 is unavoidably ambiguous. Let me offer an example of the ambiguity: one good reason for taking Aristotle to be describing human intellect in *De anima* III.5 is found in the opening thought: "Just as in the whole of nature there is something which is matter to each kind of thing (and this is what is potentially all of them), while on the other hand there is something else which is their cause and is productive by producing them all . . . so there must also be these differences *in the soul* [*en tēi psuchēi*]" (430a10–14). This suggests that Aristotle's topic concerns the *soul*, not divine mind. However, Caston offers a compelling argument for reading III.5 as introducing divine mind as the final cause of human thinking, arguing that Aristotle uses "*en*" here in the sense of "in the case of" (*Physics* IV.3 210a14–24),[41] on the basis of the parallel with "in the whole of nature." According to Caston, then, Aristotle is distinguishing *kinds* of soul, not making a distinction within an *individual* soul. Gerson, who denies that the subject of III.5 is divine intellect, simply denies that this is the correct sense of "in" on the basis that "chapter five is right in the middle of the section of *De anima* that discusses thinking in the human soul and it would be extremely odd if Aristotle were here introducing divine thinking."[42] "*En*" is doubly situated: the sense of "*en*" differs if one considers it in the immediate context or in the arc of the argument as a whole, and as a result this piece of the puzzle can be positioned in different wholes, with different implications regarding its topic.

Rather than attempt to defuse the ambiguity by deciding upon one or the other of divine intellect or human intellect as the subject, I propose to let the ambiguity stand: the subject of *De anima* III.5 is ambiguously human/divine because the nature of *thinking* is ambiguously human/divine. Because intellect is the same as its object (430a3–4, 431a1, 431b17), and its object is the universal (417b22–23), *thinking* is always the same, whoever (or whatever) the subject is. Of course, this is not unqualifiedly true—human thinking requires an image (431a16–17)—but the thinking *itself*, say, thinking the Pythagorean theorem, is identical whether Euclid thinks it or Abraham Lincoln thinks it or divine intellect thinks it. In other words, it is incidental to intellect itself that it is some particular person who thinks. If we uphold the ambiguity of III.5, we may avoid the difficulties attendant on settling the issue one way or the other: we may say that human intellect does not threaten the hylomorphism of the soul because of its dependence on the body for the images that support its thinking, but that it may be described as divine and eternal by virtue of being identical to the activity of divine mind.

I am not the first person to uphold the ambiguity of *De anima* III.5 (even if the matter is not usually put this way), and my arguments follow those of Michael Wedin (1988), Aryeh Kosman (1992), and Lloyd Gerson (2004), all of whom allow (in different ways) that III.5 is concerned with *human* thinking, but that human thinking is importantly related to the divine. Wedin allows this perhaps least of all, concerned, as he is, to provide a nontranscendentalist reading of Aristotle's account of human intellect.[43] Nonetheless, he proposes two ways of reading the passages in III.5 that most strongly suggest that the subject is divine intellect (that is, those passages that describe intellect as separable, unaffected, unmixed, and its being is activity [430a17–19], and as always thinking [430a22], and as immortal and eternal when separated [*chōristheis*] [430a22–23]). On the first reading, Wedin proposes "that we relativize ascription of divine properties, counting them as indicators of the most divine thing in us, not of anything absolutely divine."[44] The divinity features describe human intellect taken in abstraction, just as the objects of mathematics, which are not separable *simpliciter* from material objects, when separated in thought are treated as if they were separate, changeless, and eternal. "Thus, just as separation in thought is what gives the objects of mathematics apparent transcendental characteristics, so also is this the ground for attribution of immortality and eternality to productive mind . . . And just as the objects of mathematics are not extensionally separate so also for productive mind."[45] On this proposal, the subject of III.5 is simply human intellect. But Wedin countenances another reading: human and divine intellect share certain general features, while also differing in certain respects, namely, in that divine intellect is immortal and eternal.[46] On this reading, divine intellect is introduced in order to *contrast* divine intellect with human intellect. (It is worth mentioning that this is similar to the line that Victor Caston takes. He remarks, "Normally, [Aristotle] eulogizes our likeness to the divine. But he also recognizes the difference and here [in III.5] he chooses to emphasize it.")[47] Wedin concludes his reading by saying: "In short, separating is something *we* do when we consider one rather than another variant of productive mind. This means, of course, that divine mind makes an appearance in *De Anima*. But it does so by way of removing itself from the sort of productive mind that's germane to the *De Anima* account. So that account remains stubbornly naturalistic."[48]

Gerson upholds the divinity of human thinking with an intriguing proposal that there is a distinction to be drawn *both* between intellect and divine intellect *and* between intellect and human soul.[49] Intellect in itself (i.e., not as a part of a composite human being) makes possible human thinking: "It is not owing to a part of the soul that soul thinks, but owing to something distinct from soul that is, however, able to function in relation to soul when soul accesses its activity."[50] This activity, intellect, that human soul has access to, is divine without being the divine mind that is God.[51] Similarly, Kosman argues that, while Aristotle is concerned with human thinking in III.5, the principle or source of human thinking, active intellect (or, as he calls it, maker mind), is both "an element in Aristotle's psychological theory, [and] an element in his theology as well."[52] Even Caston, who offers a compelling case for taking the subject of III.5 to be divine intellect, sees it as the final cause of all human thinking.[53]

Despite significant differences in their accounts of what active intellect/productive mind/maker mind *is*, in spirit it seems that Wedin, Kosman, and Gerson *agree* that the activity of human thinking is divine by virtue of its relation (in the case of Kosman and Gerson) or likeness (in the case of Wedin) to something divine (divine intellect for Kosman and possibly Wedin, intellect in itself for Gerson). It is this spirit that I follow, too.

i. The Purpose of III.5

Let me begin with some general comments about what I, following these scholars, see to be the purpose of introducing active intellect in *De anima* III.5. As Wedin, Kosman, and Gerson argue, III.5 serves to flesh out solutions to a couple of problems that Aristotle raises at the end of III.4.[54] III.4 concludes with two questions concerning thinking:

> Given that the intellect is something simple and unaffected, and that it has nothing in common with anything else, as Anaxagoras says, someone might raise these questions: how will it think, if thinking is being affected in some way? And can it itself also be thought? For either everything else will have intellect, if it can itself be thought without this being through anything else and if what can be thought is identical in form, or it will have something mixed in it which makes it capable of being thought as other things are. (*De anima* 429b22–29)

These questions arise from the designation of intellect as nothing other than potential (*De anima* 429a21–22) and nothing in actuality before it thinks

(429a24), in order to be receptive of the form, that is, the object of thought (429a15–18). Aristotle's answers to these questions are, first, that intellect is potentially such as its objects, and this makes it possible to be affected by them, and, second, that intellect is intelligible just as its objects are, for in thinking them it is identical to them, in the case of objects without matter (429b29–430a5). But this leads to a further question, that Aristotle notes but does not immediately address: why is thinking not always happening (430a5–6)? In the case of perceiving, parallel to the case of thinking, the sense is potentially such as its object and it is impassive, but the question of how it will perceive does not arise in the same manner because there is a straightforward story to tell about how the sense comes into contact with its object—both enter the same physical space under appropriate conditions. But the story is more difficult to tell with regard to intellect and *its* objects: how is it that intellect *comes* into contact with its objects, and why is it not always being in contact with them? Unlike the objects of perception, which are external, the objects of intellect are in a way *in* the soul (II.5 417b19–23). But if this is so, what is the distinction between intellect and the objects of thought such that we should speak of thinking as a kind of receptivity or being affected?

The purpose of III.5 is to probe the distinction between intellect and the objects of thought, to provide the resources for maintaining, with respect to *human* thinking, the distinction between the active intelligible object and the receptive intellect. Again, this is a distinction that is easy to maintain in the case of perception, because the power to perceive is *within* the soul, while the object that activates that power is external. III.5 ought to provide a new distinction, parallel to the internal/external distinction that maintains a difference between the human power of intellect and the objects of intellect.[55]

So, what does III.5 introduce, and how does it resolve the question of why intellect is not always thinking? III.5 opens with these lines:

> Just as in the whole of nature there is something which is matter to each kind of thing (and this is what is potentially all of them), while on the other hand there is something else which is their cause and is productive by producing them all—these being related as an art to its material—so there must also be these differences in the soul [*en tēi psuchēi*]. (*De anima* 430a10–14)

The distinction between productive and material causes is just the *sort* of distinction required if we are to explain how intellect comes into contact with what is intelligible. We might expect Aristotle to be embarking on an exposition of the relationship between the objects of intellect, as the productive cause, and intellect, as the material cause, of actual instances of thinking. This may not be exactly what Aristotle has in mind, however. The passage continues:

> And there is an intellect which is of this kind by becoming all things, and there is another which is so by producing all things, as a kind of disposition, like light, does; for in a way light too makes colors which are potential into actual colors. And this intellect is separable, unaffected, and unmixed, being in essence activity. (*De anima* 430a14–18)

Aristotle does not seem to be talking about the *objects* of intellect as the productive cause—rather, what produces all things is *intellect*. However, we may recall that the objects of intellect are in the soul, and, furthermore, Aristotle compares the relationship between active and passive intellect to that between an art and its material. As Caston argues, art—medicine, say—is productive in the sense of being the final cause of health, that which governs the bringing into being of this instance of health.[56] Similarly, we may say, active intellect is productive of all things insofar as it is a final cause (so argues Caston), and it is the final cause because it thinks (or is) the form of all intelligible objects. The distinction thus holds between the intellect that receives the intelligible object and the intelligible object: active intellect is (or is thinking) the intelligible object, and active intellect is the productive cause.

In what sense, though, is active intellect *in* the soul? If it is simply within an individual soul, we have not resolved the problem of why thinking is not always happening; but if we take it, as Caston does, to be in the *genus* soul, that is, to refer to a *kind* of soul distinct from human soul,[57] we are indeed left with an unremarked-upon switch in topic in the middle of the argument about human thinking. It is preferable to maintain the ambiguity of this "in," in a manner close to Wedin's two readings of the subject of divine attributes outlined above. It is justified to do so if we adopt the interpretation of active intellect that Kosman offers, supplemented by Caston's argument concerning the role of divine intellect in human thinking.

ii. Kosman's "What Does Maker Mind Make?"

Kosman (1992) poses the question, "What does maker mind make?" The answer that he offers develops out of a standard answer: the standard answer, based on the analogy with light, is that active intellect/maker mind makes both what is potentially intelligible and what is potential intellect (in the first sense of potentiality) into the first sense of actuality, "that is, into what is actually *able* to think and what is actually think*able*."[58] This is a straightforward way to interpret the analogy with light: just as color is potentially but not actually visible in a dark room—even if a perceiver were in the presence of color, without light color would not be seen—so the presence of light is necessary for vision, it brings what is potentially visible into actual visibility. So too on the side of the perceiver.

Kosman takes a step beyond this interpretation, noticing that Aristotle "sometimes appears to claim not that light creates *visibility*, but that it creates *vision*" (citing *De sensu* 447a11 and *De anima* 419a7).[59] He takes this to suggest that light may produce *both* transitions, from potentially visible to actually visible, and from actually visible to actually seen (and the same on the side of the perceiver). "On this view, light is a third *hexis* necessary to the activity of vision and on par with the other two [the visible object and the potential seer]."[60]

Kosman confirms and specifies this interpretation by bringing the conversation about light in *Republic* book VI to bear on Aristotle's analogy, wherein light is said to bring together the actually visible and the actual seer (507d, 508c). What this means, on Kosman's interpretation, is that "the *primary* actualization [light] effects is from first to second actuality; it is by virtue of *that* actualization that the eye is then said to have sight, and things said to be visible."[61] We may point out, in addition to Kosman's considerations, that this accords well with Aristotle's characterization of light: it is not *light* that makes a perceiver have the capacity for vision—this capacity is present from birth (417b16). It is rather that light effects the actual vision when a perceiver and color are both present. The upshot of this analogy for intellect is that active intellect is primarily responsible for bringing what is potentially known and a potential knower into an instance of *actual* thinking.

Active intellect, then, is not *simply* responsible for the acquisition of intelligible objects—this happens through some process of discovery and learning—and therefore is not *simply* responsible for bringing about the first actuality of the ability to think in a given soul. But Kosman develops a sense in which it is *mediately* responsible for the acquisition of the intelligible objects. Becoming actually able to think—acquiring intelligible objects—requires *first* that one is able actually to think them; it is by first *actually* thinking of the Pythagorean theorem that one comes to know it in a habitual way. Analogously, it is by *actually* swimming that one learns how to swim. A lot of other things need to happen to learn—having a teacher, working on problems, and so on—but ultimately it is active intellect, that which brings the potentially known and potential knower into an actual instance of thinking, that makes learning possible.

Finally, Kosman argues that, just as light in the *Republic* is both itself most visible and the source of visibility, so too is active intellect both most intelligible, which is divine intellect, and also the source of intelligibility.[62] But this raises the further question: if intellect is the source of intelligibility, why are not all intelligible things also thinking? This is how Kosman reads the question at the end of III.4 (the more standard alternative is "why is intellect not always thinking?"), and with it he sets aside the question of why *humans* are not always thinking. As Kosman interprets it, this question is parallel to the question Aristotle raises about why perceptible things are not also perceivers (424b2).[63] The answer Kosman gives in the case of perception is that perception is a "mode of *consciousness*" while being perceptible is not; similarly, active intellect signifies "a distinction between the merely intelligible, and *nous*, which we now understand to be at once intelligible and, more significantly, capable of *actual thinking*, that is, capable of *theōria*, the fully realized second actuality of *nous*."[64] Active intellect, that is, is the faculty of *awareness* of the intelligible object.[65] This is a faculty that, like the faculty of perceptual awareness, is not a separate faculty from human intellect, but its paradigm is divine mind, that always-active thinking.[66]

In a word, Kosman takes active intellect in III.5 to be an element of the human psyche, and the element that, like light, unites the intelligible object and intellect in the activity of thinking. It is *also* divine intellect, which serves as the paradigm[67] and ultimately the source[68] of this activity. Kosman thus preserves the ambiguity of active intellect being "in" the soul. We may say, with Caston, that in one sense active intellect is in the *genus* soul insofar as it is a distinct kind of soul—divine intellect—while also saying, with Kosman and Wedin, that in another sense active intellect is an element of the activity of human thinking. Active intellect is both of these by virtue of the relationship between divine and human intellect. Divine intellect is (with Caston) the final cause of human thinking, or (with Kosman) ultimately the source of intelligibility and the paradigm of human thinking.[69] If we maintain this ambiguity of "in the soul," we may then say, with Wedin, that what is separated, divine, and eternal is *either* this aspect of human intellect taken in abstraction *or* it is divine intellect as compared to human intellect. Better, active intellect is both.

iii. Supplements to Kosman

More needs to be said if we are to make more explicit the distinction between human intellect and the objects of thought and address the question of why humans are not always thinking. Doing so will also further support the stance that the subject of *De anima* III.5 is both human and divine intellect ambiguously. Kosman's vision of active intellect is of that which joins intellect and intelligible object. Through the processes of learning, say, observing the behavior of bees, one gains possession of the form of bee by virtue of active intellect. The intelligible object, which is potentially in the bee, comes to be actually thought by virtue of active intellect. Active intellect accomplishes the identity of intellect and its object.

The obvious question to ask here is *how* active intellect joins intellect with intelligible object. This is something that Caston's interpretation of how divine intellect may operate in human thinking can answer. Just as the form of art in the artisan's soul is the final cause of the production of art, so too the divine mind—that which is eternally thinking all things—is the final cause of an individual's coming to think any particular thing, that toward which thinking yearns.[70]

On Kosman's account, active intellect in the human soul is that which accomplishes the activity of thinking, the meeting of intellect and object, and this is in a way the same as divine intellect. If we add to Kosman's account Caston's principle that active intellect is that toward which thinking strives as the final cause, we may say why a person does not always contemplate what she knows. The art of medicine, while being *in* the soul of the doctor, governs the production of health in another; the nontemporal form in the soul of the doctor governs a temporal process that aims at the form. (Being healthy is also a temporally extended condition.) Similarly, the person who has learned the Pythagorean theorem will have that form in her soul as the final cause, that is, as active intellect. But if it is in her soul *as* the final cause, it will be in the soul as that which governs a temporally extended process of thinking. Gerson points out that *De anima* III.5 emphasizes that temporality applies only to individual thinking: "Actual knowledge is identical with its object; but potential knowledge is prior in time in the individual but not prior even in time in general" (430a19–22).[71] Furthermore, Aristotle addresses the temporality of human thinking in *De anima* III.6, arguing that what is thought is only potentially divisible, even though thinking is temporally extended. Aristotle writes: "It is not possible to say what one was thinking of in each half of time; for these do not exist, except potentially" (430b10–11). He makes a similar point in *Metaphysics* IX.6, illustrating activities that have an end in themselves by saying that "at the same time we are seeing and have seen, are understanding [*phronein*] and have understood, are thinking [*noein*] and have thought" (1048b23–24). The identity of intellect and object, in human intellect, is temporal, but the temporality is an aspect of human mind, not of thinking itself. Rather, thinking is always complete, only potentially interrupted. Unlike divine intellect, then, human intellect is subject to time and therefore will not perfectly instantiate divine thinking, that is, it will not always be thinking but will be able to take up the process of thinking at will.

iv. The Consequences

In effect, this interpretation of active intellect as both divine and human permits us to take *both* of Wedin's interpretations of the separability of intellect to be true: human intellect is derivatively immortal and eternal *when taken* as separate, while divine intellect *just is* immortal and eternal. We can understand it both ways because, insofar as active intellect governs a *temporal* process that a person engages in, it is not eternal or immortal, but as an activity that is in content identical to that of divine intellect, it *is* immortal and eternal.

More importantly, what happens when a human thinks is in an important way not a *personal* accomplishment, but an accomplishment made possible by an impersonal principle that defines human intellect.[72] Kosman argues that active intellect "is simply *nous* understood in its role of self-actualization in *theōria*," by which he means that it is the principle that makes intellect *intellect*, capable of *knowing* and being *aware of* forms, rather than simply something that embodies a form.[73] Just as perception contains within itself a principle or awareness, which explains why air does not become sensitive when it takes on odor, so too human intellect contains within it a principle of awareness by which it *knows* forms rather than merely takes them on.[74] In the same way that the principle of perceptual awareness is not something that an individual *accomplishes*, yet is a principle *within* the perceptive soul, so too is the active intellect a principle that is *within* the soul but not something personal.

Separability from the Soul

This interpretation of *De anima* III.5 allows us to maintain that intellect is not separable *simpliciter* from body because of its dependence on images for thinking, while also allowing that it is separable in a different sense, in that when thought of as abstracted from the temporality necessary for human thinking, it is identical with divine intellect which *is* separable *simpliciter*. We have still to consider, however, the separability of intellect from the rest of the soul. Aristotle has already decided that the parts of the soul are separable from each other in account only, yet the other parts of the soul are clearly inseparable, *even* in account, from body. What does the conceptual separability of intellect from the body mean for the separability of intellect from the rest of the soul? I will argue that separability in account in this case expresses that the particularities of the individual are incidental to intellect, when intellect is considered in itself.

In *Metaphysics* VII.8 Aristotle argues that matter is what individuates particulars. He concludes the chapter by saying, "But the whole, this particular form in these particular bones and flesh, is already Callias or Socrates; and they are different on account of their material (since it is different), but they are the same in form (for the form is indivisible)" (1034a2–8).[75] The individuation of any particular person is the result of the differences in their matter, *hulē*, that is, their bodies. Thus, Callias may be hot tempered due to an excess of heat around his heart, and Socrates may be calm by reason of an even distribution of humors. But such physical explanations are only a part of the story.[76] Callias may be *inclined* to be hot tempered because of the disposition of his body, but that he *is* hot tempered is the result of the habits that he has formed. In other words, the individuality of Callias is not fully explained by his body alone. What makes Callias this particular human being, one who differs from Socrates, is his bodily disposition *and* his personal history: his choices, memories, education, and so on. Even though Socrates and Callias are one in form, and their form is human soul, their souls take on particular habits and encompass particular experiences and knowledge in their memories, and so on. Soul *as* form is one, but soul *as* this individual here is singular. Aristotle acknowledges just such a distinction between the form and the form *of* a particular individual in a comment in *Nicomachean Ethics* VII.4: "just as with Anthropos, the Olympic victor: in his case, the common *logos* differed little from the *logos* peculiar to him, but nonetheless it was different" (1147b35–1148a2).

What bearing do these comments have on the separability of intellect from the rest of the soul? The lack of a bodily organ suggests that intellect *in itself* is not personal or individuated: it is not directly related to matter, which is what individuates Socrates and Callias. Indeed, Aristotle tells us in *De generatione animalium* that while soul is transmitted by means of seed, intellect is generated "from outside," that is, it is not present nascently in the material of generation (736b22–29). Intellect, then, is separable from the rest of the soul in the sense that in itself it is not touched by what individuates the soul. When an individual thinks, it is incidental to the thinking that it is *this* individual that is doing the thinking.[77] In I.4, Aristotle distinguishes between the soul itself as the subject of activities and the ensouled individual that is so:

> . . . to say that the soul is angry is as if one were to say that the soul weaves or builds. For it is surely better not to say that the soul pities, learns, or thinks, but that the man does this with his soul; and this not because the movement takes place in it, but because

> sometimes it reaches as far as it or at other times comes from it; e.g., perception starts from particular things, while recollection starts from the soul itself and extends to movements or persistent states in the senses. (408b11–17)[78]

Christopher Shields (1988) explains this passage by arguing that the soul itself is not the subject of such activities because the soul is not subject to motion *kath' hauto*, and these activities either are themselves motions or involve motions (and therefore require a body, an embodied subject). We may employ this distinction to understand the separability of the intellect. Just as the soul *itself* is not the subject of pity, but instead it is the person who pities *with* her soul, so too it is not (active) intellect *itself* that is the subject of learning and thinking, but the person who learns and thinks *with* her (active) intellect.

We may infer from this that intellect is separable in the sense that thinking is the activity of a part of the soul that is not in itself affected by anything particular to the individual who is thinking; Joe's active contemplation of the Pythagorean theorem differs not at all from Alice's. By contrast, Joe's memory of his meal with Alice *does* differ from Alice's memory of the same event. On the other hand, that Joe and Alice both know the Pythagorean theorem in particular, and how they came to know it and how they recall and use the knowledge, is particular to them and their personal histories. Intellect is a part of the human soul, that is, it is still an individual who engages in the impersonal activity of contemplation. Intellect exists independently from body and the rest of the soul *only* in those nonbodily living things—gods, and especially the god of Aristotle's *Metaphysics*.[79] But it is not separable for me in my lifetime: the identity of intellect with its object is accomplished in *my* soul, but it is accomplished by a principle that is indifferent to me in my particularity.

This strange separability of intellect is expressed in a passage in *De anima* I.4:

> Intellect, however, seems to come about in us as a sort of substance [*ousia tis*], and not to be destroyed. For, though it would be destroyed most of all by the dying of light that comes with old age, in fact it is in the same case as the organs of sense: if an old man could get an eye like this one, he would see just like a youth. Thus old age consists in something that has happened not to the soul, but to that in which the soul is, just as inebriations and diseases. And indeed, thinking [*to noein*] and contemplation [*to theōrein*]

> fades away when something else within is destroyed, while it is in itself imperturbable; but being thoughtful [*dianoeisthai*] and loving or hating are conditions not of this but of what possesses this, and in the way it possesses this. Thus when the latter is destroyed, one neither loves nor remembers, for these did not belong to that other thing, but to the combination, which has perished. But perhaps intellect is something more divine and imperturbable [*apathēs*]. (*De anima* 408b18–29)[80]

Aristotle is here drawing a distinction between the deterioration of the body—that which has soul—and the deterioration of soul. Despite what one might suppose, Aristotle claims,[81] the deterioration of old age does not consist in deterioration of soul, but of the body that has soul. Thus, just as sight would be restored if one could acquire a new pair of eyes, so thinking, too, does not deteriorate in itself, but when "something else within" deteriorates. Just as seeing relies on the good condition of the organ of sight, so thinking relies on the good condition of those faculties of soul that facilitate thinking: imagination and memory. But these faculties rely on the body, and their activities belong to the composite; when the body deteriorates, therefore, these deteriorate as well and impede the activity of thinking. In itself, however, intellect is not affected by the deterioration of the body and the faculties directly entwined with it: "And indeed, thinking and contemplation fades away when something else within is destroyed, while it is *in itself* imperturbable [*apathēs*]." This is exactly because intellect is indifferent to the particularities of the individual that thinks: even if the forgetfulness of old age makes it more difficult for a particular person to contemplate what he knows, nonetheless his activity of contemplating, once achieved, is exactly the same as the contemplation of his younger self.[82]

Intellect is separable from the rest of the soul in the sense that in itself it transcends the personal and the particularities of the person thinking, by virtue of its identity with its object. Of course, this argument relies on the claim that the object of intellect is itself not particular—what is intelligible is the form, which is universal, not the particular instantiation of the form. As a result, it is both possible and, in some respects, suited to the nature of thinking that a person can think, know, and arrive at conclusions without this thinking having any bearing at all on the thinker *qua* person. Thinking by its nature is impersonal, nonperspectival, whereas perceiving is by its nature particular, personal, and perspectival. This leads to the possibility that one's knowledge conflicts with one's perception, as in the case of the akratic character; for example, one may recognize the health benefits of exercise without thereby thinking that one should exercise oneself. The akratic person *knows* the universal, but he fails to act on it because his perceptual experience, which provides the minor premise, drives him to do otherwise (*Nic. Eth.* VII.3). Because intellect is separable in the sense of being impersonal, it is possible for someone to *know* something without being impelled to action by that knowledge: because intellect is in itself impersonal, it does not necessarily implicate the individual who contemplates it. Another way of saying this is that the akratic person *has* the human form in his soul (insofar as he knows it), but he does not have the human form in the sense of *being* it (insofar as he *is not* virtuous). I will address this in further detail in section 4; for now, let it suffice to show that the separability of intellect from the perceptive part of the soul is the basis for the duality of the human soul.

3. The Duality of the Soul and the Ethical Task

In the previous chapter, I argued that human perception is characterized by an indeterminacy of significance: one perceives an object in the world as a site of possibility, both one's own individual and idiosyncratic possibilities that arise within and refer to one's perspective and also impersonal, nonperspectival possibilities. This indeterminacy is consistent with the separability of intellect, as I have interpreted it. Because intellect is separable from the perceptive part of the soul, it *need not* be brought to bear in perceptual experience: the particular is incidental to intellect. In this case, the nonperspectival context for human perception may remain merely a possibility, and one's perception will be determined by the particular desires, emotions, and so on that make up one's perspective. However, one *can* realize the possibility of perceiving intellectually; it is, after all, an individual who thinks, even if it is incidental to the thinking itself that it is *this* individual person who is thinking. In other words, one can develop the *habit* of actively perceiving intellectually, and to do so will be to integrate the perceptual and intellectual parts of the soul. In what follows, I will explain how the conflict between perception and intellect figures into Aristotle's ethics.

Arguably, Aristotle's central idea in the *Nicomachean Ethics* is that the development of habit underlies the development of virtue. This idea is sometimes expressed by calling virtue a "second nature,"[83] which succinctly suggests that the virtuous character for Aristotle is like a natural state; that is, that the virtuous person has surpassed the "neither by nature nor contrary to nature" structure of soul grounded in the separability of intellect. Moreover, Aristotle's claim that the virtuous person takes pleasure in and deliberately chooses the virtuous action suggests that her perceptive soul—the part of the soul responsible for feelings of pleasure and pain (*De anima* 413b23–24 and 414b1–5)—is aligned with the intellectual soul, which is responsible for deliberation[84] and practical wisdom (*phronēsis*).[85] If the human soul is originally dual, the development of virtue will be a transformation of soul such that it overcomes this duality and achieves a "natural" unity. I will defend this thesis by arguing that the nonrational part of the soul that Aristotle identifies as the basis for the virtues of character is the perceptive part of the soul, and that it is necessary that perception be brought under the auspices of intellect if one is to apprehend the good of any particular situation.

Aristotle attributes the virtues of character to the nonrational part of the soul that is amenable to reason (*Nic. Eth.* 1102b28–1103a10).[86] Although Aristotle decides that it is not necessary to treat the soul with precision in this work (1102a18–28) and he therefore adopts a popular division of the soul that he does not hold to be accurate, it should be clear to the student of *De anima* that this nonrational part must be the perceptive part of the soul. In *De anima* III.9 Aristotle rejects the division of the soul into a rational and a nonrational part, partly on the basis that the perceptive part "could not easily be set down either as nonrational [*alogon*] or as having reason [*logon echon*]" (432a30–31), just as the nonrational part of the soul is not *simply* nonrational because it is susceptible to reason. Similarly, Aristotle characterizes imagination, itself an operation of the perceptive part, as a kind of quasi-thinking (433a9–10). Further, the nonrational part of the soul is contrasted with the other parts of the soul familiar from *De anima*: the fully rational part, that is, intellect, on the one hand, and the vegetative nonrational part on the other (*Nic. Eth.* 1102b29–1103a3), mirroring the division of soul that Aristotle adopts in *De anima*. One might object that at 1098a1–3 Aristotle dismisses the perceptive as the basis for human virtue. This objection is met by noticing that Aristotle is not dismissing the perceptive *part of the soul*, but rather the perceptive *life* (*zōiē*) as the proper basis for virtue. This supports my earlier claim that the life governed by perception—a life that is *available* to human beings by virtue of the relative independence of the perceptive part of the soul—is not the properly human life.

Finally, in *Nicomachean Ethics* Aristotle characterizes this nonrational part as appetitive and desiring (1102b30), which corresponds to Aristotle's description of the perceptive part of the soul in *De anima* as necessarily including desire and appetite (413b22–24).[87] For these reasons, we ought to understand the nonrational part of the soul that is obedient to reason to be the perceptive part of the soul.

Clearly, virtue is accomplished when this part of the soul is obedient to reason. Aristotle indicates this as early as I.13 in *Nicomachean Ethics*:

> Yet there seems to be also a certain other nature of the soul that is non-rational, although it does share in reason in a way. For in the case of the self-restrained person and of the one lacking self-restraint, we praise their reason and that part of their soul possessing reason, since it correctly exhorts them toward the best things. But there appears to be something else in them that is by nature contrary to reason, which does battle with and strains against reason . . . In the case of the self-restrained person, at any rate, it is obedient to the commands of reason—and perhaps it heeds those commands still more readily in the case of the moderate or courageous person, since then it is in all respects in harmony with reason. (*Nic. Eth.* 1102b13–28)

For the virtuous person, this nonrational part of the soul is "in all respects in harmony [*homophōnein*] with reason [*logos*]," but initially and for the less-than-virtuous person, these elements of the soul conflict with each other. If this is ultimately a conflict between the dictates of the perceptual part of the soul and the dictates of the intellectual part of the soul, we will be better able to understand the harmony of the soul of the virtuous person by looking into the conflict between intellect and perception.

It is clear that the perceptual and intellectual modes of encounter with an object in the world sometimes conflict with one another; for example, as Aristotle notes in *De anima*, the sun does not cease to appear small even when one has knowledge of its true size (428b3–4). In keeping with my interpretation of the separability of intellect, this conflict arises because, generally, our perceptual access to the world is relative to us, reflecting and being informed by our particular desires and states, whereas intellect is not: the sun *looks* small because *we* are so far away from it; the wine tastes bitter because I am sickly; the pizza smells good because I am hungry. Broadly speaking, the objects of perception are perceived as being pleasant or painful, that is, desirable or undesirable, to be pursued or fled, according to what is (merely) apparently good *for* the perceiver.[88] This relativity is both natural and necessary for nonrational animals. It is natural insofar as the relativity derives from the physicality of perception: it is because my body is comported in a certain way that my perceptions take on the character that they do, and it is necessary because it is through the medium of perception that an animal is able to preserve its life by pursuing beneficial things and avoiding harmful things (*De anima* 434a27–b2, 434b11–25). By contrast, intellect has no bodily substratum; Aristotle argues (429a18–29) that it *cannot* have a bodily organ because bodily nature would restrict its capacity to "think all things" (429a18).

Our account of human perception contains the possibility that perception be resituated in a nonperspectival context, a possibility afforded by the presence of intellect. And indeed, Aristotle suggests that, for rational animals, there is a kind of true perception, a perception of something pleasant that is not relative to one's appetites and desires. Aristotle affords to humans alone the capacity to perceive not only what is apparently good to the perceiver, but also what is pleasant or good in itself, which is possible only by virtue of the intellect. This is a distinction Aristotle draws in the *Nicomachean Ethics* and illustrates in the *De sensu*. The *Nicomachean Ethics* passage reads: "Now, some things are pleasant by nature—and of these, some are pleasant without qualification, others are such according to various kinds of animals and human beings involved. Certain things, by contrast, are not pleasant by nature but do become pleasant, some on account of people's defects, others through habits, and still others on account of people's corrupt natures" (VII.5 1148b15–19). This distinction is illustrated in a set of comments he makes about the sense of smell in *De sensu*, where Aristotle describes what I take to be a natural harmony between perception and intellect. There are two species of smell, he tells us: one that garners its pleasantness from appetites, just as the scent of pizza is good not in itself but only because it signifies the pizza for which I am hungry, and another that is pleasant in itself, as, for example, the scent of flowers (*De sensu* 5 443b19–444a8). Scents that are pleasant in themselves "have no effect, great or small, as incitements to eat, nor do they contribute anything to appetite [*epithumia*]" (443b28–30). The pleasantness of the scent of flowers derives not from anything specific about the perceiver; rather, it reflects something true about the perceptible object. But this kind of smell "is peculiar to man, [whereas] those which correspond to flavors are perceptible to all other animals" (444a4–5).[89] This is a kind of perception that is not essentially determined by the particular condition of a particular perceiver. It operates *not* in a context introduced by the desires and states of the perceiver, but instead in an "impersonal" context: it is perceived as *anyone* would perceive it (unless one has corrupted one's sense for the scent that is pleasant in itself by too frequently adding it as perfume to our food, and coming to conflate the two pleasures [444a1–3]). As we have seen, intellect is just such an impersonal faculty. It stands to reason, then, that it is the presence of intellect, that power that distinguishes human beings from other animals, that enables human beings uniquely to perceive what is good in itself. If perception is naturally bound up with desire, pleasure, and pain, it naturally includes a reference to the perceiver; but the intellectual grasp is not so bound up and does not include such a reference. The perception of what is pleasant in itself must be a perception made possible by the presence of intellect. I propose that this is a natural instance of intellectual perception, analogous to the kind of perception that is achieved by the virtuous person.

This instance of intellectual perception can be generalized to the apprehension of all forms instantiated in material. Aristotle argues in *De anima* that the intelligible objects are present in the perceptible forms (432a3–5): just as perception receives the perceptible form of things, intellect receives the intelligible forms[90] *of those same things*. Moreover, not everything is separable from its material such that intellect *could* grasp it independently of perception, for example, the snub nose. Aristotle concludes a consideration of the mode by which the snub nose is grasped by saying, "In general, then, as things are distinct from matter, so too with what concerns intellect [*ta peri ton noun*]" (429b21–22) (where the matters concerning intellect are grasping the intelligible objects and their perceptible instantiation). Perception apprehends the particular whereas intellect apprehends the universal, exceeding the merely particular to apprehend its truth. But what is true must also be grasped in its particular instantiation, and for this to happen perception must work together with intellect: one must intellectually perceive what is true.

In a manner similar to the snub nose, what is virtuous for Aristotle is not extractable from the particular situation in which one does the virtuous thing: the ethical good is in this way not separable from its material. To grasp the good, then, intellect and perception must cooperate, just as they do to understand snubness and to perceive the pleasant scent of flowers. Yet, unlike the pleasure that we naturally take in the scent of flowers, which must be corrupted in order to perceive the pleasure relative to desire, perceiving the ethical good is a power that must be cultivated. This would take the form of a transformation of our animal nature; rather than operating within its natural context of desire and appetite, the perceptive soul will be brought to operate in the context of the intellect. The perceptive soul will be rendered *potentially* within the intellectual soul.[91] But it is up to us to forge this relationship.

4. *Akrasia*

We find confirmation that the task of ethical development is to integrate the perceptual and intellectual parts of the soul, that is, to develop the habit of perceiving intellectually, by way of contrast, in the account of *akrasia*, "lack of self-restraint." The account of *akrasia* reveals the nature of the conflict that can arise between perception and intellect; it is an account of a divided soul. In what follows, I will argue that akratic action consists in a failure of perception to supply the minor premise to the correct practical syllogism because it apprehends the present circumstance as the "mere" present, rather than a moment in a whole life. This manner of perceiving, that is, perception apprehending the mere present, is natural to nonhuman animals, but it signals a failure to integrate intellect and perception and therefore a failure to fully realize *human* perception. It is a failure to perceive intellectually.

There is a straightforward way in which *akrasia* is a conflict between intellect and perception. The akratic *knows* the good in the sense that he has apprehended the universal premise—this is an operation of the noetic part of the soul (*De anima* 417b22–23); the akratic *thinks* correctly about virtuous action. But the akratic does not *act* on his knowledge and instead pursues the present pleasure—an object of the perceptive part of the soul (*De anima* 431a10–11). Thus we may say that when the akratic behaves akratically, he is following the lead of the perceptive part of the soul instead of his reason. His perception[92] tells him "this thing here is good—pursue this," but his intellect tells him "this kind of thing is not good—avoid this," and he pursues.

One may object to this characterization of the akratic conflict because Aristotle describes the akratic action as the result of a practical syllogism, a kind of reasoning that employs a universal premise. However, of the two syllogisms mentioned at 1147a24–b19, the universal premise of the syllogism urging pursuit of the sweet is a generalized perceptual principle: all sweet things are pleasant. Indeed, Aristotle concludes *Nicomachean Ethics* VII.3 by saying, "For it is not when science in the authoritative sense seems to be present that the experience of the lack of self-restraint occurs, nor is it this science that is dragged around on account of passion, but rather that [knowledge] which is bound up with perception" (1147b15–17). What is dragged by passion in an akratic act is a generalized principle governed by perception, not by intellect. Moreover, while a practical syllogism may be used to describe the action, Aristotle's use of the practical syllogism need not describe a process of reasoning that is the activity of intellect. In *De motu animalium*, Aristotle describes the motion of a nonrational animal as a practical syllogism (701a30–33). We may, then, safely say that the akratic responds to a particular situation perceptually and intellectually, but these constitute two opposing responses, rather than one unified response.

In this straightforward way, we see that intellect and perception are operating quasi-independently of one another in the soul of the akratic person. But there is also another, deeper conflict between these two elements in the soul of the akratic: the akratic has not made the choice to live a certain *kind* of life, and in the absence of that kind of choice, he is vulnerable to the tyranny of the temptations of perception. In what follows, I will argue that this failure to make a comprehensive choice of life is the root of *akrasia*, and it results in a failure to develop the capacity for intellectual perception.

My argument will proceed thus: I will prepare my discussion of the accounts of *akrasia* given in *Nicomachean Ethics* VII.3, Aristotle's response to the Socratic position that *akrasia* is a form of ignorance, by discussing Aristotle's account of the source of animal motion in *De anima* III.9–11.[93] This discussion will establish that the desire that motivates movement is determined by the way the object of desire is apprehended, either as the good or as the merely present pleasure, according to the different faculties of apprehension. I will then turn to *Nicomachean Ethics* VII.3 and argue, first, that *akrasia* is a result of a failure of perception to supply the minor premise to the right practical syllogism, and that this failure is due to the manner in which the object is perceived. I will then argue that *akrasia* has a double aspect: it is both an inability to abide by one's choice in the moment, as a result of faulty perception, and that this inability is ultimately caused by being in a state of passion. I will conclude by considering how the akratic character is developed, and I will argue that the akratic is vulnerable to such states of passion because he has taken refuge in arguments concerning what is good rather than acting by their guidance, out of ambivalence about the sort of life he wants to lead. The akratic has failed to take hold of his own development, failed to overcome the natural duality of his soul, and as a result, his perceptual faculty operates like the perceptual faculty of a nonrational animal, beholden to the mere present, and (temporarily) without the ability to distinguish between the apparent good and the true good.

Let me offer one final remark before embarking on this argument. Generally, there are two ways of understanding the akratic's failure to act according to what she knows to be best. The first way, referred to as either the intellectualist or cognitivist interpretation,[94] understands the akratic's failure as a failure of practical reasoning, similar to a failure of theoretical reasoning.[95] The second way, the nonintellectualist or Humean interpretation, places the blame for the akratic's failure on a failure to have right desire, independently of having right reason.[96] I have framed the question of the akratic's failure in terms of a conflict between intellect and perception, which may suggest that I favor the intellectualist interpretation, but my interpretation rather falls in with the camp of interpreters who propose a third alternative, wherein having the right desire is not separable from cognizing objects of desire well and vice versa.[97] On this interpretation, having the right desire and having knowledge are intertwined states. This approach has prima facie appeal because it harmonizes Aristotle's view, on the one hand, that only the virtuous person truly desires the good, while others are deceived by the object of their desire; and his view on the other hand, that acting well because one *knows* that it is the right thing to do does not make the act virtuous—one must *be* virtuous to *do* virtuous deeds. Accomplishing virtuous acts is neither simply a matter of having knowledge, nor simply a matter of desiring rightly.

Desire and the Desired in Animal Motion

Aristotle offers two characterizations of the phenomenon of *akrasia*: (1) it is a conflict of desires, and the akratic's nonrational appetite, her *epithumia*, overpowers her rational desire, her *boulēsis*; or (2) *akrasia* is a kind of ignorance: at the critical moment of acting, the akratic is in some sense ignorant of the principle supporting her rational intention, and this leaves her vulnerable to being led to act by a present appetite.[98] Underlying both of these characterizations and linking them is Aristotle's discussion of animal motion. Indeed, we find the characterization of *akrasia* as a conflict of desires most clearly articulated in the discussion of animal motion in the third book of *De anima*.[99] Similarly, in *Nicomachean Ethics* VII.3, wherein we find the account of *akrasia* as a kind of ignorance, Aristotle invokes the account of motion when he explains, "*epithumia* leads the way, for it is able to set in motion each of the parts [of the body]" (1147a33–34). By briefly sojourning to the discussion of animal motion in *De anima* (III.9–11) I will lay the groundwork for the argument that the akratic follows the lead of an independent perceptual principle in her soul. In *De anima* III.9–11 Aristotle offers a single account of animal motion that explains the movement of both rational and nonrational animals, but he draws important distinctions between human movement and nonrational animal movement. Highlighting these differences will lay the groundwork for the argument that when the akratic person behaves akratically, she is literally moving on the basis of the animal aspect of her soul: she behaves animalistically, operating, as an animal does, on the independent guidance of the perceptual part of her soul.

At the end of *De anima* III.9 Aristotle invokes the phenomenon of *akrasia* and from it he infers, at the beginning of III.10, that both intellect (*nous*) and desire (*orexis*) appear to be movers (*kinounta*). Aristotle is here counting imagination (*phantasia*) as a kind of thinking (*noēsis*). It is clear from the discussion surrounding this remark that desire is not an independent capacity of soul that stands alone; rather, desire always accompanies imagination or practical thinking. That is, desire is present to both the perceptual part of the soul responsible for imagination and to the intellectual part of the soul responsible for practical thinking. Aristotle begins the discussion of animal movement with an invocation of the *aporia* regarding what the parts of the soul are, and he proceeds to argue that none of the parts of the soul that he posits—nutritive, perceptive, intellectual—are in themselves the causes of movement (*De anima* 432b14–433a6). Instead, Aristotle concludes

III.9 saying, "And in general we see that the man who has the art of healing does not always heal [for example], this implying that there is something else which is responsible for action in accordance with knowledge and not knowledge itself. Nor is desire [*orexis*] responsible for this movement; for the *enkrateis*, even when they desire and want things, do not do those things for which they have the desire, but they follow intellect" (433a4–8). The implication is that neither intellect alone nor desire alone is sufficient to produce movement; rather, only intellect accompanied by desire is sufficient to cause movement. Of course, Aristotle is using intellect broadly to include *phantasia*, the sort of "thinking" available to nonrational animals, and the same principle holds in their case: neither *phantasia* alone nor desire alone can produce motion; only imagination accompanied by desire does. This is hardly surprising: desire must aim at some object, present or thought of, and so it must accompany those faculties of soul that apprehend objects.

The kinds of desire that accompany these two activities, imagining and thinking, differ: *epithumia*, appetite, accompanies imagination; and rational desire, *boulēsis*, accompanies thinking. At *De anima* 433a20, Aristotle confirms that "whenever *phantasia* produces movement, it does not do so without desire [*orexis*]." He does not explicitly identify appetite as the kind of desire that accompanies imagination in these chapters, perhaps because he draws a distinction between perceptual imagination (*aisthētikē*) and rational imagination (*logistikē*) (433b30) and would reserve appetite for perceptual imagination in particular. However, the association of imagination with appetite is seen in two parallel remarks: at 433a1–3 he says, "Again, even if the intellect [*nous*] enjoins us and thought [*dianoia*] tells us to pursue or avoid something, we are not moved but we act according to appetite [*epithumia*], as do those who are akratic." Shortly afterward, Aristotle remarks that "many follow their imaginations in spite of [*para*] their knowledge [*epistēmē*], and in the other animals thought and reasoning do not exist, although imagination does" (433a10–11). These two remarks describe cases of acting contrary to reason—in one case, it is appetite that one follows; in the other, it is imagination. Because desire accompanies the parts of the soul, I take this to imply that when a person acts not according to her reason and its accompanying rational desire, she acts according to her (perceptual) imagination and its accompanying appetite.

According to the general Aristotelian principle that actuality precedes potentiality, the object of desire—whether perceived, imagined, or thought of—must be present in order for the desire to become actual. Insofar as imagination and thinking apprehend their objects differently, so too will the desires that accompany them differ.[100] It would be strange to say, for example, that one desires a cookie simply because it is a *cookie*; rather, one desires a cookie because it is sweet or smells good, or because it will satisfy one's hunger, or because it will please the friend who baked it. Desiring a cookie for these various reasons depends upon grasping the cookie in various ways: as a source of pleasure, as a source of nourishment, as an occasion for friendship. Thus, what the object of desire is apprehended *as* will determine the sort of desire that arises for it. The manner in which the object of desire is apprehended as good—what is considered good *about* it—will determine what sort of desire one has for it, and this in turn will produce the movement one undertakes. And so Aristotle offers a general conclusion at the end of *De anima* III.10, saying, "In general, therefore, and as we have said, *as* [*hōsper*] the animal is capable of desire so is it capable of moving itself" (433b27–28, my emphasis).

Of course, a person, unlike a nonrational animal, may apprehend a particular object in multiple ways simultaneously, creating a conflict of desire. Aristotle characterizes such a conflict in this way: "But desires [*orexeis*] arise which are opposed to one another, and this happens when reason [*logos*] and appetites [*epithumiai*] are opposed and it takes place in creatures that have perception [*aisthēsis*] of time (for intellect [*nous*] bids us resist on account of the future, while our appetites bid us to act on account of what is immediate [*to ēdē*]; for what is immediately pleasant appears [*phainetai*] both absolutely pleasant and absolutely good, because we do not see the future)" (*De anima* 433b5–10). With this remark, Aristotle makes us privy to the sort of object that gives rise to appetite, and, by contrast, the sort of object that would give rise to rational desire: appetite aims at an object as the source of immediate pleasure, which it takes to be simply good, whereas intellect's rational desire aims at an object considered as a moment of a larger temporal whole.[101] The nonrational animal, by contrast, has no rational desire and therefore no conflict of desires. The nonrational animal moves simply on the basis of *phantasia* and *epithumia*. Aristotle remarks that "it is always the object of desire which produces movement, but this is either the good or the apparent good" (433a27–29), but such a distinction applies only to rational animals.[102] Nonrational animals are constituted by nature to pursue what is good for them, that is, what will promote the continuance of their lives and species (434a30–b8). A person, however, can distinguish between the good and the apparent good, and both may cause motion. We may expect that one who acts contrary to her conception of the true good is, then, pursuing the merely apparent good.

This will be confirmed in Aristotle's analysis of *akrasia*, to which I now turn. Most basically, *akrasia* is an inability to act according to what one thinks or knows to be best. It is a common enough experience: one may decide, as the conclusion of deliberative reasoning about what is best, say, to get up early in the morning, but once morning comes, this decision holds no sway as one hits snooze for the fifth or sixth time. According to Aristotle, this is a uniquely human problem, and a problem made possible by the presence of intellect: a rational decision (and its attendant rational desire) can only be taken to be abandoned by means of thinking. But *akrasia* is not a universal human problem—not all people abandon their decisions—and so we must ask: what is it that renders practical thinking and rational desire ineffective when it comes to producing action? I will argue that the cause of the inefficacy of practical intellect is the independent operation of the perceptual element of the soul, that is, the failure to achieve a "natural" unity of soul. In nonrational animals, the faculty of perception is an adequate means by which an animal preserves its life. Perception is naturally sufficient to supply the guiding principle by which an animal determines what it should pursue and what it should avoid, and this principle is pleasure, the apparent good. If the human soul has not been developed so as to achieve a "natural" unity, perception will continue to supply the apparent good as a guiding principle of action, and in so doing it will come into conflict with the principle supplied by the intellect, the true good. I will argue, further, that this disorganized state of soul is the result of the failure to take charge of the development of one's character; *akrasia* is the state of soul that develops "naturally," when one fails to decide what the ultimate good is, the good which constitutes the aim of all one's actions, and shapes one's character in pursuit of that good. The result is a soul in a state of disunity: a soul that can understand the distinction between the merely apparent good and the true good, but cannot bring the appearance of the good and the understanding of the good into harmony. As a result, the akratic will be led to pursue as the object of desire what is merely pleasant.

Akratic Ignorance

I begin with a preliminary discussion of an argument Aristotle offers early in his investigation of *akrasia* and *enkrateia*, which will shed some light on the problem of the akratic's knowledge that is Aristotle's primary concern in *Nicomachean Ethics* VII.3. Aristotle begins his account of *akrasia* and *enkrateia* by considering what is distinctive about the akratic and the enkratic characters: are they distinguished by *what* they are concerned with or by the *way* they are concerned with it (1146b14–18)? He argues that they cannot be distinguished by *what* they are concerned with, because if that were the case the akratic person would, contrary to fact, be identical with the licentious person (*akolastos*)—both are concerned with pleasure. Rather, they are distinct by virtue of the *manner* in which they are concerned with pleasure: "For the licentious person is led on by what he chooses, holding that he ought *always* to pursue the present pleasure, whereas the person lacking self-restraint does not think that, but pursues the pleasure anyway" (1146b22–24, my emphasis). The akratic person differs from the licentious person in the way he holds himself toward pleasure: the licentious person *decides* that he will *always* pursue pleasure; the akratic person pursues the present pleasure without choosing it. This is an important difference: not only does the akratic person act contrary to the rational deliberation and the rational desire that constitute choice (III.3 1113a9–12),[103] but the sort of choice that defines the licentious person concerns what he ought *always* to do. The contrast between the akratic person and the licentious person is not merely that the latter chooses, in this moment, to pursue pleasure while the former does not; it is that the latter chooses the pursuit of pleasure as a *way of life*, while the former fails to abide by his choice in this *moment*. I will argue that the inefficacy of the akratic's knowledge is a result of his *lack* of choice of a way of life: the akratic is vulnerable to the seduction of the present pleasure because he has structured his life as a series of individual choices, not governed by an overall structure of the *kind* of life he thinks one ought to live. And in the absence of this comprehensive choice, the akratic is led to act upon the dictates of his undeveloped perceptive soul.

After arguing that the akratic is distinctive by virtue of the manner in which he is concerned with pleasure, Aristotle turns to address the Socratic impasse: how can a person have knowledge (*epistēmē*) of the good thing but act otherwise, without implying that this noble knowledge is "[overpowered] and [dragged] around like a slave" (*Nic. Eth.* 1145b24) by something as ignoble as passion (*pathos*)? Aristotle employs a familiar strategy in setting up his response, invoking the general point that there are different modes of knowing: knowers can be actively using their knowledge or they can have the knowledge but not be using it (1146b31–33). Aristotle then specifies one way in which one can have knowledge without using it: one can actively have the universal premise of a practical syllogism, but not have or not use the knowledge of the relevant particular premise (1146b35–1147a10).[104] In these remarks leading up to his own account of *akrasia*, Aristotle thus draws our attention to the two components of practical knowledge: the opinion that apprehends the universal and the perception that apprehends the particular. Aristotle concludes these introductory remarks by pointing out that acting contrary to knowledge is remarkable only when both these components are actively held (1147a8–10).

Aristotle proceeds to provide two accounts of the akratic's epistemic state. (1) The akratic *ordinarily* has the knowledge that, for example, one ought not to eat sweet things for the sake of one's health, but a fit of passion overtakes him that causes him to lose his grip on that knowledge. He becomes like a drunk man who recites the verses of Empedocles without understanding his own words (*Nic. Eth.* 1147a10–24): the akratic person may recite the principle that he ought not to eat sweet things while eating his cake, but this does not mean that he *knows* what he is saying. (2) The akratic has two competing universal premises, one that forbids and one that commands eating sweets, and, in the face of a sweet thing, appetite (*epithumia*) happens to be present which leads him to eat the sweet, contrary to the premise that he ought not to eat sweets (1147a24–1147b5).

Aristotle's aim in providing these two accounts of *akrasia* is to show how one can act contrary to one's *epistēmē* without directly contravening it, so that he is not committed to the absurdity that something as powerful as *epistēmē* can be overcome by something as base as passion, and (what is the same thing) to reveal the nature of the ignorance out of which the akratic acts (*Nic. Eth.* 1145b21–29). He seems to think that he is successful in achieving this aim: he concludes his discussion of the epistemic state of the akratic by saying, "And because the ultimate term [*eschatos horos*] is not universal and seems not to be knowable as the universal is knowable, it seems also that what Socrates was seeking turns out to be the case. For it is not when science in the authoritative sense seems to be present that the *pathos* occurs, nor is it this science that is dragged around on account of *pathos*, but rather that [knowledge] which is bound up with perception [*aisthētikē*]" (1147b13–17).[105] How do these two accounts warrant this conclusion?

The first account, which explains the akratic's lack of knowledge as the result of being in a state of passion, analogous to being drunk or asleep, renders the correct universal premise ("one ought not to eat sweets") dormant. In a fit of passion, the akratic "has" this knowledge only as something foreign to him and empty, just as a drunk person "knows" Empedocles's verses (*Nic. Eth.* 1147a19–20, 1147b11–12). He knows it, we may say, *only* intellectually, which is to say only impersonally and abstractly, not as something that bears on *him* personally in his present circumstances. What is affected by the state of passion is not the knowledge that one ought not to eat sweets per se, but rather the knower: one who is in a fit of passion no longer has meaningful or concrete access to that knowledge, and, indeed, to any knowledge.[106] Aristotle compares the akratic state to sleeping: in both cases, one's condition is altered such that one cannot use one's knowledge, although one still "has" it in some sense. As a result, Aristotle is not committed to the absurdity that *epistēmē* itself is vulnerable to the vicissitudes of passion ("For it is not when science in the authoritative sense seems to be present that the *pathos* occurs . . ."). It is rather that the akratic person is so vulnerable. As Moss puts it, in this state intellect is "covered over."[107]

This first account describes the general state of ignorance that the akratic is in, and this prepares Aristotle to explain more exactly what produces a particular act of *akrasia*, which is precisely what the second account supplies.[108] It is this account that warrants Aristotle's conclusion that what passion drags around is perceptual knowledge (". . . nor is it this science that is dragged around on account of *pathos*, but rather that [knowledge] which is bound up with perception [*aisthētikē*]"). The akratic, Aristotle explains, has two universal premises within his soul, one that forbids eating sweets (Aristotle does not provide a formulation of this one), and one to the effect that "everything sweet is pleasant." As I already noted, this latter premise is a generalization of perceptual experience, and it is the sort of premise that would be available to nonrational animals with experience, were they able to articulate premises. So, for example, in the *Nicomachean Ethics* III.10 Aristotle describes the behavior of a lion that smells his prey and takes pleasure in the scent because it signifies eating. This is something like operating with a universal premise generalized from perception ("things with this scent are pleasant to eat"). Since the akratic person is in a state of passion (as we just learned), he does not have proper access to the kind of knowledge that supplies the correct universal premise. His powers of thinking about what he ought to do when faced with the sweet thing are impaired by the passion; he is not able to *consider* which practical syllogism the perceptual knowledge "this here is sweet" should complete.[109] Because the intellect has been "covered over," the akratic is restricted to the present moment, similar to the manner in which a nonrational animal is beholden to his present experience.[110]

With these two complementary explanations, Aristotle has identified two aspects of the ignorance out of which the akratic acts. He is, on the one hand, in a state of general ignorance, in the same way that one who is asleep is in a general state of ignorance. But on the other hand, he is also in error concerning his perceptual knowledge. Aristotle appeals to animal motion by way of explaining how the *epithumia* produces the akratic action: *epithumia* leads the way because "it is able to set in motion each of the parts [of the body]" (*Nic. Eth.* 1147a35). As discussed above, the *epithumia* that happens to be present must arise in light of the desired object. This is where we come to realize that there is a kind of misperception at the core of *akrasia*, wherein the akratic, because of the state of passion he finds himself in, apprehends the sweet thing only as a potential source of pleasure.[111] The object of *epithumia* is pleasure, and perception offers up this object, the merely apparent good. This is a misperception in the sense of being blind to some relevant aspect of the thing seen; it is like missing the forest for the trees, or meeting a person and being unable to see beyond her appearance. It is not a misperception in the sense of being *false*—strictly speaking, the sweet *will* be pleasant, the trees are there, and the person does look this way—but it is a failure to see the whole picture. Because the akratic's experience is confined to the mere present in the absence of intellect, "an appetite [which] happens to be present" (1147a33) is able to lead the way, "dragging" the perceptual knowledge "this here is sweet" into the syllogism that would command the consumption of the sweet. Aristotle can therefore conclude that "it is not when knowledge in the authoritative sense seems to be present" that one behaves akratically, and that it is perceptual knowledge that is "dragged around on account of passion." By contrast, Aristotle remarks that when sleeping—a state similar to the passion of the akratic, wherein intellect is "covered over"—virtuous people have better dreams than nonvirtuous people (*Nic. Eth.* 1102b8–11). This suggests that the perceptual part of the soul responsible for dreams (*De insom.* 459a20–21) is in a better condition in virtuous people than in nonvirtuous people; analogously, the virtuous person would not be tempted by the present pleasure, even if her intellect lay dormant and could not instruct otherwise.[112]

This brings us back to the claim I made at the outset: that the akratic is vulnerable to the temptations of the present pleasure because he has not situated his actions within the context of life as a whole. All desire is for a particular object, but *epithumia* is for the object *as* the immediately present pleasure. The object sought after by *epithumia* is perceived in its sheer immediacy, merely as the potential for an immediate pleasure. Appetite arises when the salient thing about the perceptual object is its merely present possibilities, that is, a potential source of pleasure; intellect makes the salient thing about the perceptual object its place in one's life as a whole. The akratic is thus acting on the basis of a kind of misperception. It is not, so to speak, a *factual* misperception—the object the akratic perceives is indeed sweet; it is rather the *character* of the perception that has gone awry. The relevance of the sweetness speaks only to the pleasure to be gained by eating it: the perception is situated in the mere present. The nature of the misperception is, then, in taking the apparent good—the pleasant—to be the true good, that is, the good as it contributes to one's life as a whole.[113]

This double aspect of *akrasia* is confirmed by the contrast Aristotle draws between *akrasia* and corruption (*mochthēria*): "For corruption seems to be like such diseases as dropsy and consumption; whereas lack of self-restraint is like epileptic seizures, the former defective condition being continuous, the latter not continuous" (*Nic. Eth.* 1150b32–35). The akratic person does not persist in his state of partial ignorance; rather, his *akrasia* emerges only intermittently and then subsides, whereas the vicious person persists in his state. The structure of vice, just like the structure of virtue, is such that an act is only truly vicious if it is done from a vicious character; in a sense, all the acts of a vicious person are vicious, because vice is a persistent state of character. The episodic nature of *akrasia*, however, reveals that the state from which the akratic acts when she acts akratically comes upon her and then departs. The akratic person is she who acts contrary to her choice, but more fundamentally the akratic person is she who is vulnerable to the fits of passion within which she is *unable* to abide by her choice due to the presence of appetite. Why is the akratic susceptible to such states of vulnerability to appetite? My position is that this is due to a fundamentally passive way of living, as I hope to show, and that in the face of this kind of passivity, one's animal, that is, perceptual soul takes the lead.[114]

The Development of *Akrasia*

We will find confirmation in this interpretation of *akrasia* as a failure to develop one's intellectual perception when we consider the problem of how *akrasia* is developed.

Aristotle's general account of the formation of character uses the model of the development of an art: one *becomes* a poet by writing poems. In general, one becomes what one does, and then what one does comes naturally. Virtues and vices are *hexeis*, character states, that are developed by engaging in acts that are virtuous or vicious, just as one becomes a good or a bad carpenter by building well or building poorly (*Nic. Eth.* II.1). To a certain extent, this account explains the development of *akrasia* and *enkrateia*. *Akrasia* and *enkrateia* are also *hexeis* (e.g., 1151a27, 1151b29) that result from habit (*ethos*) (1152a25–29), yet *akrasia* is not a vice (1151a5), nor correlatively is *enkrateia* a virtue. Moreover, the *acts* that the akratic person engages in are the *same* as the acts of the licentious (*akolastos*) person (1151a5–6). Why, then, does one person who engages in licentious behavior become licentious while another merely becomes akratic? Aristotle argues that the difference between the akratic and the licentious lies in the *way* they each pursue pleasure: the latter chooses it, the former acts contrary to his choice (1146b22–24). Aristotle draws a distinction, however, between the choices that establish one's character and the choices one makes at any given time: one is responsible for a single act from start to finish, whereas one is primarily responsible for the establishment of one's character—once established, it takes on a momentum of its own (1114b30–1115a3). Did the akratic person make choices that resulted in a character whose choices are ineffective? How would these choices differ from the choices that result in licentiousness?

One response is that there is a physiological explanation for the akratic person's character. In several respects, Aristotle associates *akrasia* with certain physiological conditions or alterations. First, he considers the melancholic especially likely to be impetuously akratic (*Nic. Eth.* 1150b25–28), and he likens this character to one who gets drunk on little wine (1151a2–5), grounding at least this type of *akrasia* in a certain physiological condition. Second, he likens the passionate state of the akratic to being drunk, mad, or asleep, specifically with respect to the bodily alteration suffered in these conditions (1147a11–18).[115] The licentious person, on the other hand, is one who pursues excessive pleasures either without an appetite for them or with only a mild appetite (1148a17–20). The akratic, then, would be one who tries to achieve virtue—he comes to *learn* what one ought to do—but is prevented from developing virtuous habits by a physiological susceptibility to fits of passion. Even though the akratic engages in licentious acts, he does not develop the habits that result in that vice because, we might say, he is not himself when he engages in those acts (as signified by the regret he feels afterward).

Appeal to the physiological condition of the akratic may serve to explain why the akratic did not develop licentiousness, but it is not enough to explain the development of *akrasia*. Aristotle is quite clear that *akrasia* properly speaking is a result of habit, distinguishing between those who are akratic by nature from those who are akratic as a result of habit (*Nic. Eth.* 1152a27–31). Moreover, one aspect of virtue is to have organized and appropriate passions (1106b16–23), which is achieved as a result of habituation.[116] We are not born with appropriate passions, and no doubt one of the things that differentiates individuals is the degree to which we are susceptible to anger, desire, and so on, on the basis of our bodily conditions.[117] Why, then, does the akratic not habituate his passions? What are the acts by which a person develops *akrasia*, if he neither develops licentiousness through his licentious acts, nor habituates his passions so as to develop virtue?

The answer, I believe, is to be found in a remark that Aristotle makes in *Nicomachean Ethics* II.4, when he is elucidating his claim that people become virtuous by engaging in virtuous acts. He concludes the chapter with the following remark:

> It is well said, then, that as a result of doing just things, the just person comes into being and as a result of doing moderate things, the moderate person; without performing these actions, nobody would

> become good. *Yet most people* [hoi polloi] *do not do them*; *and, seeking refuge in argument* [logos], *they suppose that they are philosophizing and that they will in this way be serious*, thereby doing something similar to the sick who listen attentively to their physicians but do nothing prescribed. Just as these latter, then, will not have a body in good condition by caring for it in this way, so too the former will not have a soul in good condition by philosophizing in this way. (*Nic. Eth.* 1105b9–18, my emphasis)

The many have some sense that they ought to be virtuous, and they develop some *logos* of what virtue would entail, but they *fail to act*. As a result, they leave their souls in bad condition, just as one who fails to heed the prescriptions of one's doctor will be left in poor health. Both the soul and the body require active care if they are to be healthy, not merely lip service. This point reflects Aristotle's hylomorphic view of body and soul: to a certain extent, caring for the soul and caring for the body are one and the same project. One is caring for one's nutritive soul by caring for one's body when one follows the doctor's orders. However, as we have seen, intellect occupies a unique position in the soul and requires special cultivation through learning. One might mistakenly suppose, on the basis of intellect's special position, that to bring the soul into good condition one need only educate oneself. The development of *akrasia* would then stem from a basic folly; Aristotle accuses those who do not see what is obvious of extraordinary carelessness: "To be ignorant, then, that the corresponding *hexeis* come from engaging in a given activity is exactly the mark of someone who is insensible [*anaisthētos*]" (*Nic. Eth.* III.5 1114a9–10).

Perhaps we can take the analogy further. What it means not to follow the prescriptions of the doctor is to allow one's body to follow its natural course: if one fails to take the medicine prescribed by the doctor, one's illness will worsen. Similarly, what it means not to actively care for the soul is to let the soul follow its natural course, that is, to allow oneself to act on whatever desires one happens to find within oneself. Wouldn't habitually taking such a passive stance lead to the condition of *akrasia*? Such a person would fail to habituate her passions, while at the same time (intellectually) learning what she ought to do. When this person comes to act, she will find within herself two competing impulses: the impulse that has developed naturally (i.e., without interference or supervision) to pursue pleasure, and the impulse to follow her rational account of what she ought to do—this person is akratic. The poor condition of soul that results from this practice of the *hoi polloi* is the akratic condition, and it is developed precisely by failing to act. Moreover, this failure to act while learning about the good is to embody an ambivalence toward what kind of life one will lead: it is to halfheartedly choose both the life of virtue and the life of ease, and in choosing both, one chooses neither. In the absence of a serious choice about what kind of life one will live (which is the same thing as choosing what kind of character one wants to develop), one develops *akrasia* as if by default, and this failure to choose has the consequence of restricting one's *ability* to choose, that is, to act according to one's rational desire.

Conclusion

In summary, I have argued that human beings, as rational animals, are initially and naturally characterized by a duality of the soul, having both a perceptual soul and an intellectual soul, both supplying principles sufficient to govern one's life. The virtuous person, however, is characterized by a harmonious soul, which, I argued, means a soul in which the perceptual and intellectual parts are integrated with one another. In the terms set forth in the previous chapter, this is to say that the virtuous person's perception is informed by intellect; it is an intellectual perception in the sense that the particular object apprehended perceptually is apprehended in light of what it really is, not merely in light of what it is to the perceiver. In terms more common in the ethical context, the apparent good offered by perception represents what is truly good. I then confirmed, by way of contrast, that the nonvirtuous soul suffers from having a perceptual principle independent from an intellectual principle by examining the phenomenon of *akrasia* and Aristotle's explanations of it. In the following chapter, I will further confirm the harmony of the virtuous soul in terms of intellect and perception by examining the intellectual virtue of *phronēsis*, "practical wisdom" or insight. I will argue that *phronēsis* is a power for good practical reasoning because it enables a person to rightly apprehend her particular circumstances, and that this right apprehension *is* intellectual perception.

CHAPTER 4

Phronēsis

I have offered an account of human perception, that is, an account of the nature of perception considered as a part of an intellectual soul. I argued that human perception is shaped by one's habits of understanding, one's intellectual habits, as, for example, a botanist's sight of a tree will hold a significance that differs from a hiker's sight of the same tree. What this shows is that the character of one's perception may be shaped by one's intellectual habits—one may come to perceive intellectually. In an ethical context, I argued that becoming virtuous consists precisely in developing the capacity to perceive intellectually; the aim of ethical development is to accomplish a harmony of soul, a result that is achieved by bringing the perceptive part of the soul under the guidance of intellect. As our analysis of *akrasia* showed, what this means, concretely, is to develop the capacity to perceive the present as a moment in the broader temporal context of a whole life. An akratic agent is beholden to the mere present, whereas a virtuous person apprehends the greater significance of what she perceives at present. In this section, I will confirm this analysis of the psychological underpinnings of virtue by addressing the virtue of *phronēsis*, "practical wisdom." I will argue that *phronēsis* is, in part, the developed capacity for perceiving well.

Naturally, perception occurs within and is shaped by the contingent features of the perceiver: the pizza smells good when one is hungry; the wine tastes bitter when one is ill. In its natural (i.e., undeveloped) state, then, perception gains access to the apparent good, distinct (for humans, at least) from the true good that is understood intellectually (*Nic. Eth.* 1139b12–13). For nonrational animals, nature assures that the apparent good—what appears good to the animal—is in fact good for the animal, for the most part and for healthy whole creatures. My cat does not have a problem with overeating because her hunger accurately leads her to eat a sufficient and only sufficient amount of food. For humans, though, there is no such guidance (or at least such guidance is severely limited and easily overturned); instead (or for the most part) we must guide *ourselves* to pursue what is truly good for us.

Nothing assures the coincidence of the apparent good with the true good for humans except the virtue that we ourselves develop. Indeed, we have so little assurance about the cohesion of these two goods that we do not even have a secure idea about what the nature of the true good is—is happiness fame and fortune? or pleasure? or honor?

This distinction between the apparent good and the true good corresponds to the distinction between perception and intellect: perception grasps the apparent good and intellect grasps the true good. The problem is to bring the apparent good into alignment with the true good, the perceived good into correspondence with the intellected good. Not only is it expedient to align the perceived good with the intellected good so as to avoid the akratic state of being of two minds about how one ought to act, it is also necessary if the true good is to be realized in action in the first place. The proper object of intellect is the unchanging universal, but the realm of action—the realm of ethics—is particular and variable. In order for the true good to be realized in action it must be adjusted and particularized. *Phronēsis*, I will argue, fulfills precisely this function: it is knowledge particularized, or, what is the same thing, it is the capacity for intellectual perception. Specifically, *phronēsis* is a manner of perceiving that is both articulate enough to be sensitive to and discerning of the ethically relevant features, and flexible and open enough to be determined by deliberation.

Introduction: The Limit of *Logos* and the Apprehension of the Particular

The task Aristotle sets for himself in book VI of the *Nicomachean Ethics* is to define the *orthos logos*, the "right reason," that identifies the middle course (*to meson*) at which virtue aims (1138b18–20, 1138b32–34; see also 1106b14–18, 1106b27–28).[1] Immediately upon introducing this question, Aristotle turns his attention to the intellectual virtues (1139a1). Although this seems to some to be a detour, by the end of book VI Aristotle identifies *phronēsis* as the *orthos logos* of virtue: "For virtue is not only the characteristic that accords with correct reason [*kata ton orthon logon*], but also the one that is *accompanied* by [*meta*] correct reason. And *phronēsis* is the *orthos logos* concerning such sorts of things" (1144b26–28). In what follows, I will address the question of how and in what sense *phronēsis* is the answer to the opening question of book VI. I will argue that *phronēsis* is a state of soul characterized by the *orthos logos* in the sense of being the power or condition for good practical reason, and it is such by being perceptively sensitive to the particulars of the situation in which one must act.

The reason it is necessary to define the *orthos logos*, Aristotle tells us at the opening of book VI, is to specify the knowledge of the sorts of things virtue aims at (*Nic. Eth.* 1138b25–34). It is rather empty to know only that one ought to act according to right reason—if all one knew was that virtue aims at the mean that accords with the *orthos logos*, "he would be no further ahead in his knowledge—for example, he would not know what sorts of things ought to be applied to the body if somebody should say, 'so many things as the art of medicine commands and as he who possesses that art commands.'" However, it seems that we are left with exactly this kind of thing: if the *orthos logos* is *phronēsis*, then we are left with the result that what sorts of acts are virtuous are just those that the *phronimos* identifies. This is exactly what Aristotle already gave us in the definition of virtue in II.6 1106b36–1107a2. The question, then, is: how does an understanding of *phronēsis* provide content to the understanding of virtue?

If one is keeping in mind what the middle course consists in, what Aristotle means to do by defining the *orthos logos* may seem a bit of a puzzle. Aristotle introduces the idea that virtue aims at a middle course in book II, after reminding his listener that arguments (*logoi*) concerning ethics do not admit of precision since "matters of action and those pertaining to what is advantageous have nothing stationary about them" (*Nic. Eth.* 1104a4). This imprecision of ethical arguments is due to the nature of action, which is concerned with particulars (1141b16),[2] yet "still less precise is the argument [*logos*] concerned with particulars, for it does not fall under an art or any sort of precepts" (1104a6–7).[3] There is, in other words, a limit to what *logos*, argument or reason, can attain concerning the particulars with which virtue is concerned, yet the middle course that the virtuous act attains must be determined with reference to the particulars the virtuous agent faces.[4] Aristotle goes so far as to say that, rather than follow an argument, "those who act ought themselves always to examine what pertains to the opportune moment [when it presents itself]" (1104a8–9). Because action is tied to flexible particulars, it seems more important that the virtuous person be able to read (so to speak) the virtuous middle course off the present particulars than to have the right reason or argument about—an *orthos logos* of—the middle course. One may reasonably decide, for example, to be courageous in battle by standing one's ground, but being courageous may end up requiring abandoning that plan (and the reasoning that led to it). Perhaps paradoxically, virtue requires the flexibility *not* to abide by one's own reason, should the situation call for it. It is not *irrational* to abandon one's plan, should the situation call for it; rather, the rationality that determines the middle course is broader than having the right argument because it includes the flexibility to decide or determine whether one's reasoning applies in particular circumstances. But this raises the question: if the *orthos logos* identifies the middle, which—because it is wrapped up with particulars—cannot be precisely determined by argument, what is Aristotle after in defining the *orthos logos*?

I propose that what Aristotle aims to specify is the *power* or *capacity* for right reason in ethical matters: what makes it possible to reason well about action and what produces such reasoning.[5] "*Phronēsis* is the *orthos logos*," then, does not mean being in possession of good and true arguments; rather, it means being the condition for and power of (good, correct) practical thinking.[6] It is such a power, at least in part, I will argue, by being receptive to particulars as significant in specific ways to the present situation and the ethical decision to be made; by correctly apprehending the particulars *about which* one thinks and *with respect to which* one chooses the middle course and the virtuous action, one is able to reason well about what to choose. There is flexibility to the way that a situation appears to one, and as a result one can simply *fail to notice* or fail to be struck by relevant details.[7] Good practical reasoning requires an initial sensitivity to the circumstances one finds oneself in, and I will argue that *phronēsis* makes possible good practical reasoning just by providing this correct apprehension of particulars.

The sensitivity to the particulars of one's present circumstance exceeds being receptive to new reasons that figure into one's practical thinking, and abandoning one's plans in the appropriate moment does not necessarily mean that one discovers new reasons when one is called upon to act that one failed to anticipate. Rather, the present moment has ethically relevant features that *cannot* be anticipated and therefore fall outside the realm of argument. Generally, the point that the present in which one acts has features that cannot be anticipated is recognizable from ordinary experience: it is the reason an actor gets nervous before a performance or a speaker fears becoming tongue-tied at the crucial moment. Despite having decided and prepared in advance exactly what to do, one simply is not guaranteed that one will successfully execute the performance.[8]

This general feature of action seems to be what Aristotle is pointing toward in his rejection of universal ethical rules and his emphasis on the variability of the particulars of action. For example, Aristotle does not consider Sophocles's Neoptolemus to be akratic for failing to abide by his decision to lie to Philoctetes (*Nic. Eth.* 1151b17–22). Neoptolemus had been persuaded by Odysseus that the right thing to do was to lie to Philoctetes, which is to say that Neoptolemus had decided upon the right course of action as the conclusion of an argument. But when it comes to the moment of action, Neoptolemus does not lie to Philoctetes. The reason this does not constitute an akratic abandonment of reason, Aristotle explains, is that Neoptolemus fails to abide by his reason on account of a noble pleasure, pleasure in telling the truth. Aristotle does not say that Neoptolemus was *wrong* to have been persuaded by Odysseus to lie to Philoctetes and he does not explain his new course of action as adopting a *new* argument or a new reason. Rather, it seems, Neoptolemus's sensitivity to Philoctetes's suffering brings into relief the pain of lying to him and prompts Neoptolemus to act on account of the pleasure of truth telling. Neoptolemus may have even taken into account Philoctetes's suffering and his own distaste for lying in making his decision to lie, but the way the *present* situation *actually* speaks to him dictates a different course of action. If the situation speaks well to Neoptolemus, he is right to answer its call. Aristotle does not consider it *irrational* for Neoptolemus to abandon his plan at this appropriate moment, and this shows that the rationality that determines the middle course is broader than having the right argument because it includes the flexibility to see whether one's reasoning applies in particular circumstances. Were he less insightfully sensitive to Philoctetes's character and suffering, he would not have been led to abandon his decision to lie. If he had seen Philoctetes as a dangerous, deranged, cursed person (as Odysseus had led him to believe), he would not have been prompted to the noble act that he in fact undertook.[9] A contrasting example is that of Jane Austen's Emma Woodhouse, who, because she views the particulars of her circumstances (particular expressions, conversations, behaviors, etc.) with a certain interpretation already in mind (that Mr. Elton loves Harriet), is blind to the particular acts and intentions of those around her and as a result causes great suffering to those she cares about most. Having decided in advance what one ought to do may interfere with seeing the particulars truthfully.

Several times in *Nicomachean Ethics* VI, Aristotle emphasizes that *phronēsis* is concerned with the particular (1141b14–16, 1142a14–16, 1142a23–30, 1143a25–29, 1143a32–35).[10] Apprehending particulars is the defining mark of perception, according to Aristotle's account of this power in *De anima* (II.6 417b21–23, 417b27), and carried over into the *Nicomachean Ethics* (1112b34–1113a2, 1142a26–27, 1143b4–5), and as a result we might expect *phronēsis* to involve some sort of perception. Aristotle makes good on this expectation when in VI.9 he likens *phronēsis* to a kind of perception (1142a23–30). A couple of questions arise, however, if *phronēsis* is a kind of perception: first, what sense does it make to say that *phronēsis* is the power to *perceive* particulars in an ethically significant way? The proper objects of perception are such things as colors and shapes, not such things as the goodness or badness of a particular. Moreover, *phronēsis* is an *intellectual* virtue, not a virtue of the perceptual part of the soul.[11] Second, if *phronēsis* is a kind of perception, in what sense is it an *orthos logos*?

I will argue that the correct apprehension of the ethical particular is a function of the combined powers of intellect and perception, and specifically that *phronēsis* transforms the mean of perception that characterizes perception as a whole (*De anima* 431a20) into an *ethical* mean of perception.[12] This will answer both the question of how an intellectual virtue crosses into the territory of perception, and the sense in which *phronēsis* is the *orthos logos*. The mean of perception is also a *logos* in the sense that it is an appropriate ratio of the terms that define each sense—the mean of vision, for example, is an appropriate ratio of white and black—and *phronēsis* is a *logos* in the same sense. In sum, my thesis has two parts: (1) *phronēsis* is the *orthos logos* of virtue because it enables the virtuous person to correctly perceive the particulars with respect to which she acts; and this means perceiving particulars in their relevance to one's particular ethical aims, and (2) *phronēsis* does this by providing perception with the terms by which it is receptive of ethical particulars, operating as an intellectually informed mean of perception.

1. *Phronēsis*

Let me begin with some initial remarks about Aristotle's discussion of *phronēsis* in VI of the *Nicomachean Ethics*. Aristotle's primary focus in book VI seems to be on intellect's contribution to action. That this is his concern is indicated, first, by the reason he offers for needing to define the *orthos logos* of virtue, referred to above: one who knows only that she ought to act according to the *orthos logos* will not know how, specifically, to act at all (1138b29–32). Second, the work of VI.2 is to introduce practical thinking as distinct from theoretical thinking and as necessary for action: "Now, thinking itself moves nothing, but thinking that is for the sake of something and concerned with action does, for it rules over [*archein*] production as well" (1139a35–b1).

Having marked out practical thinking as his focus, Aristotle proceeds to identify and discuss the intellectual virtue responsible for *good* practical thinking.[13] *Phronēsis* is just such an intellectual virtue. *Phronēsis* is "a true *hexis* bound up with action, accompanied by reason, and concerned with things that are good or bad for a human being" (*Nic. Eth.* 1140b4–6). *Phronēsis* is a state of soul that *makes possible* the sort of thinking necessary for good action.

What sort of state makes practical reasoning possible? It is telling that *phronēsis* is a state of soul *accompanied by* reason: this suggests that *phronēsis* is not *simply* the activity of practical reason, but also the condition for it.

Aristotle acknowledges that *phronēsis* is something more than reason when he notes that "*phronēsis* is not solely a state accompanied by reason, a sign of which is that it is possible to forget such a state, but not to forget *phronēsis*" (*Nic. Eth.* 1140b28–30). By using the term "state" (*hexis*) Aristotle seems to be referring to the person who has learned, say, geometry, that is, a person with the first actuality of geometrical knowledge. It is possible for a geometer to *forget* his knowledge of geometry, regressing to the stage wherein he has only the first potentiality for knowledge of geometry. To lose one's geometry *hexis* would just be to forget the content of geometry, its axioms and proofs. But it is not possible to forget *phronēsis*, and this suggests that it is a different sort of *hexis* than the geometry *hexis*, a sort of *hexis* that exceeds the content of reason. I take this to mean that *phronēsis* offers a *way of seeing* that makes possible good reasoning. In this way, *phronēsis* is rather like the state of mind that makes it possible to enjoy visual art: one may forget what Picasso's *The Old Guitarist* looks like, but the way of seeing that makes one appreciate such a work is not forgotten. Similarly, one may forget the *reasons* one chose to stand one's ground in battle, but the way of seeing that made those reasons salient is not forgotten.

That *phronēsis* is a state of seeing well in addition to a state with reason is borne out in the discussions of *phronēsis* that follow. Aristotle maintains, on the one hand, that *phronēsis* is a supposition (*hupolēpsis*)[14] of the principle of action, in the sense of being a supposition of that for the sake of which the action is undertaken (*Nic. Eth.* 1140b11–17). At a later moment, he connects this supposition with deliberation: *phronēsis* is a true supposition of the end with respect to which one deliberates well (1142b31–33). Similarly, the *phronimos* is described, on the one hand, as one who is able to deliberate well (1140a25–28, see also 1141b9–10). On the other hand, Aristotle maintains that *phronēsis* is a kind of perception because it is concerned with particulars, which are not captured by *logoi* (1142a23–30), and he describes the *phronimos* as one who *sees* correctly the particulars of action (1143b4–14, esp. 1143b11–14). It appears, then, that *phronēsis* is a state of soul with a twofold ability: to see the particulars well, and to hold the true supposition of the aim of action.

Aristotle addresses the gap between having a *logos* and acting well with respect to particulars in the distinction he draws between experience (*empeiria*) and art (*technē*) at the opening of the *Metaphysics*. Experience is oriented toward the particular, whereas art is possession of a universal:

> And art comes into being whenever, out of many conceptions from experience, one universal judgment [*hupolēpsis*] arises about those

> things that are similar. For to have a judgment [*hupolēpsis*] that this thing was beneficial to Callias when he was sick with this disease, and to Socrates, and one by one in this way to many people, belongs to experience. But the judgment that it was beneficial to all such people, marked out as being of one kind, when they were sick with this disease . . . belongs to art. (*Met.* 981a5–12)[15]

Those with experience, he goes on to say, are more effective in action than those who have a *logos* but have no experience (*Met.* 981a12–15), for the reason that action concerns the particular:

> Experience is familiarity [*gnōsis*] with things that are particular, but art with those that are universal, while actions [*praxeis*] and all becoming are concerned with what is particular. For the doctor does not cure a human being except incidentally, but Callias or Socrates or any of the others called by such a name, who happens to be a human being. So if someone without experience has the reasoned account [*logos*] and is familiar with the universal, but is ignorant of what is particular within it, he will often go astray in his treatment, since what is treated is particular. (*Met.* 981a15–24)

What is important for art is the way many particulars are the same, but what is important for treating a sick person is the way that person is unique: one treats "human being" only incidentally to treating Socrates. This is not to say that Socrates is not amenable to certain kinds of *logoi*—he *is* a human being, with certain features and a certain history—and having these *logoi* will help one treat him. But neither is Socrates identical with these *logoi*, and a treatment that was successful once may not be successful again. The matter is similar in the case of ethical action. One will have certain *logoi*—certain principles, certain aims, certain familiarity with people, and so on—but these *logoi* will only *aid* in acting well, they will not ensure it. One must also be open to the particular as it exceeds what is captured in a *logos*. Again, the case of Jane Austen's Emma is illustrative here: Emma's *logos* of her circumstances, her hypothesis that Mr. Elton is in love with her friend Harriet, obstructs her vision of Mr. Elton's behavior. But being attuned to behaviors that signify esteem or love—having a *logos* of love—would ordinarily be an aid to seeing what is happening.

The twofold character of *phronēsis*, I will argue, has this kind of structure. The *phronimos* perceives the particulars well and has the right supposition of the aim, and these are mutually informing: for the aim to be right, it must be responsive to particulars, and to perceive the particulars well, one's perception must be informed by one's aims. It will be in this sense that *phronēsis* is the *orthos logos*: a state of soul wherein perception is informed by an ethical mean.

2. Virtue and *Phronēsis*

It may seem more natural to assign the capacity to apprehend ethical particulars to the nonrational part of the soul and say that one perceives well by virtue of having good character. Virtue of character is the good state of the nonrational part of the soul that makes one apt to feel passion appropriately (*Nic. Eth.* 1106b16–18), and it is natural to think of the kind of sensitivity that is necessary for ethical reasoning to be a matter of feeling appropriate passions—being struck with horror at the sight of violence, for example. Moreover, passions are those things that are accompanied by pleasure and pain (1105b21–23), and the latter are activities of the perceptual part of the soul (*De anima* 431a10–11, see also 413b23). Finally, Aristotle defines virtue of character as a state of soul that makes one apt to hit the middle course (*Nic. Eth.* 1116b15–16). For these reasons (and perhaps others), one might hold that it is virtue of character, not the intellectual virtue of *phronēsis*, that gains sight of the significance of ethical particulars.[16]

However, Aristotle's discussion of *phronēsis* in VI challenges the thesis that it is virtue of character that is responsible for perceiving well in two respects. First, Aristotle explicitly identifies *phronēsis* with perception (*Nic. Eth.* 1142a23–30), and, second, Aristotle characterizes virtue without *phronēsis* as a blind person, stumbling toward what she thinks is good but causing harm instead (1144b8–12); similarly Aristotle characterizes *phronēsis* as the "eye of the soul" (1144a29–30). Both of these suggest that it is *phronēsis* that provides the sight of the practical good in its particularity, not virtue of character.[17] (I elaborate both of these points below.)

Aristotle addresses the issue of the relationship of virtue of character and *phronēsis* at the conclusion of book VI, when he considers the question of why *phronēsis* is useful in producing right action (*Nic. Eth.* 1143b18–19). He offers two justifications for the question. First, good actions are the deliverances of having the right state (*hexis*), that is, the right virtue, and "we are not more skilled in the actions that correspond to [for example] health by possessing the arts of medicine and gymnastic training" (1143b21–28). If, for example, it is because one is courageous, having been habituated to endure frightening things, that the courageous person is especially capable of performing courageous actions (1104a35–1104b3), there seems to be no role for *phronēsis* to play in effectively producing good actions.

Second, even if one were to claim that *phronēsis* is not necessary for the *performance* of the courageous action of the courageous person, but that it is nonetheless necessary for the *development* of courage, it would then not be necessary to become *phronimos* oneself: one could simply obey one who is *phronimos*. "For it will make no difference whether they themselves have *phronēsis* or obey others who have it, and that would be enough for us, just as it is also in what concerns health: although we wish to be healthy, nonetheless we do not learn the art of medicine" (*Nic. Eth.* 1143b28–33). If nonrational virtue is itself sufficient to produce virtuous actions, this renders *phronēsis*, understood as an *intellectual* state concerning the good and the bad for human beings (1140b4–6), superfluous.

Aristotle rejects the idea that *phronēsis* is not useful for producing virtuous action; he will argue, to the contrary, that there is no nonrational virtue *without phronēsis* (1144b30–32). Both of the objections to the utility of *phronēsis* for the production of virtuous action that he raises stem from a particular vision of nonrational virtue that Aristotle must reject, as I will argue that he does. The objectionable vision of nonrational virtue is that according to which nonrational virtue contains its own measure and serves as its own guide, just as a simply natural living creature does. An oak, for example, has its measure internal to it in the sense that it grows to maturity on its own; even if it had the capacity of intellect, it would still do it no good to *know* that it ought to grow to forty feet high because that measure is already programmed (so to speak) in its nonrational soul. On this view, if nonrational virtue contains its own measure, it is enough to *be* courageous, that is, to have the nonrational habit of facing fearful situations, in order to stand one's ground in battle when appropriate. It will not help to also *know* that courage dictates standing one's ground in this particular situation. If one adopts this vision of nonrational virtue, the utility of *phronēsis* will indeed be cast into doubt. Furthermore, if one accepts this vision of nonrational virtue, then it would be immaterial whether one follows one's own *phronēsis* or that of another in developing virtue; *phronēsis* will, in any case, be rendered superfluous by the accomplishment of virtue of character, and so it is not necessary to have it oneself. Nonrational virtue, on this vision, is self-guiding *in itself*—it need not draw on another power in order to determine or produce the actions that manifest virtue—and so the development of this self-guiding capacity need not be the implementation of some other power in one's own soul rather than that of another person.

This question of the utility of *phronēsis*, and the vision of nonrational virtue that gives rise to it, are consequences of an important move that Aristotle makes at the outset of his account of virtue in book II of the *Nicomachean*

Ethics. In the second chapter, Aristotle sets aside the qualification that virtuous action is *kata ton orthon logon*:

> It is necessary to examine matters pertaining to actions, that is, how one ought to perform them. For these actions have authoritative control over what sorts of characteristics come into being, just as we have said. Now, "acting in accord with correct reason" is commonly granted, and let it be posited for now—what pertains to it will be spoken of later, both what "correct reason" is and how it relates to the virtues. (*Nic. Eth.* 1103b29–34)

Aristotle's account of virtue in books II–V thus *seems* to say that virtue of character in itself produces virtuous action, without the intellectual input that supplies the *orthos logos*. In II.4, for example, Aristotle argues that a virtuous act is one that proceeds from a certain condition, namely, (a) acting knowingly, (b) choosing and choosing the act for its own sake, and (c) being in a steady state. But he continues by noting that for virtue of character "knowledge has little or no force, whereas the other two criteria amount to not a small part but rather the whole affair—criteria that are in fact met as a result of our doing just and moderate things many times" (*Nic. Eth.* 1105b2–5). This pronouncement appears to support the notion of virtue of character as self-sufficient, in the absence of intellectual input. Yet Aristotle finds it necessary to invoke intellect even in the account of the virtues of character: choice is, of course, a rational desire productive of action that results from deliberation (III.2–3). Moreover, when Aristotle defines virtue in II.6, he includes the *phronimos* in the definition: virtue is "a state marked by choice [*hexis prohairetikē*], residing in the mean [*mesotēs*] relative to us defined by reason and as the *phronimos* would define it" (1106b36–1107a2). And so we see that Aristotle does indeed invoke intellectual input even in the account of virtue of character, and this unsettles the appearance of virtue of character as sufficient *in itself* to produce virtuous action.[18]

In order, then, to show that *phronēsis* is indeed useful for producing virtuous action, Aristotle must reject the vision of virtue in which virtue of character contains its own measure and serves as its own guide. Aristotle's response does so and more. His response to the question of the utility of *phronēsis* is that virtue and *phronēsis* mutually require one another: *phronēsis* cannot be what it is in the absence of virtue, nor can virtue be what it is in the absence of *phronēsis*. "It is clear, then, on the basis of what has been said, that it is not possible to be good in the authoritative sense in the absence of *phronēsis*, nor is it possible to be *phronimos* in the absence of moral virtue"

(*Nic. Eth.* 1144b30–32). I will for the moment only address the insufficiency of virtue without *phronēsis*.[19] Aristotle argues for the necessity of *phronēsis* by introducing a distinction between natural virtue and virtue in the authoritative sense (*kuria*). Natural virtues are present in children and beasts, but "they are manifestly harmful in the absence of intellect . . . just as a strong body moving without eyesight will end up stumbling with considerable force because it is without sight, so it is also in this case" (1144b8–12). Aristotle specifies that the form of intellect that transforms this blind natural virtue into true virtue is *phronēsis* (1144b16–17). Clearly, then, Aristotle envisions *phronēsis* as a sort of sight by which the motive force of virtue is guided (see 1143b11–14).[20]

Natural virtue, as Aristotle depicts it, seems to be a right intention that goes wrong; a disposition to be just that fails to deliver just acts (or if it succeeds, it does so on the basis of chance rather than virtue). Such a good-hearted yet foolish disposition is a familiar trope in literature (my example of Jane Austen's Emma, who, despite good intentions, causes harm to a dear friend, fits the bill): one who tries to do right but, due to a failure to understand the specificities that define the situation within which one acts, goes terribly wrong. Aristotle describes just such an occurrence in his consideration of acting on account of ignorance in *Nicomachean Ethics* III.1. Ignorance of particulars may cause great harm, as occurs if "one suppose[s] that his own son is an enemy, just as Merope did, that the pointed spear has been blunted, or that the stone is pumice. Or, by giving someone a drink to save him, one might kill him. Or wishing only to touch, as sparring partners do, someone might land a blow" (1111a11–15). If *phronēsis* is that which provides the sight of a well-meaning intention that otherwise goes wrong, as Merope goes wrong, we may infer that the sight that *phronēsis* provides is a correct apprehension of such particulars of action, which Aristotle lists generally as "who acts, what he does, with respect to what or in what circumstances, and sometimes also with what (for example, with an instrument), for the sake of what (for example, preservation), and how (for example, gently or violently)" (1111a3–6).

That it is *phronēsis* that apprehends the particulars of action is confirmed by Aristotle's repeated insistence, throughout VI, that *phronēsis* is concerned with particulars (*Nic. Eth.* 1141b14–16, 1142a14–16, 1142a23–30, 1143a25–29, 1143a32–35). What sort of apprehension is this? The correct apprehension of particulars may be understood as correctly identifying objects, that is, correctly subsuming the particular blunted spear under the genus "practice weapon." Of course, this kind of identification must be involved in the correct apprehension of particulars, but it cannot be the whole story. As we saw above, there is a gap between having the *logos* and acting well, which Aristotle expresses in terms of the difference between experience and art (*Met.* I.1 981a12–24). Aristotle makes a similar point in the *Nicomachean Ethics* VI discussion of *phronēsis* (1141b14–21), offering as a case where experience is more effective than art that of the experienced person knowing that poultry is healthful, whereas the artist knows that light meats are healthful. In order to produce health, it is necessary to identify the meat that is light, which is to identify poultry in general and also particular pieces of poultry; but this identification is not achieved by having the *logos* "light meat is healthful" by itself. Moreover, it is also necessary to determine whether in this case light meat is the right choice, how much the sick person ought to eat, or whether it would be better to refrain from eating at all. In other words, identifying the "with what" of action is inseparable from identifying the "how," and the "how" in any particular case is a matter of judgment, not *technē*. Aristotle insists that these are matters of judgment concerning the particulars of action, and this kind of judgment is a matter of perception, not a matter of *logos* (1109b20–24). This suggests that *phronēsis* is not merely the perception *that* this meat is chicken, but an ongoing perceptual responsiveness to the particularities of the patient that dictate whether and in what quantity this chicken ought to be consumed. Having experience or *technē* opens up the context within which a judgment is made, but it does not determine the judgment itself. For example, having experience healing people or having the medical art will offer chicken as a solution to Socrates's illness, but it is up to the judgment of the healer to appropriately apply (or refrain from applying) this solution.

We may see this point more clearly if we take Aristotle's example of the sparring partners. The sparring partners understand that the "how" of practice sparring is "not too hard, not too soft; a touch, not a hit." They will also be able to inspect their spears to be sure that the "what" they are operating with are blunted spears. But achieving the touch appropriate to sparring (as opposed to battle) will depend upon other factors, such as how heavy the weapon is, how quickly the sparring partner moves, how far away he is, and so on. These are things that one can understand in a general way, but achieving the right level of force will require that one be perceptively responsive to the particulars as they occur. We see a similar point in learning how to dance, especially a partner dance such as swing: one may be told to hold oneself a certain way, to move one's feet a certain way, and so on. But actually dancing well will require that one respond to one's partner's movements *as they occur* and that one dance as the music moves one to dance. To identify these particulars is not only to subsume them under their genera, but also to be responsive to them in their particularity in the moment. Nussbaum offers a further example, that of telling a joke—following a rulebook to tell a joke would inevitably fail, because a joke is successful only in being tailored to the concrete situation.[21] The phronetic apprehension of particulars is an apprehension of them as an element of a present, ongoing situation, and discerning, perceptually, their appropriateness to the ongoing situation.

Phronēsis is especially concerned with one kind of particular named in Aristotle's list: the "for the sake of what" of action. In VI.5 Aristotle indicates, in a somewhat roundabout way, that *phronēsis* identifies that for the sake of which one acts. Moderation, he asserts, the virtue concerning pleasure and pain, preserves *phronēsis*, "for it is not *every* supposition that the pleasant and painful ruin and distort . . . but rather those suppositions concerning action. For the sources of action are that for the sake of which the actions are undertaken, but to someone who has been ruined on account of pleasure or pain, the *principle immediately fails to appear*—it is not manifest to him that he ought to choose all things and to act for the sake of this and on account of this" (*Nic. Eth.* 1140b13–19, my emphasis).[22] *Phronēsis*, the supposition protected by moderation, is a supposition about that for the sake of which the action is undertaken.[23]

It might seem a little surprising to find the for-the-sake-of-which on the list of the particulars in which action consists. Aristotle's example of preservation is not obviously particular; rather, it is that at which all living things aim. Similarly, virtuous actions are undertaken for their own sake, that is, for the sake of virtue, for the sake of acting well, for the sake of the *kalon*, and for the sake of *eudaimonia*. To act for the sake of virtue, then, seems to require a general conception of what virtue *is*, perhaps what *eudaimonia* is.[24] In what sense, then, is the for-the-sake-of-which of action a particular? It is particular insofar as action itself is particular—an action *of* a particular person *in* a particular situation, and all the rest of the particulars listed in III.1—and since the for-the-sake-of-which of virtuous action is internal to the action itself, *it too* is particular. Similarly, that for the sake of which one builds a house is a *particular* house; a particular instance of the universal, house.

The difference between that particular house, however, and the particular virtuous action is that the variation in particular qualities of the house does not alter its being a house—whether the house is red or yellow, two stories or four, open concept or railroad layout, whether wood or brick—whereas the particularities of the action *do* alter the nature of the action. To land a blow when sparring is a different act than merely to touch one's partner. The particular house does not *consist* in its particularities—it will be a house even if gutted and redesigned—but the virtuous action *does* consist in its particularities—to alter the particulars is to alter the action. As Aristotle says, *phronēsis* must be especially acquainted with particulars (more than universals), because "it is bound up with action, and action concerns the particulars" (*Nic. Eth.* 1141b14ff.).

In the case of virtue, the Lesbian rule is a fitting model: the rule must bend to fit the particulars, not the particulars to the rule. "For the rule [or measure] of something indeterminate is indeterminate too, just as is the case with the lead rule used in house building in Lesbos: the lead rule changes in relation to the shape of the stone and does not stay the same; and so too the specific decree changes in relation to the matter at hand" (*Nic. Eth.* 1137b30–32).[25] The parallel with virtue runs as follows: determining the aim of a virtuous act requires the flexibility to adjust one's aim to fit the particulars, rather than to adjust the particulars to fit one's universal ethical dictum. To accomplish such flexibility, one must let the particulars *speak* to one, and it is this that *phronēsis* accomplishes.

I conclude from these considerations that *phronēsis* guides virtue by identifying the for-the-sake-of-which of action in *specific* circumstances. Virtue provides (at least)[26] the general inclination to be, say, just, and *phronēsis* specifies this inclination by identifying the *particular* aim of action here and now (for example, not giving back a sword to one in a frenzy [as in *Republic* I]).[27]

3. *Phronēsis* and Perception

I will return later to the idea that *phronēsis* guides virtue by identifying the particular for-the-sake-of-which of action, and turn now to the thesis that *phronēsis* is good or true perception. There are two textual justifications for pursuing the hypothesis that *phronēsis* is perceiving well. First, there is Aristotle's insertion of the *phronimos* into the definition of virtue as the arbiter of the mean (*Nic. Eth.* 1106b36–1107a2), understood as the appropriate respect, manner, time, and so on in feeling and action (1106b16–24). Aristotle later remarks that whether a person is blameworthy for departing too much from the mean is discerned by perception (1109b20–22).[28] If departure from the mean is discerned by perception, it stands to reason that the discernment of the mean is also achieved by perception. Second, Aristotle explicitly likens *phronēsis* to perception on the basis of its being concerned with particulars more than with universals (1142a23–30). If *phronēsis* is perceiving well it will, of course, not be perception in the sense of perception of special or common perceptibles, but a rather new and sophisticated kind of perception, one, I will argue, that is informed already by intellect. We will see that the kind of perception at play in this passage is an intellectually informed perception.

We may reiterate at the outset that perceiving well is only one of the accomplishments of *phronēsis*. To be *phronimos* is to be skilled at acting virtuously, and to decide upon the right action requires more than good perception. In VI.7, Aristotle notes that *phronēsis* is said to be concerned with "the human things about which it is possible to deliberate" (*Nic. Eth.* 1141b8–9), and in this passage we are about to examine he says that it is *of* the ultimate particular (*tou heskatou*) of which there is no *logos* but only a perception. These two objects are distinct: in III.3, Aristotle expressly declares that there is no deliberation about the objects of perception (1112b32–1113a2). This indicates that *phronēsis* has two functions: to be receptive of the particulars *with respect to which* one deliberates, and to thereby deliberate well about *how to act* with respect to those particulars.

Phronēsis Is a Kind of Perception (*Nicomachean Ethics* 1142a23–30)

Aristotle characterizes *phronēsis* as perception in a (much discussed) passage in VI.8:

> And that *phronēsis* is not science is manifest: *phronēsis* concerns the ultimate particular thing [*to eschaton*], as was said, for the action performed is of this kind. Indeed, *phronēsis* corresponds to [*anti-keisthai*] intellect, for intellect is of the defining boundaries [*horos*], of which there is no rational account [*logos*]; and *phronēsis* is of the ultimate particular thing [*eschaton*], of which there is not a science but rather a perception [*aisthēsis*], and a perception not of things peculiar to one of the senses, but a perception of the sort by which we perceive that the ultimate particular thing [*eschaton*], in mathematics, is a triangle. For here too there will be a stop. But this is perception rather more than *phronēsis*, though perception of a form different from that [of one of the senses]. (*Nic. Eth.* 1142a23–30)[29]

This passage declares that *phronēsis* is of those things of which there is only perception, but not perception in the strict sense of the faculty receptive to proper perceptibles like color, sound, smell, and taste. It is, instead, an intellectually informed perception. It would be absurd to attribute a perception of a triangle *as* the ultimate figure in mathematics to a nonrational animal.[30] To perceive the triangle in this way requires, at least, that one be familiar with mathematics as a science, perhaps especially with geometry as a subset of mathematics. Analogously, then, to perceive the particulars of one's circumstances as relevant to how one decides to act requires, minimally, some conception about what it is to be or do good.

We may perhaps push the analogy even further. If to perceive that a triangle is the ultimate figure in geometry is to perceive it as foundational in that science, in the sense that other figures may be built from the triangle, to perceive an ethical particular is to perceive it as that with respect to which one must act. The perception that the triangle is ultimate is a perception of a certain kind of significance that the triangle bears: the triangle is a basic term that marks off the field of geometry. A triangle is more than the ingredients of geometry—points, lines—it is the first figure, the first instance of a rectilinear shape with which geometry is concerned. The triangle is the minimal configuration of lines that has an intelligible structure; it is the first arrangement of (straight) lines that we can call a shape, and it signals the emergence into a new mathematical domain. In this sense, it is a stop.[31] Similarly, *phronēsis* is the perception of a particular as having foundational significance in *its* domain, the domain of action.[32] It will be more than perception of special or common perceptibles; it will be perception that a particular is a basic term in a situation requiring action. What this would amount to is perceiving a particular in terms of good and bad: one perceives not only a certain configuration of shapes and colors, but that this configuration is a person; and not only does one perceive that this is a person, but that this is a person in distress; and not only does one perceive that this is a person in distress, one perceives that it is bad for this person to be in distress and it would be good to remedy the distress.[33]

This is a complex kind of perception, and it may be helpful to distinguish between the different levels of perception occurring here. There are, of course, the basic levels of perception operative here: perception of the special and common perceptibles such as colors and shapes, and the perception of the incidental perceptibles such as Philoctetes. Included in such perception of incidental perceptibles is the fact that Philoctetes is wailing. There is, further, the perception that Philoctetes is distressed—that he is not, say, putting on an act for the sake of his visitor, Neoptolemus, but is truly in distress. This may seem like a matter for judgment—one may, upon reflection, decide that Philoctetes was putting on an act. But to raise that question in the first place, one must be initially struck by something off about Philoctetes's wailing (unless one is generally suspicious of others, in which case the question reflects more upon one's own attitude than upon the other's expression). Finally, Neoptolemus perceives Philoctetes's wailing as an occasion for action. We may call this kind of perception a "caring perception." One may perceive a person in distress without perceiving this as a situation in which one is oneself implicated; in order to *act* with respect to some particular, one must perceive this particular in a caring way, not as a matter in the world which has nothing to do with oneself. It may seem that these latter, complex levels of perception are not perceptions at all, but judgments. But let me point out that nonrational animals exhibit behaviors that would require such "judgments" without having the capacity for judgment. For example, when in heat a female cat will wail. Male cats will hear this, and will hear it not only as a sound, not only as a wail, but also as an occasion for mating. The male cat, too, has a kind of "caring perception." This is not to say that the way Neoptolemus perceives Philoctetes's wailing is simply the *same* as a cat's perception—the sorts of actions that are available to Neoptolemus are more sophisticated and variable than those available to the cat—but it is consistent with it, which shows that the perceptual capacity makes the sorts of discernments we might be tempted to assign to intellectual judgment.

These kinds of perception, both the mathematical and the ethical, are not simple perceptions, not merely the reception of perceptible properties of some object of sense, but instead a perception informed by some knowledge or idea. The knowledge of geometry is not transmitted *by* the sight of the triangle, but it informs the perception of the triangle and enables the recognition of the triangle in its foundational position in geometry. In general, there is no perceptual awareness[34] *without* such organizing coordinates; perception is always informed by *some* contextualizing factor. This is true of perception in both rational and nonrational animals. Neither humans nor nonrational animals experience bare sensory qualities, but instead perceive objects as they bear upon the perceiver. For the nonrational animal, the objects of perception are informed by its project of self-preservation and reproduction. For example, in the *Nicomachean Ethics* Aristotle describes animal perception thus:

> It is not the smell of hares that hounds enjoy but their meat, and the smell produces the perception [of the meat to be enjoyed]. The lion too enjoys not the sound of the cow's voice, but the eating of the cow, though the fact that the cow was nearby he perceived through the sound of its voice, and so he appears to enjoy this. And, similarly, the lion does not take enjoyment because he sees "a deer or a goat in the fields," but because he will have its meat. (*Nic. Eth.* III.10 1118a18–23)

The mere perception of smell (of the hare), or sound (of the cow), or sight (of the deer), is perceived by the animal in light of its desire to eat the source of such perceptions. Of course, the nonrational animal's perceptions are not informed by intellect, but they *are* informed by that animal's aim, the for-the-sake-of-which of the activity of hunting and eating the animal.[35] Thus, in *De anima* Aristotle identifies the activity of perceiving with the activity of feeling pleasure and pain, and the part that perceives and feels pleasure and pain with the part that flees and desires (III.7 431a8–14).

Insofar as the human's aim, the that-for-the-sake-of-which of action, is identified by intellect in the form of *phronēsis*, it is intellect that informs perception. Insofar as *phronēsis* is a kind of perception itself, we may understand it to be such intellectually informed perception of ethical particulars, that is, of particulars in their relevance to ethical action. So, just as the hound, upon encountering the scent of the hare, perceives it as a prompt to hunt because of its aim of self-preservation, so too a virtuous person, upon encountering, say, a person in distress, will perceive this as a prompt to virtuous activity because of her aim of acting virtuously. Or, in other circumstances, for example, our virtuous person is running into a burning building to save someone, seeing the person on the sidewalk outside who is in distress will not weigh upon the virtuous person as an occasion for virtue in the same way. Notice, however, that the identification of the specific for-the-sake-of-which of action is not other than perceiving the particular in a certain way, that is, *as* the prompt to a specific action. Having the right aim and perceiving the particulars *as* relevant to that aim are not two different states of mind (although they may be different in account, as Aristotle would say): the perception of the particulars *just is* the supposition of the aim as realized or specified in some circumstance.

It may seem that identifying *phronēsis* with a kind of perception is unnecessarily opaque. Why call *phronēsis* a kind of *perception* of particulars, rather than, say, a judgment *about* particulars? Why say, as the analogy suggests, that one *perceives* a particular as an occasion to enact a virtue, rather than that one *judges* thus? Why say that intellect operates *within* perception (by informing it) rather than say that intellect operates on the (neutral) material provided by perception? It is worth noting that, insofar as this question tracks the fact-value distinction—perception offers the fact, intellect judges the value—the question must be taken with a grain of salt. As Joseph Owens (1991) has argued, the fact-value distinction does not fit easily with Aristotle's moral and epistemological views. Based on Aristotle's principle that "the origin of all human cognition is located in sensible things,"[36] Owens argues that "known first of all in particular instances by anyone who has been brought up in the proper moral habituation, the aspect of the *kalon* is universalized by the mind just as is any other aspect commonly in the plurality of things."[37] In other words, what is good is *already* cognized in the particular before one comes to have an *idea* of goodness with which to judge the particular. This allows Aristotle to say in *Nicomachean Ethics* VI.11 that "one ought to pay attention to the undemonstrated assertions and opinions of experienced and older people, or of the *phronimos*, no less than to demonstrations, for because they have an eye derived from experience, they see correctly" (1143b11–14).

In keeping with the ability of those who have experience but not knowledge of the good to apprehend the particular good, the answer to why one would claim that *phronēsis* is a *perception* may be that Aristotle wants to maintain a degree of continuity between animal behavior and human behavior, and to speak of *phronēsis* as a kind of intellectual perception permits that continuity. In VI.7, Aristotle emphasizes the mundane nature of the human good, our likeness more to beasts than to gods. Unlike *sophia*, which is concerned with the highest things, *phronēsis* is concerned merely with the *human* good. "All would say that what is wise is the same thing but that what is *phronimos* differs: they would assert that that which observes the good condition for each sort of thing is *phronimos*, and they would entrust such concerns to this. Hence they assert that certain beasts too are *phronimos*, namely, all those that manifestly have the capacity for forethought concerning their own life" (*Nic. Eth.* 1141a24–28). If animals have something like *phronēsis* without having intellect or judgment, *phronēsis* ought to be, at least in part, a perceptual operation.

Another part of the answer rests in Aristotle's position that perception is inherently evaluative, as Moss has persuasively shown (2012). As I will discuss in more detail below, the objects of perception are perceived as pleasant or painful, which is to say that they are perceived as good for or bad for the perceiving animal. Moreover, this perceiving an object as good (pleasant) or bad (painful) motivates the animal's action with respect to it: "to feel pleasure or pain is to be active with the perceptive mean towards the good or bad as such. Avoidance and desire, as actual, are the same thing, and that which can desire and that which can avoid are not different either from each other or from what can perceive" (*De anima* 431a10–14). Perception is itself evaluative, and since the objects of perception are present particulars, this is what perception evaluates.

That the nature of perception in nonrational animals is evaluative already suggests that in the case of rational animals, too, perception will do at least some work of evaluating particulars as good or bad. We can see further that it is necessary that intellect operate *through* perception rather than make judgments *about* it if we consider another feature of perception: in addition to being evaluative, perception must also be selective. Aristotle does not make this feature explicit, but it is too obvious a fact of experience that *not* all objects of perception are perceived pleasantly or painfully—many are not even noticed, or are noticed as irrelevant to the perceiver—for Aristotle (great observer that he is) to deny. Moreover, this feature is implicit in the evaluative nature of perception: if an animal perceives something as pleasant, it will pursue it; in order to pursue it, the animal cannot be distracted by the myriad of other perceptible objects. So, for example, our lion that smells that cow (*Nic. Eth.* 1118a18–23) and begins hunting it will not notice, that is, perceive pleasantly or painfully, the grass at his feet. The principle of perception's selectivity is supplied by the animal's aims, the general aim of self-preservation as specified in this particular situation in which there is a cow to hunt.

If the relationship between perception and intellect were such that intellect proffered judgments upon the neutral information provided by perception, it would be necessary that perception be indifferently attentive. What I mean is that, if *intellect* alone decides what is good or bad, what is an occasion for action, then perception would have to impartially present to intellect *all* the particulars of one's situation. In our example of the person in distress outside of a burning building, perception would not only present these aspects of the situation as equally worthy of noticing, but also the heat on one's skin from the fire, the hunger in one's belly, the way one's clothing feels, that there are many people watching the fire, and so on; if perception were not selective, intellect would decide on the comparative importance of *all* perceived data. This not only seems implausible based on experience—it does not seem that one makes judgments about what is worthy of attention from among a myriad of perceptual objects—but it also supposes that perception offers a kind of view from nowhere, as if the perceiving animal (rational or nonrational) were not already invested in pursuing goals that dictate which particulars are relevant. This contradicts the limited and particular nature of perception—in fact, it makes perception more like intellect, which is impartially receptive of all things.

To call *phronēsis* intellectual perception is to recognize that the aims that one adopts influence the way that things *appear* to one. This is something that Aristotle emphasizes with respect to habit and character in the *Nicomachean Ethics*. The manner in which one habitually faces fear, for example, will alter the way fearful things *appear* to one, either as occasion to flee or occasion to stand one's ground. This is why it is only the virtuous person to whom the practical good appears (III.4 1113a22–31).

In sum, then, *phronēsis* is an intellectual virtue concerned with particulars, that is, objects of perception. It is nonetheless an *intellectual* virtue because perception of particulars is *informed* by the rational agent's projects and aims, of which *phronēsis* is a true supposition (see *Nic. Eth.* 1142b32–33). More accurately, *phronēsis* is the identification of the aim of action called for by the particulars of the situation.

The Mean of Perception

So far, I have argued that *phronēsis* is the capacity to correctly apprehend ethical particulars with respect to which one acts, and such an apprehension is accomplished by intellectually informed perception. But this requires some clarification: in what manner does intellect inform perception? Also, our original question remains: in what sense is *phronēsis* thus understood the *orthos logos* of virtue? These two questions will be put to rest by the same answer: I will argue that intellect informs perception by adjusting the perceptual mean that determines pleasure and pain, transforming it into an *ethical* mean. A distinctive mark of Aristotle's virtuous person is that she feels pleasure and pain at the right things—she takes pleasure in doing courageous acts (or at least is not pained by it) (*Nic. Eth.* 1104b3–8). Insofar as pleasure and pain are active states of the perceptual mean (*De anima* 431a10–11), this suggests that in the virtuous person the perceptual mean is altered so as to discern not only which perceptual qualities are pleasant and painful but which scenarios call for virtuous acts—the perceptual mean becomes an ethical mean. The ethical mean will provide an answer to the question of how intellect informs perception. It will also provide the sense in which *phronēsis* is the *orthos logos* of virtue: the perceptual mean is itself a *logos*, and the *ethical* mean will similarly be the *right logos*.

The person of genuine virtue is one who is appropriately sensitive, one who responds to her circumstances emotionally and actively in the right manner, at the right time, with respect to the right person, and so on. This receptive discernment, I will argue, is accounted for if we understand *phronēsis* as intellectually informed perception. To be receptively discerning requires that one be determinately open: on the one hand, one must be capable of appreciating unpredictable elements that are significant to one's situation, or, in Nussbaum's words, be capable of being surprised.[38] On the other hand, one must be able to distinguish between what is and what is not relevant or significant. In order to be receptively discerning, one must have a basic measure by which one can discern the relevance of things—this is the determinateness—but a measure that does not predict in advance what will and will not be significant—this is the openness. Perception by itself is receptively discerning insofar as it is defined by a perceptual mean, and insofar as *phronēsis* is a kind of perception, I suggest that *phronēsis* is the *orthos logos* of the *ethical* mean by providing to perception the terms within which to receive ethical particulars.

Aristotle's general account of perception in *De anima* II.5 introduces the determinacy of perception in a basic way: perception is a developed potentiality, analogous to the potential knower who has already learned, say, mathematics, but is not actively using that knowledge (417b16–19). Perception is not an undifferentiated potential, as the child's potential to be a knower is undifferentiated, but an already determinate potential for specific modes of perception—vision, hearing, touching, tasting, smelling, perceiving common and incidental perceptibles. That perception has this structure of having five senses determines what sorts of things are to be perceived—colors, sounds, tangible qualities like hot and cold, tastes, odors, sons of Diares and Cleon—but not which *specific* things are to be perceived. In this sense, perception is determinately open.

There is, however, a more sophisticated sense in which perception is determinately open: perception is a mean (*mesotēs*), both with respect to each of the five senses (*De anima* 424a4–7), and with respect to the unity of perceptual experience (431a20). With respect to each of the five senses, Aristotle introduces the mean to explain how the sense discriminates its object and the sense in which it receives its form. Ultimately, the perceptual mean of each sense and of perception as a whole is invoked to explain the awareness included in perception. Aristotle first introduces the idea that perception is a mean at the conclusion of his analysis of the sense of touch:

> Their sense-organ, that of touch, in which the sense called touch primarily resides, is the part which is potentially such as they are. For perceiving is a form of being affected; hence, that which acts makes that part, which is potentially as it is, such as it is itself actually. For this reason we do not perceive anything which is equally as hot or cold, or hard or soft, but rather excesses of these, the sense being a sort of mean [*mesotēs*] between the opposites present in objects of perception. And that is why it discriminates [*krinein*] objects of perception. For the mean is capable of discriminating; for it becomes to each extreme in turn the other extreme. And just as that which is to perceive white and black must be neither of them actually, although both potentially (and similarly too for the other senses), so in the case of touch that which is to perceive such must be neither hot nor cold. (*De anima* 423b30–424a10)

This passage tells us that the structure of sense as a mean explains the capacity of the sense to be acted upon and receive the sensible qualities. In order to be receptive to sensible qualities, the sense itself must not actively be any particular quality already, but potentially any one of them; in order to be potentially but not actively any one of a particular set of qualities (defined by the opposites relevant to each sense, e.g., hot and cold with respect to touch), the sense must be a mean, a balanced ratio between the two opposites that can become weighted in one direction or another by the object at work on the sense. The mean is a determinate structure, a *logos*, that enables the sense to receive a specified range of qualities (*De anima* 424a25–28). Perception is not merely a blank slate, receptive of anything that happens to come its way; rather, it is receptive in particular ways of particular things. In order for the sense to be so discerningly receptive, it must have its own determinacy, its own particular structure that governs how it is receptive.[39] This is, of course, completely understandable: perception is a mode of engagement with the physical world, and any such engagement must be determinate.[40]

Moreover, it is by virtue of being a mean that the sense discriminates (*krinein*), that is, includes an awareness of, its objects. Shortly after the introduction of the mean, Aristotle remarks: "It is also clear why plants do not perceive, although they have a part of soul and are affected by tangible objects; for they are cooled and warmed. The reason is that they do not have a mean, nor a first principle of a kind such as to receive the forms of objects of perception; rather they are affected by the matter as well" (*De anima* 424a32–b3). Because plants do not have a mean, the way they are affected by sensible objects is to simply take on those qualities, rather than to become aware of them. What plants lack is a structure that maintains a distinction between the plant itself and what it is being affected by; the mean supplies this structure. This implies that, in discerning the perceptible object, the sense maintains its mean state while it is moved from it in receiving the sensible quality: the sense becomes *aware* of heat because it remembers, so to speak, its natural state of balance. The perceptual mean is a persistent state that enables receptivity and discernment of its object, both with respect to each of the five senses and with respect to perception as a whole.

Finally, the mean of perception, by governing the range of items to which a sense is receptive, determines whether an item will be pleasant or painful. In *De anima* III.7, Aristotle notes that perception discerns what is pleasant and what is painful: "to feel pleasure or pain is to be active with the perceptual mean towards the good or bad as such" (431a10–11). Aristotle has already argued that the mean of perception governs a range of things of which it is receptive (425a25–28), explaining that this is the reason why a sense is destroyed by an excessively strong object: "for if the movement is too violent for the sense-organ, its *logos* is destroyed—and this we saw the sense to be—just as the consonance and pitch of the strings are destroyed when they are struck too violently" (424a30–32). He later adds that this range also determines whether something will be pleasant or painful: painful if the object falls at the extreme of the range, pleasant if it falls near the middle (426a27–b7). Being pleased or being pained, then, arises just with the perception of pleasant or painful objects, that is, of objects that fall within or without the range governed by the mean of perception. The mean of perception, then, is a persistent state that enables receptivity and discernment both of the perceptual object and at the same time of the goodness or badness of that object (where perceptual goodness or badness, in nonrational animals, is the pleasure or pain caused by a perceptual object).

The Ethical Mean

For nonrational animals, determinations of pleasure and pain are sufficient determinations of what is good (beneficial) and what is bad (harmful), for the reason that nonrational animals seek only the preservation of their own life and the continuation of their species. Rational animals, however, seek not only the preservation of life, but also the achievement of a *good* life. If, then, the good life differs from the pleasant life, there will be a distinction to be drawn between what is pleasant and what is good. And indeed, the good life is distinct from the life of pleasure (a life, Aristotle remarks, suited to beasts [*Nic. Eth.* 1095b19–22]), and the good is distinct from the pleasant (II.4 1113a25–b2).[41] What is pleasant *appears* good, but it may or may not be truly good. This distinction is especially evident in the phenomena of *akrasia* and *enkrateia*: what appears pleasant to such people are things they *think* are bad. This distinction between what is pleasant and what is good is a distinction that is unique to rational animals. This suggests, and the cases of the akratic and enkratic confirm, that the power that discerns what is truly good, rather than apparently good, is an intellectual power. The (undeveloped) mean of perception, for humans, is not sufficient to determine what is good or in what the good life consists; intellectual operation is required.

However, despite distinguishing what is truly good from what is pleasant, Aristotle insists that pleasure and pain are of the highest concern to virtue (*Nic. Eth.* 1104b8–9, 1105a4–7), "for taking delight and feeling pain make no small contribution to our actions' being well or badly done" (1105a6–7). In II.3, Aristotle emphasizes the importance of feeling pleasure and pain at the appropriate things, for "it is on account of the pleasure involved that we do base things, and it is on account of the pain that we abstain from noble ones" (1104b9–11). Moreover, "pleasure has been a part of the upbringing of us all from infancy; it is difficult to remove this experience, since our life has been so ingrained with it" (1105a1–3), and as a result it is necessary to be well brought up with respect to pleasure and pain (1104b11–12), habituated to feel pleasure and pain in the appropriate things.[42] Further, Aristotle makes the case that "the pleasure and pain that accompanies someone's deeds ought to be taken as a sign of his characteristics: he who abstains from bodily pleasures and enjoys this very abstention is moderate, but he who is vexed in doing so is licentious" (1104b3–7). Evidently, Aristotle recognizes that what a person finds pleasant or painful is variable, subject to habituation,[43] and in accordance with one's character—one's virtue or lack thereof.

The mean of perception determines whether some object is perceived as pleasant or painful, and on this basis nonrational animals perceive what is good or bad. Rational animals, however, can and do distinguish what is pleasant or painful from what is good or bad (see *Nic. Eth.* I.4 1095a20–28, II.4 1113a25–b2). The phenomena of *akrasia* and *enkrateia* make this distinction especially obvious: such people take pleasure in something despite thinking that thing is bad. The virtuous person, by contrast, takes pleasure in things that are truly good, and only in these. Pleasure and pain, it seems, follow upon the goodness or badness of the object, not vice versa. Pleasure and pain, in general, are relative to the subject's state (for example, what is pleasant or painful differs according to whether one is healthy or ill) and signify the apparent good.[44] The virtuous person is in such a state and has a character such that the pleasant and painful match up with good—the apparent good and the truly good align. This is why the virtuous person is a "rule and measure" (1113a33).

We have, then, a distinction between what is pleasant and what is good, yet what is pleasant at least *appears* to be good (even if it is not, in fact, good). This distinction suggests that, in nonvirtuous rational animals, (a) there is a principle in addition to the (undeveloped) mean of perception by which the good and the bad are discerned, and (b) that in virtuous people these two principles are aligned. The principle that distinguishes the good from the bad is an intellectual principle, as indicated by the akratic and enkratic people who *think* what is good while taking pleasure in something else. In the virtuous person, then, the perceptual mean and some sort of intellectual principle are in harmony. As we saw, pleasure and pain are subject to habituation: what one takes pleasure in and the manner in which one does so are the results of education in upbringing.

There is a significant difference between the way a nonvirtuous person experiences pleasure and pain and the way a virtuous person does. In III.4, Aristotle addresses the question of whether the object of wish (*boulēsis*) is the good or (merely) the apparent good (*Nic. Eth.* 1113a15–22). The reason the question arises is because "different things appear good to different people, and, should it so happen, even contrary things" (1113a21–22). As a result, either the merely apparent good is the object of wish and there is "no object of wish by nature" (1113a21), or what is truly good is the object of wish, and those wish for the merely apparent good do not in fact wish for the true object of wish (1113a17–18). Aristotle resolves this problem by allowing that the object of wish is what appears to be good, but that what appears to be good is truly good for one in a good condition, that is, to a serious or virtuous person, and to a base person what appears good *merely* appears to be good (1113a22–29). He concludes:

> For the serious person judges [*krinein*] each case correctly, and in each case what is true appears to him. For with respect to each characteristic, there are noble and pleasant things peculiar to it; and the serious person is distinguished perhaps most of all by his seeing [*horāin*] what is true in each case, just as if he were a rule and measure of them. But in the case of most people, a deception [*apatē*] appears to occur on account of the pleasure involved, for what is not good appears to them as good. They choose the pleasant, then, on the grounds that it is good, and they avoid pain on the grounds that it is bad. (*Nic. Eth.* 1113a29–b2)

For the nonvirtuous person, pleasure and pain are *deceptive*. The deception that the nonvirtuous person suffers on account of pleasure, in a straightforward way, is to be deceived in thinking something good that is not good. But there is also a structural way in which pleasure is deceptive to the nonvirtuous: the nonvirtuous person wrongly identifies the goodness or badness of something with the pleasure or pain she takes in it. Even if she happens to take pleasure in something truly good, she thinks it good *because* of the pleasure involved.[45] The virtuous person, by contrast, correctly sees what is truly good, and takes pleasure in it on that basis. In the discussion of pleasure in *Nicomachean Ethics* X.6, Aristotle argues that "what appears to a serious person seems to be the case in fact; and if this is nobly stated, as indeed it seems to be, and [if] virtue and the good human being, insofar as he is good, are the measure of each thing, then the pleasures that appear to him would be pleasures in fact, and the pleasant things would be those in which he delights" (1176a15–19). Thus, whereas pleasure is deceptive for the nonvirtuous, it is a true appearance of the good for the virtuous.

For the true and apparent good to coincide, the virtuous person must take pleasure in what she determines by intellectual exercise is good. But intellectual exercise does not by itself alter the appearance of the good. In order for the *appearance* of the good to change, the mean that determines what is pleasant and what is painful must itself be altered: the explicit idea of the good must come to inform the perceptual mean, transforming it into an ethical mean. The ethical mean of perception would be a steady state that enables the discernment and receptivity of perceptual objects *as* good or bad, and *as* occasions for virtuous action (and passion). What I mean is this: *phronēsis* provides the terms of apprehension of the ethical particular, just as the mean of vision provides the terms black-white that define the range within which visual objects are perceived. The supposition of the for-the-sake-of-which of action that *phronēsis* provides sets the terms for the reception of particulars by attuning the virtuous agent in particular ways, just as the cardiologist is attuned to certain symptoms of heart disease. The *phronimos*, similarly, has a set of terms that attune her to occasions for virtue, and this informs her perception of such particulars.

Let us mine the idea of the mean of perception: the terms that define the mean (e.g., black/white) are established by the prior work of the parents; like the soul itself, perception is a natural first actuality. As a result, black and white are pre-empirical terms *of* experience: experience of color is made possible by these terms and others like them. Ethical experience is not preprogrammed in the way perception is preprogrammed because of the distinction between pleasure and the good.[46] Instead, ethical experience must be worked up and developed. Once developed, however, the terms that condition ethical experience take on the role of pre-empirical terms, like black and white. For example, a child must learn to concern herself with others; she must learn to share, for example, or to ask about the well being of others. Once learned, however, the child's experience is colored by a general concern for others. Having concern for others is no longer an option; it becomes a term of experience of others. However, being concerned for the well-being of others *in general* will only accomplish natural virtue—such a person may free a dangerous criminal out of such concern. In order to be *phronimos*, a person will have to have the terms of concern for others in the right balance; *phronēsis* harnesses such terms into a mean. Just as the mean of perception discriminates what is, for example, hot from what is *too* hot, so too the *phronimos* will discriminate what is concern for others from what is *too* concerned for others (or deficient concern for others).

Recall that *phronēsis* is an intellectual perception of particulars as occasions for virtue. This kind of perception, I argued above, is perception informed by the agent's virtuous aims. Now that we have seen the connection between pleasure as the appearance of the good and what is truly good for the virtuous person, we should understand *phronēsis* as the ethical mean responsible for the unity of the appearance and the reality of what is good. And if it is a mean, it is an *orthos logos* that enables the receptivity of particulars in their goodness (or badness).

4. *Phronēsis* and Deliberation

Phronēsis is sometimes taken to be the process of practical thinking, or to be equivalent to good deliberation. Aristotle does, indeed, articulate an intimate connection between deliberation and *phronēsis*: he begins his inquiry into *phronēsis* through its connection to deliberation ("As for what concerns *phronēsis*, we might grasp it by contemplating whom we say to be *phronimos*. It seems to belong to the *phronimos* to be able to deliberate nobly about things good and advantageous for himself" [*Nic. Eth.* 1140a24–27]), and he repeats the sentiment later, that the *phronimos* will be one who deliberates well (1141b9–10). Similarly, he concludes the chapter devoted to deliberation by saying, "So if having deliberated well belongs to those who are *phronimos*, good deliberation would be a correctness that accords with what is advantageous in relation to the end, about which end *phronēsis* is a true conviction" (1142b31–33). Rather than identify *phronēsis* and good deliberation, however, Aristotle speaks of good deliberation as what *phronēsis* makes *possible*. The person *with phronēsis* will deliberate well, and *in general* one who deliberates well will also be *phronimos* (1140a30–31); good deliberation is in accord with the end that *phronēsis* identifies.

In the discussion of deliberation in *Nicomachean Ethics* III.3, Aristotle sets limits to what may be deliberated about: we deliberate only about things that are up to us and subject to action (1112a30–31), we do not deliberate about ends (*telos*) but only about things toward the end (1112b11–12), and we do not deliberate about particulars, such as "whether this is a loaf of bread or whether it has been baked as it ought to have been—for these belong to perception" (1112b34–1113a1). In VI, we see *phronēsis* identified with *both* these limits of deliberation: *phronēsis* is the true supposition of the end with respect to which one deliberates (1142b31–33), *and* it is of those particulars of which there is no *logos* but only a perception (1142a23–30). If we understand *phronēsis* as the ethical mean of perception, we can accommodate both of these characterizations, and see how *phronēsis* contributes to good deliberation. The ethical mean of perception provides the terms within which particulars are perceived in their relevance to ethical choice and action, and such relevance is, in turn, determined by the aims and projects of the agent. If *phronēsis* is such a power to apprehend ethical particulars, it is *both* a supposition about the end or aim of action, for example, staving off one's hunger, *and* a perception of particulars such as this bread that is baked well. The *phronimos* may nevertheless have to deliberate about how to go about procuring the bread (buying it or baking a similar loaf), but the limits between which she deliberates will already be provided. For a more obviously virtue-related example, we might think of the generous person. She will have the aim of acting generously, and this enables her to perceive the destitute person as an occasion for enacting virtue. It is by virtue of having the aim (of which *phronēsis* is the true supposition) that she perceives the particular (this person here) in the way that she does. She may still deliberate about how best to be generous to this person, but the limits between which she deliberates will be set by *phronēsis*. As I claimed above, the supposition of the limit and the perception of the particulars relevant to it are not two separate states: the perception of the particulars *just is* the supposition of the aim as realized in some circumstance. And so the *phronimos* will in general also be a good deliberator because she is right with respect to the defining terms about which one deliberates.

5. *Phronēsis* and Virtue

There is one final issue to be addressed before closing. Twice at the end of *Nicomachean Ethics* VI Aristotle seems to say that *phronēsis* is concerned only with the things toward the end or aim of action, and virtue of character secures that end. (a) In VI.12, in the context of developing the question of whether *phronēsis* is useful for action, Aristotle notes, "It is possible for someone to perform each thing in turn while being in a certain state, with the result that he is good—I mean, that is, through choice and for the sake of the actions themselves. As for the choice involved, then, virtue makes it correct; but as for doing all that is naturally done for the sake of that choice, this belongs not to virtue but to another capacity" (1144a18–22). At the conclusion of VI.13, he says, "It is clear too there will be no correct choice in the absence of *phronēsis*, nor in the absence of virtue; for the latter makes one carry out the end, the former the things conducive to the end" (1145a4–6).[47] If we understand virtue to attune one *generally* in a virtuous way—to enable one to *be* concerned with the well-being of others—and *phronēsis* to be the *specific* attunement to particulars in light of such a general attunement, these comments mean that virtue sets the broad aim, and *phronēsis* specifies that aim in its receptivity to the particular.

Recall that in *Nichomachean Ethics* VI.5 Aristotle remarks that pleasure and pain may *corrupt* the supposition of the principle of action, that is, what the aim is that *phronēsis* grasps. This corruption, I suggest, may occur in two complementary ways: pleasure may corrupt the supposition of the principle of action simply by deceiving the agent about what is good, or pleasure may corrupt the conviction of the principle of action by focusing too much of the agent's attention on one feature of a practical situation. In X.5, Aristotle notices that pleasures are closely bound up with particular activities, such that "those who engage in an activity with pleasure judge [*krinein*] each particular better and are more precise about it" (1175a31–32). Furthermore, Aristotle continues, "given activities are impeded by the pleasures arising from other activities: those who love the aulos are incapable of paying attention to speeches if they overhear someone playing the aulos, because they take greater delight in the art of playing the aulos than they do in the activity before them. The pleasure derived from the art of aulos playing, then, spoils the activity concerned with speech" (1175b2–6). If it is the mark of the *phronimos* to identify correctly the particular aim of action, it is necessary that the *phronimos* be innocent of both these kinds of corruption: what she takes pleasure in must correspond to what is truly good, and she must not take too much pleasure in any one thing, which would blind her to other important elements by which to determine a good action. So, for example, a person with *phronēsis* should not take too much pleasure in listening to the aulos, which would blind her to the elements of her situation that would engage her generosity. Moderation moderates the pleasures so that the agent is neither deceived by them nor too taken by particular pleasures.

Conclusion

The problem that the akratic faces is that her perceptual experience is governed by a principle that differs from the principle that she explicitly adopts intellectually. So, for example, an akratic may reasonably hold that one ought to treat other people with respect, but nevertheless angrily uses violence upon a friend because her perception is informed only by a principle of pleasure and pain. As I argued in the previous chapter, this means that the akratic perceives her friend only as a source of pain, which is to say that she is perceived as a merely present particular, not in the larger context of the good life or even in the context of their friendship as an ongoing relationship. This requires some intellectual input to transform mere perception into understanding perception.

This problem is compounded by another, which has been the focus of this chapter, namely, that one must be sensitive to the particulars of the situation such that one can discern when and how one's aim to act virtuously is to conform to the particular circumstance in which one acts. If one operates too intellectually, so to speak, operating on the basis of an explicit rule, one will not have the resources to discern when what usually ought to be done should not be done here and now. For example, if one holds that respecting other people amounts to telling the truth, but one is not sensitive to the specificities with respect to which one acts, one will not be able to discern that respect is better accomplished by lying or keeping silent in this case.

Both of these problems point to the necessity of perceiving well, where perceiving well means not being beholden to the pleasures and pains of the mere present and also not being blinded by one's own adherence to principles. Perceiving well means being receptive of particulars as they truly are, not merely as sources of pleasure or pain and not merely as one judges them to be by subsuming them under universal categories. But these two problems also seem to require opposing things of perception and intellect—intellect must enrich perceptual experience without rigidly determining it. Intellect must resituate perception while maintaining perception's sensitivity to the particular. If the understanding of *phronēsis* offered here is right, we can accommodate both requirements of perceiving well. Learning, reflection, and thought open up perceptual possibilities, analogous to the way that learning to walk opens up the possibility of running and dancing without dictating which dances and runs one will undertake. Similarly, developing a friendship with a person enables one to see things about that person that she may not even see herself. Learning about the kinds of behaviors that elicit and manifest generosity opens up the possibility of recognizing new expressions of generosity. But the way that learning opens up new ways of seeing is not by introducing new categories—adhering too strictly to these categories can cause a person to be blind to new particulars—but rather by structuring the perceptual mean with new terms of receptivity, in the way that "white" and "black" structure our receptivity to color.

Aristotle insists that the aim of virtuous action is only apparent to the fully virtuous person. As we have seen, the aim is a particular in the sense of being internal to the particular action undertaken. Furthermore, this particular aim cannot simply be decided upon in advance, but must instead be sensitive to the unpredictable reality of the present situation of action. To have the virtuous aim be apparent to one, then, means that one must be maximally receptive to ethically relevant features of the situation of action. In other words, one must be able to see broadly—not to be confined to one's categories of understanding—and to see deeply—to be able to comprehend the significance of something that is not subsumed under one's categories of understanding.

Neoptolemus sees in this broad and deep way. Were he like Emma Woodhouse, the thesis that Odysseus persuaded him to adopt (namely, that Philoctetes was a cursed and vile man) would have prevented him from seeing Philoctetes's suffering as an occasion for the virtues of friendship and honesty. Instead, Neoptolemus's good character enables him to see

Philoctetes's suffering in its relevance to virtuous action. Being prepared to see one thing did not prevent Neoptolemus from seeing what was actually in front of him, and it was this sight that caused him to alter his chosen course of action. To be able to decide whether one's reasoning applies to one's current circumstances is the mark of the *phronimos*, and it is accomplished by the virtue of intellectual perception.

CONCLUSION

Recapitulation

We set out to offer an account of ethical perception in Aristotle's philosophy, drawing primarily on the *De anima* and the *Nicomachean Ethics*. In order to do this, it had to be established first that perception is a robust enough capacity to apprehend particulars in their relevance to ethical life, which was the work of the first two chapters. We saw in the first chapter that perception is a part of the soul consisting in the basic powers to perceive special, common, and incidental perceptibles—colors, shapes, and concrete particulars—which make possible secondary powers, especially *phantasia* and memory. Furthermore, these secondary powers enrich the content of the basic powers of perception, situating the present perception in a temporal context of a continuous life. Most importantly, memory and *phantasia* make it possible to perceive concrete particulars as occasions for action. This understanding of the perceptual part of the soul established that perception is a robust capacity that far exceeds the bare perceptions of sensory objects which is to be interpreted by another faculty. Rather, perception is inherently interpretive and interpreted.

The work of the first chapter established that perception is a faculty that in principle can apprehend particulars in their ethical significance, but it is not the whole story. The account of perception offered there covers both human and nonhuman animals, but ethics is a uniquely human concern. The second chapter took up the question of how human perception might differ from nonhuman animal perception by taking a step back and looking at the perceptual part of the soul from the perspective of the soul as a whole. Here it was established that, in a fully developed soul, the perceptual part of the soul is *potentially* in the intellectual soul. This means that human perception is informed by intellect in the sense that it influences what a perceptual object is perceived *as*; one's understanding influences the way one perceives. Moreover, the intellect's influence on perception frees perception from being simply relative to the perceiver, as it is in nonrational animals. A nonrational animal is confined to perceive concrete particulars as pleasant and painful for it, whereas a rational animal may perceive concrete particulars as they are in themselves, including whether they are good or bad, rather than merely good or bad *for* the perceiver.

The first two chapters established that Aristotle's account of perception is able to accommodate the perception of particulars in their ethical significance, as good or bad in themselves and as occasions to act. The following two chapters sought to secure the importance of ethical perception in Aristotle's *Nicomachean Ethics* by showing that virtuous action requires ethical perception, and that ethical development consists in the achievement of the harmony of the intellectual and perceptual parts of the soul. The third chapter undertook the latter task. It was established that humans are uniquely ethical creatures because they are uniquely responsible for the completion of their own natures. The psychological ground for this unique feature is the separability of intellect—intellect is not necessary for mere living, but it is necessary for living a good life. As a result, one can come to *know* the sort of acts that virtue consists in, but one may still be unable to *do* it because one's perceptual soul is fully capable of producing action independently of intellect. This interpretation of the natural separability of intellect from the perceptual part of the soul was confirmed in the phenomenon of *akrasia*. The akratic suffers from a divided soul, and we saw that akratic action stemmed from perceiving in a way divorced from intellect. Specifically, the akratic perceives concrete particulars as merely pleasant or painful, not as good or bad, and as a result she perceives them as occasions for acting on the basis of the mere present, rather than on the basis of the good life.

The final chapter further confirmed the importance of ethical perception by addressing that virtue necessary for all the rest: *phronēsis*. It was established there that *phronēsis* is, in part, the ability to perceive particulars correctly as the site for virtuous action. Furthermore, the nature of intellect's impact on the perceptual part of the soul was clarified: ethical perception consists in the transformation of the mean of perception that marks out a range of pleasure and pain into an *ethical* mean, such that what is perceived as pleasant or painful accords with what is good or bad.

Ethical Development

Ethical perception, then, is the capacity to perceive particulars accurately as occasions for virtuous action. It is accomplished by bringing the perceptual part of the soul into harmony with the intellectual. Of course, this raises the question of *how* such a transformation is accomplished. It would take another book to answer this question fully, not least because the answer requires a careful study of Aristotle's *Politics* and an account of the precise relationship between that work and the *Nicomachean Ethics*, and an account of the relationship of the *polis* to the individual. Nevertheless, it is appropriate to make some general remarks about how ethical perception may be developed.

The difference between an undeveloped, "natural" perception and a developed, ethical perception is the difference between an idiosyncratic perspective in which what happens to *appear* good (i.e., pleasant) is assumed to actually *be* good and a more sophisticated perspective in which what appears good *is* good, and not merely pleasant. This is a difference between a person who is blind to her perspective—who thinks something is good because it appears so to her, regardless of whether or not she is in a good position to make such a determination—and one who is aware that she operates with a perspective. The former is a person who insists that there is something wrong with her food despite the fact that she has an illness that affects the way things taste to her; the latter is she who understands the distortions illness brings about, even when she herself is ill. To develop the capacity for ethical perception, then, requires that one be brought out of the naturally self-relative orientation that serves well for the survival of nonrational animals but hinders the pursuit of the good life of human beings.

Aristotle expresses how important being habituated well in one's feelings of pleasure and pain (which, as we have seen, are activities of the perceptual part of the soul) is to the development of virtue many times in the *Nicomachean Ethics* (1095b3–6, 1103b22–25, 1104b8–13, 1142a11–22, 1179b4–31). Generally speaking, Aristotle espouses two mechanisms by which this childhood habituation of passion happens: by the force of law and by imitation (especially musical imitation). Law and imitation share one feature: both serve to draw a person out of her personal perspective. Law does this by orienting an individual toward the good of the whole, and by insisting that the good of the whole is better and more important than the good of any individual part. In *Politics* I.2 Aristotle argues that the city (*polis*) as a whole is prior to the families and individuals that are its parts (1253a18–28). In III.4, he defines the virtue of a citizen relative to the good of the whole (1276b20–31), and finally in VIII.1 Aristotle argues that the legislator ought to concern himself with education because "the whole city has one end [*telos*] . . . [and] of common things, the training too must be common" (1337a21–27).[1] Following the law, then, requires that one recognize a good that is distinct from one's private feelings of pleasure and pain, and, rather than take one's own idiosyncratic perspective (i.e., feelings of pleasure and pain) to determine what is good or bad, obedience to the law requires adopting a perspective from which one is beholden to a greater good. Obedience to the law requires that one act not out of one's naturally selfish perspective, but out of a perspective on the good of the whole.

Aristotle introduces the importance of good laws with regard to the development of virtue at the conclusion of the *Nicomachean Ethics*, where he reiterates that being habituated well to feel pleasure and pain rightly is a necessary condition for developing virtue, just as it is necessary to till the soil for it to be receptive of seed (1179b23–26). He continues, "In general, passion seems to yield not to speech [*logos*] but to force. So there must first be an underlying character that is somehow appropriate for virtue, one that feels affection for the noble and disgust for the shameful" (1179b28–31). Law, Aristotle argues, has the force necessary to train the passions because it offers no object for the passions to direct themselves against (1180a18–24). In the *Rhetoric* Aristotle determines that anger is necessarily addressed to a particular person, "such as Cleon, and not just at a human being, and because that person has done something" (1378a32–b1).[2] For this reason, if an individual were to compel a young person to act contrary to her passions, the young person would get angry and this would obstruct the habituation to feel pleasure in what is noble and good. But the law offers no such object for anger, and so has the kind of force appropriate to habituate the passions (*Nic. Eth.* 1180a18–24).

Law is an impersonal force, which is why it is suitable to shape the passions. On the one hand, this is because rebellious passions require a person against whom to act, if they are to produce actions contrary to the law. The law is not the sort of thing one can be angry with and so purposively act against. On the other hand, breaking the law exacts punishment, so if one *does* break the law in order to pursue one's personal pleasure, one is then made to suffer pain. As a result, one comes to associate pain with the acts contrary to the law, and pleasure with the lawful acts. If the laws are good ones, this amounts to becoming habituated to feel pleasure in the right things and pain in the wrong ones.

However, this habituation takes two forms. A young person may either be habituated to follow the law out of a desire to act for the sake of the noble (*Nic. Eth.* 1180a5–8) and out of a sense of the shamefulness of acting contrary to reason (*logos*) (1179b7–11), or out of a sense of fear of retribution (1179b10–16) and pain (1180a8–12). If one is habituated only in the latter way, one is only superficially good and not truly virtuous. One maintains the self-relative perspective, where breaking the law is bad because it appears so to oneself, that is, causes one pain. If one is habituated in the former way, one is prepared for virtue because one sees that to act contrary to the law (assuming the law is good) is to act in a way that is *bad*, not merely in a way that causes pain.

What accounts for these distinct manners of habituation caused by the law? Two answers can be gleaned from Aristotle's text. First, one may be habituated only to fear punishment simply because of having a deficient nature:

> For the many obey the governance of necessity more than of speech [*logos*], and of punishments more than of what is noble. Hence some suppose that legislators ought to encourage people in the direction of virtue and exhort them to act for the sake of what is noble, on the grounds that those who have been decently guided beforehand by means of habits will be obedient, whereas those who are disobedient and *too deficient in nature* [*aphuēs*], they suppose the legislators ought to inflict on them various chastisements as well as acts of vengeance; the wholly incurable, they ought to banish. For, they suppose, someone who lives decently, with a view to what is noble, will be obedient to the governance of speech [*logos*], whereas someone who strives for pleasure in a base manner must be chastised by means of pain, *like a beast of burden*. (*Nic. Eth.* 1180a4–12, my emphases)

The second reason for the difference in how the law habituates different people can be gleaned from Aristotle's discussion of education in the *Politics*. In *Politics* VIII, Aristotle argues that childhood education ought to be legislated (1337a11–27), and he distinguishes between the education appropriate for the leisured class and the education appropriate to the wage-earning class (1337b4–21). Those of the leisured class are educated in music, which contributes to the formation of character by virtue of being imitative (1340a70b13). The imitative character of music is an agent of habituation of the passions because

> music happens to be something pleasant, and since virtue concerns taking pleasure aright and liking and disliking, then it is clear that there is need of nothing so much as learning and getting habituated to judging aright and taking pleasure in decent characters and noble deeds; there are likenesses to be found in rhythms and tunes that are very close to real natures—likenesses of anger and mildness, of courage too and moderation, of all their opposites as well, and of the other qualities of character (the facts themselves make the matter clear, for we undergo changes in the soul when we listen to such rhythms and tunes); and getting used to taking pain and pleasure in likenesses is close to being in the same state with respect to the reality (for instance, if someone takes pleasure in seeing another's

> image for no other reason than that form is the same, then he must also find pleasant the view of that very thing whose image he is viewing). (*Pol.* 1340a14–28)

There are two important claims here about how music habituates the passions. First, music operates directly on the passions, without the mediation of *logos* or law. Hearing music of a certain sort produces feelings of pleasure while music of another sort produces feelings of pain. Second, music *imitates* real things, and so habituates the soul not only to feel pleasure and pain at certain kinds of music, but also to feel pleasure and pain at the sorts of things the music imitates. For example, a violent piece of music will produce feelings of pain, and as a result real violent episodes will similarly produce feelings of pain. But by law only the leisured class will receive this musical education, and so only the leisured class will be habituated by law in the appropriate manner.

Aristotle singles out imitative music as an especially important element in character development, but he considers imitation generally to be an important educative tool. In the *Poetics* he remarks, "For just as to imitate is natural to human beings from childhood (and in this they differ from the rest of the animals in that they are the most imitative and do their first learning through imitation), so also is it natural for everyone to take pleasure in imitation" (1448b5–9).[3] In this text, Aristotle is speaking primarily about looking at imitative art, rather than imitating another's behavior, and the pleasure taken in imitation is because "in their contemplating there is a coincidence of learning and figuring out what each thing is, for example, 'That's him!' since if by chance one has not seen it before, it will not *qua* imitation produce pleasure" (1448b15–18). The pleasure taken in seeing an imitation derives from the recognition that an appearance signifies a reality, that a photograph is of one's father, for example. It is a pleasure in seeing through the mere appearance, and insofar as imitations are pleasant in this way, one who learns through imitation will become habituated to take pleasure in the reality of things, rather than the mere appearance. Imitation, then, also draws a person out of her private, personal perspective that takes mere appearance to be the whole truth and initiates that person into a perspective from which what is true can be identified through its appearance.

Of course, being law abiding (for the right reasons) and taking pleasure in imitation are not the same as being virtuous—these are the tools by which to develop virtue. Learning through imitation and abiding by the law cultivate the soul so that it is ready to be brought into harmony with intellect—to be obedient to reason—as one comes into maturity. Both law and imitation prepare the soul for becoming virtuous by changing the person's attitude toward what appears to her to be true. Law does this by introducing the distinction between what is merely good for oneself and the greater good of the whole, and by habituating one to pay heed to that greater good, regardless of the pleasure and pain to oneself; and imitation does this by directly habituating one to feel pleasure and pain at the right things, and more generally by habituating one to take pleasure in seeing what is true behind appearances. Being habituated in this manner clears the path for intellect to inform the perceptual part of the soul—the part responsible for the way particulars appear—by removing the authority of mere appearance. Thus, when a well-habituated person learns that it is truly bad to overindulge on sweets, she will not be persuaded by the appearance of the present doughnut as pleasant. Instead, she will be ready to see beyond that appearance and to pay heed to the true good, health. With further learning and further habituation, she will cease to even see the doughnut as something good and desirable.

I conclude with a comment about what I see to be the central insight of Aristotle's ethics. The insight is expressed in Aristotle's observation that virtue comes about neither by nature nor contrary to nature, but is present in those who are of a nature to receive it and is completed through habit (*Nic. Eth.* II.1 1103a24). This insight captures the unique nature of human life, which exceeds what is natural while being irrevocably situated within nature. What this means is that human life is neither simply up to us nor simply granted to us. Instead, living a good human life requires navigating the natural, taking up what is granted to us, and making it human and thereby good. The perceptual part of the soul is the centerpiece of this ambiguity of human nature: it is a natural capacity, shared with other natural creatures, but it is called upon to exceed its nature in perceiving particulars in their ethical significance. Ethical perception is just such a natural capacity that has been transformed into something human and something good.

NOTES

Introduction

1. Translations of *Nic. Eth.* taken from Bartlett and Collins (2011), occasionally modified.

2. Moss (2011), 205, cites Cooper (1975), 64; Hardie (1968), 213; Broadie and Rowe (2002), 49; McDowell (1998), 30; Joachim (1951), 218; Greenwood (1909), 51; and Irwin (1975), 578.

3. Gendler (2008), 642.

4. There is recent work that attempts to soften the opposition between Aristotle and Kant. Korsgaard (1996) argues that Kant has a similar concern with emotions that Aristotle does, and that Aristotle's notion of acting for the sake of virtue itself is similar to Kant's account of moral worth.

5. Even Adam Smith, for whom morality is largely manifest in one's sentiments and emotions, the privileged perspective is that of the "impartial spectator" (*The Theory of Moral Sentiments*, III.i.2).

Chapter 1

1. Moss (2012) argues that Aristotle is an empiricist concerning practical life in the same way that he is an empiricist concerning theoretical learning. In both cases, perception is the source of the principles from which thinking and reasoning happen. This is a very promising way of interpreting Aristotle's thinking about the role of perception in human life. I would like to add to this thesis the corollary that for ethical life, perception continues to serve as a necessary and irreducible component of cognition. One will not be able to reason and act well unless the particulars with respect to which one acts are perceived *as* calling for action.

2. Jennifer Whiting, "The Locomotive Soul" (2002); Klaus Corcilius and Pavel Gregoric, "Separability vs. Difference: Parts and Capacities of the Soul in Aristotle" (2010); and the third chapter of Thomas Johansen's *The Powers of Aristotle's Soul* (2012).

3. Whiting (2002) takes the parts of the soul to be separable *both* in *logos* and in magnitude, by virtue of being realized in different "nonoverlapping" parts of the (single, unified) body (152); Corcilius and Gregoric (2010) reject this and instead understand separability in magnitude to require independently existing magnitudes. According to Corcilius and Gregoric, different capacities realized in, say, the heart and the brain do not mean that they are *separable* in magnitude, only that they are different (114–16). Johansen (2012) takes Corcilius and Gregoric to task on the question of *why* these capacities are parts of the souls of which they are parts, and complements their reading by considering the relationship of the part to the whole (see 57n31). Johansen argues that the parts *are* parts by virtue of distinguishing different *kinds* of soul—plant, animal, human, divine (59–62).

4. See Whiting (2002), 142–45; Corcilius and Gregoric (2010), 96–103; and Johansen (2012), 54–59.

5. Translations of *De anima* II–III are taken from Hamlyn (1968), occasionally modified slightly.

6. Translations of *De memoria* are taken from Sorabji (1972), occasionally slightly modified.

7. Corcilius and Gregoric (2010), 100.

8. Ibid., 95–108.

9. Johansen (2012), 56–59.

10. Whiting (2002) takes a different position. She takes separability in magnitude to be the distinguishing feature of the parts of the soul, and separability in definition to distinguish the basic from the derivative powers housed in a part of soul (152–55). As a result, she takes the *locomotive* capacity to be a part of the soul, consisting of the capacity for desire (*to orektikon*), the capacity for perception (*to aisthētikon*), and the capacity for *phantasia* (*to phantastikon*). Although her argument is quite ingenious, the position is problematic for at least two reasons. First, it seems to make the bodily makeup of an organism prior to and determinative of the nature of the parts of the soul, whereas Aristotle says that the soul is the ruling element of the body (*De anima* 410b11–13). Second, it seems more difficult to disentangle the bodily system that supports nutrition and reproduction from the systems that support perception than it might at first seem. If the capacity for perception is ultimately located in the heart (as Aristotle claims at, e.g., *De somno* 455b34–456a6), it is located in an organ that is also a part of the nutritive system (*De partibus animalium* 647a24–31). Rather than take the nutritive part and the perceptual part of the soul to be separable *both* in place *and* in account, as Whiting does, I take it that they are separable *only* in account from one another, and that what distinguishes the relationship between the parts of the soul from the relationship between the powers of a single part of soul is that the powers of the part of soul are *not* separable even in account, but are merely different in account. See Corcilius and Gregoric (2010), 114–18, for other criticisms.

11. Whiting (2002), 145.

12. Johansen (2012), 54–55.

13. There is some controversy concerning exactly what the common sense (*aisthēsis koinē*) referred to here amounts to. See Everson (1995 and 1997), 148–57; Modrak (1987); and Gregoric (2007).

14. As Hamlyn (1968) says, "Commentators usually object to the notion of seeing that something is sweet, but there can be no valid objection to speaking in this way; the objection presumably stems from the prejudice that there must be an intrinsic connexion between sight and its objects if we are to speak of seeing at all. The phenomenon in question is no doubt a product of learning or experience, but this does not make it any the less a case of seeing" (118–19).

15. Modrak (1987) makes a similar point (70).

16. See Everson (1997), 187–93.

17. See Merleau-Ponty (1962), "Introduction."

18. Citing *De insomniis* 458b31–459a3 on perceptual error, "to see or hear incorrectly can only happen to one who sees or hears something real, although not what he supposes" (Everson's translation), Everson argues that "here, the subject does not perceive what he takes himself to perceive. What he does actually perceive he does not recognize—so recognition cannot be a condition for it to be true that someone perceives an accidental sensible" (191). But to misrecognize is to misperceive—*some* incidental perceptible must enter into the content of the perception in order to be a *mis*perception—and the real thing

one perceives may refer to the special sensibles. Similarly, one may mis-see that the white is sweet—sweet enters into the content of the perception—and this is only possible when one sees what is really white.

19. Translations of *De insomniis* taken from Hett (1936).

20. Modrak (1987), 69.

21. Cashdollar (1973), 168–70.

22. I discuss incidental perception in Rabinoff (2015a).

23. Reference to a unified perceptual faculty is found four times in *De anima* (425a30–31, 426b21, 427a9, and 431a20), three times in a long passage in *De sensu* (449a7, 449a14–16, 449a17–18), three times in a passage in *De memoria* in which Aristotle is identifying the faculty to which memory belongs (450a10–11, 450a11–12, 450a14; summarized at 451a15–18), and three times in a passage in *De somno* (455a15–16, 455a19, 455a20).

24. For the former, Modrak (1987), 62–65; Johansen (2005), 271; for the latter, Everson (1997), 144–57; Gregoric (2007).

25. As do Kahn (1966), 67; Kosman (1975), 517–18.

26. In construing the question of perceiving that we perceive as a question of awareness, I am following Kosman (1975) and Caston (2002), who construe the argument of *De anima* III.2 as concerning perceptual consciousness. Johansen (2005) criticizes both these positions, and he particularly criticizes Kosman's position that perceiving that we perceive accounts for the awareness that distinguishes the *perceptual* effect that (for example) an odor has on a perceiver from the nonperceptual effect that the same odor has on an inanimate object that becomes stinky (507–8). Johansen argues that it "is implied by Aristotle throughout Book II that first-order perception is a form of awareness (*aisthanesthai*) of its object," and at issue in the question of perceiving that we perceive "is the different question by what faculty we are aware of our first order perceptions. This is a question not about perceptual awareness as such; it is specifically a question about our awareness of our own perceptual processes" (257). (See also Osborne [1983], 405, although she takes the question of III.2 differently than Johansen.) It surely *is* implied in book II that the perception of sensible objects is a way of being made aware of them, but it is not *explained* there (as Kosman [2005], 279, also says, in his reply to Johansen). In other words, one can read III.2 as making explicit what was implied all along: that perception is a mode of awareness. The opening of III.2 explains how. This sequence of topics accords with Aristotle's methodological principle, articulated in II.4: one must first speak of the objects of perception, then the activity, and only then the capacity. *De anima* II.6 concerns perceptual objects; II.7–11 focuses more specifically on one kind of object, special perceptibles; and II.12 discusses the activity of perception, namely, the reception of the perceptible form without the matter, and raises the question of what makes this activity specifically *perceptual*. This question, as Kosman asserts, is answered in III.2. (Caston [2002] offers a very compelling "activity reading" of the III.2 passage, wherein Aristotle is concerned not with the capacity of perception, but with instances of active perceiving. Johansen [2005] vigorously defends the "capacity reading," wherein Aristotle is concerned with explaining how the perceptual capacity afforded by the five senses accounts for higher-order perceptions.)

I take Aristotle to be concerned in III.2 with first-order perceptual awareness, not second-order perceptual awareness. For one thing, he takes *perceiving* that we see and hear to be an obvious phenomenon, and (as it seems to me) it is much more obvious that we are (first-order) perceptually aware in general than that we are *perceptually* (second-order) aware of our perceptions. Osborne argues that the question Aristotle is asking in the opening lines of III.2 is "how we are aware that we are seeing (as opposed to hearing, for example) or hearing (as opposed to tasting, for example)" (406). However, later in the chapter he *argues* that it must be by perception that we distinguish seeing from hearing (e.g., *De anima* 426b14–15), which seems to indicate that he has a different concern at the chapter's opening. Caston argues that "Aristotle opts for a more basic form of awareness" in part because "we are not constantly undergoing a kind of double vision" (772). I have something similar in mind here.

27. Why this follows is discussed in Caston (2002), 763–73; Johansen (2005), 241–44. Osborne (1983) considers Aristotle to be surveying possibilities here, notes that this consequence follows from both options (seeing that one sees by sight or by another sense), and doesn't take it to be an immediate problem (401–2).

28. See Caston (2002), 773–75, for a different articulation of the assumptions underlying the regress argument. He identifies two (774): (a) "A perception of a perception is also of what the earlier perception is of," to block the possibility of perceptual loops, and, more substantially, (b) "Whenever we have a perception, we have a perception of that perception," to get the regress started. The way I've construed it, the regress gets started because, if the initial perception of an object does not explain awareness, no subsequent perceptual activity of the same kind will explain it, either. The question just gets pushed back to the new act of perception: what makes the perception of perception *awareness* of that perception?

29. Though Johansen (2005) takes the issue in this argument not to be general perceptual awareness, but specifically higher-order awareness of the change undergone in perceptual awareness. See pp. 249–50.

30. Perhaps Johansen's formulation, referred to above, captures some of this: there is a difference between receiving a perceptual object (seeing color) and monitoring whether or not such an activity is happening at all. It would be odd to say that what is perceived in the discernment of darkness, either darkness itself or the *in*activity of the sense of sight, is an object. Whatever form this monitoring takes, it must differ from the object-oriented form of perceiving, for example, red.

31. See Gregoric (2007), 99–111, for a detailed analysis of this passage. He also takes *koinē aisthēsis* in this passage to refer to the primary perceptual faculty.

32. Trans. Hett (1936).

33. Translations of *De sensu* are taken from Hett (1936).

34. Kahn (1966), 67.

35. Kosman (1975), 518.

36. In his discussion of incidental perception, Everson (1997) distinguishes between perceiving an object and *recognizing* that object, and argues that something is incidentally perceived "because it forms an accidental [i.e., incidental] unity with some special sensible which does act on the sense organ. Just as the special sensibles are *kath' hauta* causes of the change in the organ, and hence the perception, so the accidental sensibles are accidental causes of perception" (188). If, however, awareness is inherent to the perceptual system, this distinction cannot be upheld. To perceive an incidental sensible is to become aware of it.

37. Trans. Ross (1984).

38. See Caston (2004) and Sisko (2004) for opposing interpretations of this "by the way."

39. See Tuozzo (1996), Block (1961), and Kahn (1966) on this issue.

40. Kosman (1975), 518–19.

41. Moss (2012) has recently and brilliantly argued for the central importance of *phantasia* in ethical action and thinking, and while this is right in many significant respects, since *phantasia* is essentially dependent upon the more basic perceptual powers, it is of utmost importance that one first of all learn to *perceive* well.

42. See also Everson (1997), 158, which interprets the passage similarly. Modrak (1987), 82–87, holds a similar position.

43. Caston (1996), 46–52.

44. Moss (2012) offers a similar account, as does Everson (1997), 175; and Lorenz (2006), chaps. 9–11.

45. See Wedin (1988), chap. 3, and discussions there.

46. So Wedin (1988), Everson (1997) (arguing that Aristotle uses *phantasia* in a broad and a technical sense, 184–85), Modrak (1987), and Moss (2012), 51–57, all argue that Aristotle offers a single account of *phantasia* that covers all the features he attributes to it and the functions it serves.

47. See Schofield (1978). Everson (1997) defends a modified form of Schofield's position: *phantasia* is introduced to account for features of perceptual experience that fall outside what the perception strictly speaking can accomplish—and he takes perception strictly speaking to be the effect of the special and common perceptibles on the sense organ. This does not imply, however, that *phantasia* has a primarily skeptical function (Modrak [1987], 86, makes a similar point), nor that it operates only when perception strictly speaking either is not or is not operating well (see 165–86).

48. See Wedin (1988), chaps. 2–3; for a clear statement of the contrast between perception *sans phantasia* as falling short of awareness and perception with *phantasia* as including awareness, see 41–42. In some moments, Modrak (1987) seems to attribute a similar role to *phantasia*, but at others she seems to give it a role closer to the one Schofield (1978) argues for; see 83 for the former, 87, for the latter.

49. See Nussbaum (1978).

50. Everson (1997), 165–78; Moss (2012), 51–57.

51. See Moss (2012), chap. 3.

52. In general, however, I find Nussbaum's account problematic because the interpretive function she attributes to *phantasia* makes the perception of incidental perceptibles redundant—these are already interpreted perceptible objects (see Everson [1997], 158–65, for a similar criticism; see also Wedin (1988), chap. 2, for a thorough refutation of the view). Wedin's (1988) position (and Modrak's [1987], insofar as she defends the same point) that *phantasia* is necessary for awareness of an object seems problematic for a similar reason: Aristotle *also* attributes perceptual awareness to perception itself. Schofield's position is problematic for teleological reasons: *phantasia* is necessary for animal motion and the animal's successfully avoiding predators and attaining prey. If *phantasia* were primarily a skeptical operation, it would not be able to successfully guide an animal's motion. See Wedin 65–71 and Everson 165–72 for other critiques of Schofield's position.

53. Caston (1996), 48–52.

54. *Phantasia* is also said to be true or false in the context of being distinguished from *epistēmē* and *nous*. Because these latter are not false in *any* sense, that *phantasia* is false in the sense established by the contrast with veridical perception is enough to distinguish *phantasia* from these two things.

55. Schofield (1978), 108–10, offers a similar reading of this passage, as does Everson (1997), 178–79 (despite the differences in their interpretations).

56. This is not to say that *phantasia* need accompany *all* perception, only that it *may* be concurrent. Schofield (1978) espouses a similar position. See Nussbaum (1978) for the alternative position that *phantasia* is involved in every perception of an object *as* something (259), and Wedin (1988, 51–57), who argues that *phantasia* accompanies *all* perception.

57. See similarly Lorenz (2006), chaps. 9–11.

Chapter 2

1. See Vasiliou (1996), 777, who argues that the first principles of ethics are "the that" with which ethical reasoning begins (rather than a general principle), and suggests that, for this reason, it is necessary to develop a perceptual capacity to see "the that."

2. See Cashdollar (1973) and Modrak (1987), who argue similarly. See Kahn (1992) and Everson (1997) for opposing accounts.

3. See Cashdollar (1973), note 22: "That moral principles are sometimes gained through aisthesis (EN 1098 b 21) surely presupposes incidentally perceiving x as good, just, bad, unjust, etc." (165). Incidental perception will be further addressed in section 2 of this chapter. Moss (2012) devotes an original and intriguing study to this question, arguing that it is by *phantasia* that the good is apprehended.

4. *Post. An.* 86a30: "Universal demonstrations are objects of thought [*dianoia*], particular demonstrations terminate in perception"; *Post. An.* 100b12: "There will be a comprehension [*nous*] of the principles"; *De anima* II.6 417b21–23.

5. Of course, Aristotle frequently comments that thinking requires *phantasia* (*De anima* 431a17) and that there is no learning without perception (427b16–17, 432a7–8). But the manner in which he conflates these two powers in the following passages does not suggest merely a relationship of dependence of one faculty on another.

6. Trans. Barnes (1993). In this case, it is clear that Aristotle means to refer to the perceptual faculty, although not any specific perceptual power. *Post. An.* II.19 addresses the question of prior "knowledge" that makes possible knowledge in the robust sense, and identifies perception as the faculty that houses this prior "knowledge." That this is a literal use of perception is clear: Aristotle introduces perception as that which is shared with animals, and mentions various secondary perceptual powers (99b34–100a9).

7. Translations from the *Nicomachean Ethics* are from Bartlett and Collins (2011), occasionally modified. I take *aisthēsis* here to be meant in the same sense as in *Post. An* II.19, above. In *Post. An.*, perception contains the universal in the particular that is its object, and this is what makes it possible to come to know. In this *Nic. Eth.* passage, similarly, the universals arise from the particulars of which there is perception. Because of this similarity—the universal in the perception—I take *aisthēsis* in the *Nic. Eth.* passage in a literal unspecified sense, that is, referring to the activity of perception generally, not a specific perceptual power. The difference between these two passages is that in the *Post. An.* passage Aristotle is addressing the acquisition of universals, whereas in this passage he is addressing the developed capacities (*hexeis*) that apprehend the particulars of action. Rather than *nous* acquiring the universal *from* perception, as in the *Post. An.* passage, here *nous/aisthēsis* is apprehending the particular.

8. Translations of *Metaphysics* taken from W. D. Ross in Barnes, ed. (1984), modified.

9. Charles Kahn (1992) notices a similar ambiguity, distinguishing four senses of perception: broader and narrower senses of *aisthēsis* both on the objective and subjective sides (365). He argues that the broader conceptions of *aisthēsis* are informed by noetic elements—human *aisthēsis*. My intention is to supplement and support this conception

of *aisthēsis* with an argument about the priority of the whole soul to the part, and then to draw out the consequences of this conception with regard to ethics.

10. Humans are distinguished from nonhuman animals precisely by the presence of *nous*, the capacity for thinking (*dianoia*), or reason. Aristotle places the difference between kinds of living things in the configuration of soul: plants have only the nutritive power, animals have perception in addition, and some animals (i.e., humans) also have the capacity for thought and reason (*De anima* 415a2–14). Both *dianoētikon* and *logistikon* are associated with *nous* in *De anima*, for example, at 414b18–19 ("Some things have in addition the faculty of movement in respect to place, and others, e.g. men and anything else which is similar or superior to man, have that of thought and intellect") and at 432b26 ("the calculative part [*to logistikon*], which is called mind [*nous*]"), respectively. See Johansen (2012), chap. 3, for a discussion of the parts of the soul as the differentia of species of living thing.

11. Similarly, perception is often contrasted with things that are properly human: with the acquisition of virtue through habit at *Nic. Eth.* 1103a25–30; with deliberation at 1112b34–1113a1; the vice that renders one most animal-like, dissipation, is an excess concerning the pleasures of the sense touch (1118b1–2); it is ruled out as a source of action (*praxis*) by virtue of its being shared by animals (1139a17–20); animal-like people are identified as those who lack reason and live by perception alone at 1149a9–11.

12. The sense of *aisthēsis* in these passages *could* be taken to be metaphorical—one simply sees in the sense of understanding how far of a deviation from the mean is blameworthy. However, the contrast with what can be determined by *logos* challenges this. Aristotle generally identifies two capacities that supplement what can be determined by *logos*, *aisthēsis* and *nous*, and generally *aisthēsis* is the capacity concerned with particulars, *nous* with first principles. For this reason, it is best to read *aisthēsis* here as, again, referring to the perceptual capacity in an unspecific way.

13. Similarly, perception is identified as one way of grasping first principles (*Nic. Eth.* 1098b5); the verb *aisthanesthai* is used at 1100a20 as that faculty which can grasp good or evil; at 1126a5–6 as that faculty which grasps proper occasions for anger; most importantly, it is closely associated with *phronesis* at 1142a26; and with *nous* at 1143b6; in the practical syllogism at 1147a26 and 1147b10; associated with a kind of knowledge at 1147b17; with understanding (*sunesin*) at 1161b25; at 1170a17, human life is defined by the powers of thinking (*noēsis*) and perception.

14. Charles Kahn (1992) articulates a similar position when he says, "More generally, our perceptual experience is penetrated through and through by conceptual elements derived from *nous*. This is a point which Aristotle frequently takes for granted but rarely discusses in any detail" (365). However, Kahn means by this that perception strictly speaking must be accompanied by *nous* smuggled in through what is incidentally perceptible (369). I differ from Kahn in that I take the incidental perceptibles to be genuine objects of perception, and perception to be *informed by* intellect, rather than supplying data for intellectual operations. Kahn goes too far in his insistence upon the special perceptibles being the *only* things given by perception, and I side with Deborah Modrak (1987) on the issue of the complexity of the perceptual capacity, because animals without reason also perceive meaningful wholes that are incidentally perceptible.

15. Modrak (1987), 119.

16. Ibid., 123.

17. For example, Modrak (1987), 35–37.

18. Kahn (1966) calls the analytic treatment of the five special senses as independent of each other a "methodological fiction" (63); I will be making a similar claim with regard to the parts of the soul. Their independence, too, is a methodological fiction. See Johansen (2012), chaps. 2–3 for a quite different but in many ways complementary account of the structure of the soul. My position is similar to the position Pavel Gregoric (2007) defends when he remarks, "in reality there is only one soul in each case, which is what ensures integration and co-operation of various parts or aspects of the soul, as when perception helps an animal to take nourishment or move about. Thus the soul is responsible for all the activities that a living being with this soul manifests" (38–39).

19. Translations of *De anima* I are taken from Shiffman (2011), occasionally modified.

20. Polansky (2007) rightly explains the importance of deciding whether the account of the whole or the account of the parts is to be addressed as an issue of metaphysical priority, that is, whether the parts are dependent on the whole (individual) soul or whether the parts are independent of any individual or species soul (46–47). I address this issue in this and the following subsections.

21. See Whiting (2002), 146.

22. Tuozzo (1996) offers a similar interpretation of parts of a body.

23. It seems to me that the placement of this argument, following as it does upon laying out the sequence of powers, invites wariness about the presumption that parts of the soul are the same regardless of the kind of soul they are parts of. The question of the relationship between parts is complicated by this succession because what is in some cases a whole soul—the nutritive soul of the plant—is in other cases a part of soul. With the argument of *De anima* 413b11–414a1, Aristotle distinguishes between kinds and parts of soul, and this should caution his audience against treating the parts as if they were kinds, that is, independent of the whole and of the other parts.

24. To be separable means to be, in *some* way, independent. Corcilius and Gregoric (2010) distinguish three kinds of separability for Aristotle: to be separable *simpliciter*, separable in place/magnitude (*topōi* or *megethei*), and to be separable in account/being (*logōi* or *tōi einai*). To be separable *simpliciter*, they argue, means to be capable of separate existence. Something is separable in place/magnitude when "*x* can have a location independent of the location of *y*, i.e., *x* can be found at a place at which *y* is not found." Similarly, something is separable in *logos* when "the account of *x* is independent of *y*, i.e., there is an adequate definition of *x* which makes no reference to *y*." Corcilius and Gregoric take this to be the same as to be "separable in being," namely, "what it is to be *x* is independent of what it is to be *y*, so the *x* can be adequately defined without *y*" (section 4). See Whiting (2002) and Johansen (2012) for discussions of separability. See the previous chapter for a discussion of the parts of the soul.

25. Polansky (2007) comes to the similar conclusion that the evidence of the divided insect establishes that the soul is a unity of parts, and that the unified soul is the organizational principle of the parts (179–80). See also Brentano (1897, reprint 1977), 36–37.

26. This kind of priority of the whole to the parts corresponds to one of the senses of priority that Aristotle identifies in *Met.* V.11. This sense of priority is characterized as a kind of independence: "Some things then are called prior and posterior in this sense, others in respect of nature and substance, i.e., those which can be without other things, while others cannot be without *them*" (1019a1–4). The whole soul must be prior to its parts in this sense—the parts of the soul cannot be separated in such a way that they could subsist without the whole; but, as the plant and divine souls show, whole souls can exist without

particular parts. If the parts of the soul *were* separable in place or *simpliciter*, this priority would not attain.

27. Kosman (1987) eloquently discusses numerical identity and difference in being or account, in the context of distinguishing accidental being from substance (369–71).

28. Aristotle often remarks that a body part ceases to be what it is when severed from the whole: *Met.* 1035b23, 1036b30; *De anima* 412b21–23; *Part. an.* 641a3–4; *Pol.* 1253a20–25. Whiting (2002) similarly takes the relationship between the parts of the soul to the whole soul on the model of the parts of the body to the whole body.

29. See also *Parts of Animals* II.9. Ackrill (1972–73) seems to take the parts of the body to be similar to other sorts of parts that may function differently in different contexts (128), suggesting that Aristotle "recognize as a possibility the re-use of severed organs and the re-activation of dead bodies." Charlton (1980) raises problems with Ackrill's interpretation of *dunamis* and *entelecheia* that lead him to this point. Ackrill's point seems to me to contradict Aristotle's insight that souls belong to bodies of particular kinds (*De anima* I.4 407b13–26)—soul is not the sort of thing that can be *applied* to a body, it is the sort of thing that essentially *determines* what a body is. See Kosman (1987) and Brentano (1867, reprint 1977) for such an account, and Bos (2010) and Everson (1997), 69–78, for alternative accounts of the relation between soul and body.

30. Tuozzo (1996) sees a similar kind of functional incompleteness of parts in wholes in teleologically unified entities: the parts of a body have functions that are only fully intelligible with respect to a single higher function to which they are subordinate, analogous to the hierarchy of crafts (148–51). I would like to emphasize a corollary of this incompleteness of the parts, namely, that what ultimately is operating is the body (or soul) as a whole; it is only when conceived in isolation from the body that it is true to say that the hand alone grasps, or the eye alone sees. Rather, it is the body that grasps by means of the hand, and the soul that sees by means of the eye. As Tuozzo notes (154–55, and citations there), some commentators see a tension in Aristotle between the idea that there is an ultimate organ of perception and the idea that perception operates through various parts. I agree with Block (1961) that "the attribution of an activity to a complex body as a whole is not incompatible with the claim that one part of that body is more directly the cause of the activity than another" (53). See also Kahn (1966), especially 56, for a similar view about the common sense power.

31. I take this to be similar to Kahn's (1992) claim that, regarding the hierarchy of natural bodies, living things, sentient animals, and rational animals, "since each level is qualitatively distinct, each calls for its own autonomous level of understanding and explanation" (360).

32. Johansen (2012) notes that ultimately Aristotle seeks an integrated view of the parts of the soul and that *De anima* takes steps in that direction, but argues that definitionally the parts are prior to the whole and make no reference to it (71–72).

33. Discussions of the common account of soul given in *De anima* II.1 can be found in Ackrill (1972–73), Bolton (1978), Charlton (1980), Whiting (1992), Menn (2002), Polansky (2007), and Johansen (2012), chap. 1.

34. Matthews (1992) addresses the variety and unity of these life activities, arguing that what unifies these senses of "life" is that they are necessary for the perpetuation of particular species (191); Bolton (1978) offers a related discussion about how the definitions of soul mark off living things appropriately; Johansen (2012) rejects the idea that there is a general notion of life (51).

35. Kahn (1966) similarly notes, with respect to the figure-soul analogy, "Even in the case of animals, which are by definition sentient and must therefore possess a sensory *psuchē*, this faculty is not concretely separable from their sheer capacity to live" (47–48).

36. In this passage (*De anima* 414b28–32) Aristotle uses the adjectives *proton*, *aisthētikon*, and *threptikon* substantially, without specifying whether he means these as parts, souls, or simply powers. The comparison with the sequence of geometrical figures suggests that he means souls, since the triangle and the quadrilateral are both *kinds* of geometrical figures, and it would not be natural to take the triangle to be primarily a part of the quadrilateral. However, Aristotle might have intended to maintain the ambiguity, given that what are in some cases kinds of soul (nutritive, perceptive) are in other cases parts of soul.

37. This analogy between the sequence of figures and the sequence of souls is often interpreted in light of questions about whether or not there is a genus of soul that can be the subject of a definition properly speaking. See, for example, Ward (1996) and citations there. My concern is not with the definition of soul per se, but rather with the internal complexity of souls, and as a result, I take from this passage a description of the relationship of parts of soul within a complex soul. This approach is consistent with concerns about definitions, and I am persuaded by Ward's argument that there is no proper definition of soul over and above the kinds of soul. Just as there is no "life" over and above kinds of life, so there is no "soul" over and above kinds of soul. See Johansen (2012) for an alternative account of the definition of soul (chaps. 1–2, esp. pp. 62–63).

38. Ward (1996) makes a similar point (124), although in the end she thinks that Aristotle has not explained what unifies a soul (127). Johansen (2012) also makes a similar point (69), although he sees the potentiality of the part in two ways: as providing the potentiality for the higher capacity—there is no perception without nutrition—and as potential because it is a part of a soul defined by the higher capacity. And, contrary to Ward, he sees the unity of the soul accomplished in the figure-soul analogy when the parts of the soul are understood on the model of matter (potentiality) to form (actuality) (70).

39. Relying on an analogy to interpret Aristotle's views concerning the structure of the soul will have its limitations—it is, after all, only an analogy, with the limitations that analogies carry with them. However, necessity dictates arguing this way here—it is here that Aristotle discusses the internal complexity among the parts of the soul. We may also be sure that he is serious that the parts of the soul are present potentially because he reiterates this thought in *Met.* 1040b6–15, discussed above. Moreover, Aristotle discusses the ways that mathematical objects are potentially within others (which I will point out). Furthermore, the nature of the soul is generally analogous to mathematical objects insofar as both are nonmaterial but are inseparable from bodies. In the absence of any definitive statement concerning the relationship between the parts of the soul, it is justified to mine this analogy in answering the question of the structure of the soul.

40. Contrary to Brentano (1897, reprint 1977), 42.

41. This is consistent with Johansen's (2012) understanding of potentiality (*dunamis*) as a way of being that does not in itself "make one exercise that capacity" (20). I will argue that the activity of a subordinate part of the soul is mediated by the higher and defining part, and similarly Johansen argues that "the reason why a capacity is not in itself sufficient for its own exercise is that other factors are required, such as one's desire and the opportunity to exercise the capacity in the case of active capacities, or external agents or prompts in the case of passive capacities" (20).

42. See Brentano (1897), 44.

43. Distinguishing between efficient cause and final cause may be helpful here. Gotthelf (1987) offers compelling reasons for accepting that the final cause (that-for-the-sake-of-which), the form (soul or life in this case) is not reducible to its material elements, the efficient cause, elements that are nonetheless necessary for the form's realization. I extend this principle to the subordinate life processes of an animal: such processes as breathing and a beating heart are necessary for the life of the organism, but necessary in the sense of being an efficient and not a final cause, for what it is to be an animal is not reducible to the nutritive functions. Similarly, in Gotthelf's argument, the material elements of an organism do not sufficiently account for it (220–22). See also Tuozzo (1996) for the incompleteness of parts. See also Kosman (1987) for an account of the instrumentality both of the body and the parts of the body as being for the sake of the whole (376–37). Similarly, I argue, the parts of the soul are for the sake of the whole, and the whole is defined by the highest capacity. For opposing views, see Ackrill (1972), 126–28; Bos (2010), who argues that the instrumental bodies are the four elements, not the organized body; and Everson (1997), 60–69, who argues that the soul is the soul of the bodily organs that are the loci of capacities, not the body as a whole.

44. See chapter 1. See also Modrak (1987), 81; Wedin (1988), 61n48; and Gregoric (2007), chap. 3.

45. Lorenz (2006) makes a similar point (197–99).

46. Similarly Kahn (1992) asks: "We are sentient in virtue of our hylomorphic soul. Are we rational animals in virtue of two distinct souls, the one that makes us animals and 'a different kind' that makes us rational? Is human nature constituted by one essence or two?" (361). Of course, my thesis is that the perceptive faculty *does* change, that the virtuous person is not merely an animal with extra powers—that humans are constituted by a single, if fractured, essence.

47. Parts of what follow appear in or inform Rabinoff (2015b).

48. See Russon (1996). In a certain way this point is intuitive. What it means to be aware of some object is to have some distance from it and some freedom in relating oneself to it. In Aristotle's account of perception, then, the passivity of the perceptive power (being *receptive* of the form of the perceptible object and in a certain way determined by it) is the condition for a more fundamental agency. In being so effected by the perceptible object, the animal is given some initiative in responding to it, fleeing or pursuing it, for example.

49. Aristotle makes the point most clearly with respect to perception in the narrow sense, but the point can be extended to the perceptual faculty as a whole, which is also characterized as a mean (*De anima* 431a20).

50. Trans. Sachs (2001).

51. A note must be made regarding what it is that is happening in the event of perceiving. Sorabji (1992) famously argues that the sense organ literally takes on the qualities (red, round, etc.) that are perceived. Similarly, Slakey (1961), and more recently Everson (1997) offer literalist accounts of sense perception. Burnyeat (1992), at the other extreme, argues that there is no physical change accompanying perception. Lear (1988) takes a middle ground, arguing that there is a physical change in the organ of sense, but that it does not literally take on the quality being perceived; instead, the perceptible form, which is "an irreducible reality," is transmitted by means of some physical change, such as the air hitting the eardrum (113); and Bradshaw (1997) follows his lead in developing "dual-*logos* theory" in which perception is defined both by a fixed ratio of elements in the sense organ and a flexible ratio that takes on the *logos* of the object of sense. This is a difficult question,

but I find Bradshaw's and Everson's accounts most compelling; although they might disagree on some details, I find their accounts quite similar. The important thing to explain is how the power of perception which has no magnitude is related to the change in the sense organ (*De anima* II.12), and Bradshaw's dual-*logos* theory provides the resources for such an explanation, while Everson's account of the material change in the sense organ leaves room for such an explanation.

52. Moss (2012), 22–29, argues that the perceptions themselves are pleasant or painful, and that this is what it means to perceive a pleasant or painful object. Her account is based on the physiological underpinnings of motivation for motion (the heating and cooling of the area around the heart, for example) expressed in *De motu animalium*. Similarly, Johansen (2012) conceives of "appetite as the emotive side of the perception of pleasure, withdrawal or repulsion as the emotive aspect of the perception of pain. The emotive and the cognitive are here two sides of the same coin, one in number" (249). This seems to me to be a good way of understanding Aristotle's claim that pleasure and pain are activities of the perceptual part of the soul with respect to the good or bad as such. Hamlyn (1968), on the other hand, claims "the assertion that the existence of sense-perception necessarily implies the existence of pleasure and pain has no claim to conceptual necessity" (90).

53. I leave aside the problematic case of the "imperfect" animals (*De anima* 433b31) without locomotion that receive nourishment "from the source from which they have been born" (434b1–2). Polansky (2007) argues that animals that lack locomotion "are merely shortchanged in bodily endowment" (509). Whether or not this is the right explanation of such animals, it seems clear that Aristotle thinks of the animal with locomotion as the paradigm animal.

54. I say "merely" because, of course, some aspects of animal physiology *are* constituted like the plant—my skin also absorbs vitamin D whether or not I take pleasure in suntanning. But the nutritive functions most necessary for the continuance of life—eating, drinking, sleeping, reproducing—are constituted differently than the plant's are; these functions invoke and require some degree of voluntary action on the basis of what is or appears good or pleasant.

55. *De anima* III.9 clearly considers the discussions of perception and intellect to be concluded: "The soul of animals has been defined by reference to two potentialities, that concerned with discernment, which is the function of thought and perception, and secondly that for producing motion in respect of place. Let so much suffice about perception and the intellect; we must now inquire what it is in the soul that produces movement" (432a15–20).

56. The "good or bad as such" (*De anima* 431a12) that the perceptive part is in relation to when it perceives pleasure or pain transforms into "either the good *or* the apparent good" when we are considering *all* creatures with perception, both those that have and those that lack intellect. I interpret this shift to mean that the intellect opens up possibilities that are not available to the animal that lacks it, that is, the possibility to transcend the limits of one's own perspective—to have access to the good as such, rather than the good in relation to oneself.

57. That is, it brings the *orektikon* into activity.

58. Moss (2012), 104–5, characterizes the passage similarly; see also Richardson (1992) and Johansen (2012), 250–51.

59. Two competing interpretations of this passage are represented by Kahn (1992) and Modrak (1987): Kahn argues that the perceptive faculty *only* perceives the hot and the cold, not the flesh itself and its *logos*. As a result, it is either by the perceptual faculty or

nous differently disposed that we discern the compound flesh (370). By contrast, Modrak (1987) argues that, rather, because the perceptible object is on a continuum with the noetic object, what discerns the essence, *nous*, is the same faculty, perception, differently disposed (119). Hamlyn (1968) similarly takes this passage to show that "the intellect by which one judges essences, 'what it is to be F,' is not after all utterly distinct from the senses" (138). I end up siding more with Modrak/Hamlyn. Based on Aristotle's insistence that essences do not exist anywhere separate from the concrete individuals of which they are the essence, while not being identical to them, it seems to me that intellect and perception are, in a very real sense, concerned with the *same* object, considered in different ways. Polansky (2007) makes the point that, just as what distinguishes the special perceptibles must be one, so too what distinguishes flesh from being-flesh must be one (447). I also reject Kahn's restriction of perception to merely the special perceptibles.

60. Modrak (1987) employs a similar strategy for interpreting the relationship between the noetic and perceptive faculties (117–24). She comes to a different yet, I believe, compatible interpretation. She considers the perceptual faculty to operate as the material cause of the noetic—the noetic faculty works on the object of the perceptual faculty, abstracting the essence from the particularizing elements of the perceptual object (123). Johansen (2012), 228–29, takes a similar stance. I conclude that perceptual experience is affected by the very possibility of performing such an operation.

61. Bradshaw (1997) puts the point well: "The picture presented here is that of a sense as inherently a mean between sensible extremes, but one capable of adjusting itself to match whatever deviations from the mean are presented to it. Strictly speaking, what it perceives are these deviations; that is why "we do not perceive (*ouk aisthanometha*) what is equally hot and cold or hard and soft. As has often been noted, by 'equally' Aristotle must mean equally to us (or to our sense organs), rather than equally in itself (i.e., tepid or moderately hard)" (146).

62. The difference between the way the plant is affected from the way the sense is affected is sometimes taken as support for a nonliteralist interpretation of the way the sense takes on the perceptible form (e.g., Burnyeat [1992], 21–22; Modrak [1987], 59n15). Everson (1997), 86–89, argues that it is evidence for the literalist interpretation, because the bodies of plants are not even such as to take on the perceptible form at all—plants do not take on heat, for example, but come to feel hot to touch.

63. See Modrak (1991b). I address this issue more fully in the next chapter.

64. Similarly Johansen (2012): "I take the comparison of perception with a bent line and *nous* with a straight to be that it is by *nous* that you can see how long the line really is" (228).

65. This is how Sachs interprets the perplexing passage 429b11–23. He says in a footnote to his translation of the passage: "This rich and difficult paragraph implies that intellect pervades all human experience . . . The same perceptible form that acts incidentally on the various sense organs acts directly on intellect, but is not the only sort of form that the intellect takes on" (141). Modrak (1987) similarly emphasizes the inherence of the intellectual object in the sensible particular, but focuses not on the bodily component, but on the continuity between the perceptible object and the noetic object, on the one hand, and between the perceptual faculty and the noetic on the other (119).

66. I take this perceiving-as to be included in the perception of incidental perceptibles, discussed in the previous chapter as perceiving-that. These two locutions (perceiving-as, perceiving-that) amount to the same thing: to say one perceives that the tall brown cylin-

der is a tree trunk is the same as saying that one perceives the tall brown cylinder *as* a tree trunk. See below for more discussion of incidental perceptibles.

67. *De anima* 429a5–7 confirms that animals live according to *phantasia*, and 433a10–21 confirms the connection between *phantasia* and desire, by the analogy set up at the beginning of the chapter between *phantasia* and *nous*.

68. Modrak (1987) makes a similar point (100) by means of Aristotle's description of *phantasia* as a kind of thinking.

69. At *De anima* 433b30 he calls it *logistikē* and at 434a *bouleutikē*.

70. Kahn (1992), 369.

71. Modrak (1997), 69–71.

72. Everson (1997), 187–93, distinguishes between the question of how such objects as the son of Diares is *perceived* and how such objects are *recognized*, dismissing the latter as not what Aristotle is concerned with in the project of *De anima* of explaining how perception works. But it seems to me that if Aristotle is concerned to explain *life*, he must explain how perception serves the life of animals, and the perception of the special perceptibles without their being articulated into recognizable wholes seems insufficient to support that life. See Cashdollar (1973), who argues that incidental perception is as important to Aristotle's account of perception as the special and common perceptibles are.

73. Kahn (1992), 367–69.

74. Ibid., 367–68.

75. See Corcilius and Gregoric (2010) for the argument that these capacities are not themselves *parts* of the soul, but functions of the perceptual part. For an alternative account that reaches compatible conclusions, see Johansen (2012), chap. 2.

76. Modrak (1987) makes a similar argument (70), and gives a compelling argument for attributing the perception of incidental perceptibles to the common sense power.

77. Kahn (1992), 369n17.

78. See Heidegger's *Being and Time* distinction between the present-to-hand and the ready-at-hand.

Chapter 3

1. See *De anima* III.4 429a27–29: "Those who say, then, that the soul is a place of forms speak well, except that it is not the whole soul but that which can think, and it is not actually [*entelecheia*] but potentially [*dunamis*] the forms."

2. I do not mean to say that the individual is identical to its form, but that insofar as it is anything at all, as opposed to a mere heap (*Met.* VII.16 1040b9), it *is* its form.

3. See also *De anima* II.4 415a26–b7.

4. Trans. A. Platt in Barnes (1984).

5. Except, perhaps, in the case of things like health. This is perhaps the reason that Aristotle favors health and sickness as a metaphor for virtue and vice (e.g., *Nic. Eth.* III.5 1114a11–19).

6. The status of this statement is the subject of much discussion; see Barnes (1971–72), Ackrill (1972–73), Bolton (1978), Ward (1996), and Johansen (2012). My argument here does not rely on whether this constitutes a definition or not.

7. Russon (1995) gives an insightful account of the soul as the governing principle and expression of life.

8. To my knowledge, Aristotle does not use this phrase. It is, however, implied by the nature of virtue, which is the excellence at being what one is. Virtue names excellence of form.

9. See MacIntyre (1999) for a similar characterization of human nature (68–69); and Irwin (1988), 374–75, for a discussion of virtue completing human nature.

10. See also *De anima* 429b3–9: "But when intellect thinks something especially fit for thought, it thinks inferior things not less but rather more. For the faculty of perception is not independent of the body, whereas intellect is separable. When the intellect has become each thing in the way that one who actually knows is said to do so (and this happens when he can exercise his capacity himself), it exists potentially even then in a way, although not in the same way as before it learned or discovered; then it can think by itself." Both of these passages show that intellect is what "has" the forms. See also *Metaphysics* IX.5: intellect is a rational potentiality, capable of bringing about contrary effects.

11. This is a tension that is widely acknowledged. Modrak, for example, writes: "Aristotle seems to be fully cognizant of the tension between the two tendencies in his theorizing about the human soul—(a) the desire to give a unified treatment of all the faculties of soul such that the internal unity of the soul and the unity of the living being who is an ensouled body is assured, and (b) the desire to give an account of the intellect that captures its uniqueness and divinity. The first desire issues in the attempt to encapsulate the core concept of soul in the general definition and the second in the attribution of separability to active *nous* in 3.5" (Modrak [1991b], 758). See also, for example, Wedin (1988), Sisko (1999), and Broadie (1997).

12. Kahn (1966) writes that perception is "any capacity possessed by living animals for obtaining information concerning the outside world—for entering into contact with, and hence responding to, their food, their enemies, their mates, their offspring" (46).

13. Caston (1999) eloquently expresses Aristotle's hesitancy with respect to this kind of problem in terms of whether or not intellect falls under the study of natural science (206–7).

14. See *Nic. Eth.* book X.7.

15. Lear (1988), 165.

16. As Barnes (1971–72), 104 and n4 puts it: " 'X is separate' is an incomplete expression, and its sense will depend upon the intended completion 'separate from r.' Talk about the separation of psychic elements is not always talk about the relation between soul and body," citing *De anima* 413b14–414a3 as an example of separation from other parts of the soul.

17. See Wedin (1988), 186–87, and Politis (2001) for a similar thought about the unlimitedness of intellectual objects implying lack of a bodily structure. Gerson (2004), 358 offers a different account.

18. Caston (1999) offers a compelling case for the former, Gerson (2004) for the latter.

19. Kosman (1992), 353.

20. Cohoe similarly argues (2013) that, unlike perception, intellect's objects are not spatiotemporal, and neither is understanding/thinking (349, 372).

21. *De anima* I.1 403a3–15, I.5 411b17–18; II.1 413a4–7, II.2 413b24–27, II.3 415a11–13; III.4 429a10–13, 429a24–26, 429b3–5, 429b15–17, 429b20–22, III.5 430a 21–25, III.7 431b18–19.

22. See also *De mem.* 450a6–15, where Aristotle describes the necessity to think, for example, of a triangle by means of a finite magnitude even though in thinking of the triangle as such the magnitude is irrelevant. He goes on to attribute the image of the finite triangle to the primary sense faculty (*prōton aisthētikon*).

23. See Modrak (1991b) for a detailed argument that shows that human intellect is inseparable from the body, and that discusses many possible attributes or activities thought to belong to the intellect independently of the body. See also Wedin (1988), Politis (2001), and Broadie (1998), who points out that Aristotle finds many physical features of the human body suited for intellectual life (168). For various dualism arguments, see Barnes (1971–72), Heinaman (1990), Robinson (1983), Shields (1988), and Sisko (1999).

24. See Miller (1999).

25. See Bronstein (2012).

26. On the way that experience emerges from memory, see Engberg-Pedersen (1983), 145–50, and Gregoric and Grgić (2006).

27. Trans. Barnes (1993).

28. So Modrak also argues (1991), 759.

29. D. Frede (1992) argues similarly at 288–90.

30. D. Frede (1992), 291.

31. Ibid., 292.

32. Caston (2009), 325. See also Caston (1998) and Wedin (1988), 136–41.

33. Wedin (1988), 106–9.

34. Broadie (1998) takes this question to be primarily concerned with separation from other parts of the soul, not the body. She takes this to be a question of whether there is a *type* of soul consisting of intellect alone.

35. Politis (2001) makes a similar point (378).

36. See Caston (1999) for a recent and compelling defense of this interpretation.

37. Wedin (1988), chaps. 5 and 6, offers this interpretation.

38. See, for example, Barnes (1971–72), Modrak (1991b), and M. Frede (1992) for expressions of this problem.

39. This charge is leveled by, for example, Gerson (2004), 348–49. Caston (1999) argues that it is not out of place to invoke divine intellect because divine intellect is ultimately the cause of all thinking (217).

40. See Wedin (1988) and Modrak (1991b) for answers to this kind of difficulty.

41. Caston (1999), 206.

42. Gerson (2004), 362n7.

43. Wedin (1988), 160–61.

44. Ibid., 192.

45. Ibid., 192. Sisko (1999), 252n10 identifies two problems with this suggestion: (1) that *De anima* III.5 does not say "as-if" separable and eternal, and (2) that active intellect is an efficient cause of thought. Answers to both problems can be found in Caston (1999) (although not in defense of Wedin): (1) Aristotle describes things in terms of being divine when he means that they are derivatively divine (216), and (2) active intellect is a final not efficient cause of thought (219–22).

46. Wedin (1988), 193–94.

47. Caston (1999), 214.

48. Wedin (1988), 194.

49. Gerson (2004), 356–57.

50. Ibid., 356.

51. Ibid., 370.

52. Kosman (1992), 370.

53. Caston (1999), 222–23.

54. Wedin (1988), 168, Kosman (1992), 353, and Gerson (2004), 360. Barnes (1971–72), 111 sees one of the functions of *De anima* III.5 as resolving the question of the separability of intellect from the body.

55. I set aside the question of how intelligible objects are *acquired*, despite Aristotle's reminder at *De anima* 429b3–5 that intellect has two stages of potentiality, because Aristotle's method dictates that he address what is actual prior to what is potential, and so he seems to be doing here.

In reading *De anima* III.5 to contribute to the explanation of how human thinking happens, I follow Wedin (1988), Kosman (1992), and Gerson (2004). Wedin argues that the active and passive intellects in *De anima* III.5 are introduced "to account for the fact that S is able to think of its (in principle) unlimited objects *autonomously and spontaneously*" (185). Gerson similarly sees *De anima* III.5 as advancing an "explanation of how the intellect is acted upon in order for there to be intellection" (360). Kosman argues that maker mind is responsible for explaining how potential knowledge and what is potentially knowable become actual knowledge and actually known (354–56). Even Caston (1999), although he is a proponent of the divine intellect reading, offers an account of the role that divine intellect plays in thinking that ends up sounding similar to Kosman's. Kosman says: "The paradigm of this *activity* of mind is that divine mind whose substance is *energeia*, and specifically the *energeia* of *theōria*—*noēsis noēseōs noēsis* as it is called in the *Metaphysics*: thinking thinking thinking. It is finally, I suggest, that active thinking, thinking as *theōria*, which maker mind makes, a thinking most fully exemplified in the unremittingly active thinking of the divine mind" (356). Similarly Caston: "But if the Divine Intellect makes only a cameo appearance in *De anima*, it is nevertheless a significant one for Aristotle. For a complete explanation of thought (or indeed any actualization) will ultimately make reference to God when pushed to its furthest limits: the heavens and all of nature depend upon God as a principle or source of change (*ek toiautēs archēs ērtētai*, *Metaph.* 12.7, 1072b13–14). In this sense, God can correctly be described as a 'mover,' as something that is responsible for change taking place" (217). For both Kosman and Caston, then, the active intellect that is named in *De anima* III.5 is the ultimate principle of thinking, that which serves as the perfect instantiation of thinking (and, as Caston points out, living in general). The difference is that Kosman sees active intellect in *De anima* III.5 as the principle of *human* thinking primarily, which implicitly refers to and is derived from the perfect thinking of divine mind, whereas Caston sees it as divine mind, which is ultimately a necessary explanatory principle.

56. Caston (1999), 220–21. Caston cites *Metaphysics* VII.7.

57. Ibid., 206. See also Broadie (1998).

58. Kosman (1992), 347.

59. Ibid., 348.

60. Ibid., 349.

61. Ibid., 350.

62. Ibid., 353–54.

63. Ibid., 355.

64. Ibid.

65. Compare Gerson (2004), 356.

66. Kosman (1992), 356.

67. Ibid.

68. Ibid., 353.

69. Gerson (2004) argues, similarly, that intellect itself (distinct from human soul) is "the entity with which each individual is ideally identical. So, for a composite individual, access to intellect is possible only because that individual is ideally intellect" (356–57). I prefer Kosman's interpretation because it seems that divine intellect fits well with what Gerson wants intellect itself to do, and the principle of parsimony would dictate avoiding the introduction of a third term when two will do.

70. Caston (1999), 220–21.

71. Gerson (2004), 355.

72. See Gerson (2004), 356.

73. Kosman (1992), 356.

74. Ibid., 355.

75. Trans. Sachs (1999).

76. Aristotle makes a similar point in the first book of *De anima* (403a24–403b16), where he notices that anger (for example) has both a physical explanation (boiling blood around the heart) and a formal explanation (desire for revenge).

77. See Caston (1999), 215–16, for a similar understanding of this passage.

78. Trans. Hamlyn (1968).

79. See Bolton (1978) for an argument showing how Aristotle's definition of soul can include divine, nonembodied intellects.

80. Trans. Shiffman (2011).

81. That Aristotle is speaking in his own voice here, rather than expressing one side of an *aporia*, is indicated by the fact that he takes these things to disprove the position that gave rise to the *aporia* (408b30–31): "From these things it is clear that the soul is not such a thing as to be moved."

82. Compare Gerson (2004), 350–51.

83. See, for example, Broadie (1991), 91, citing *Nic. Eth.* 1152a30–33; and McDowell (1998), 192. Vasiliou (1996) is especially clear in his development of this idea.

84. Choice is distinctive of rational animals (*Nic. Eth.* 1111b12–13), and deliberation is a kind of reasoning (*logos*) and thought (*dianoia*) (1112a15–16).

85. *Phronēsis* is one of the intellectual virtues, and it is concerned with right action.

86. Similarly, Aristotle distinguishes between good deliberation and mere cleverness, with the difference being that the former is "able to attain to the good" whereas the latter is correctly deliberating about whatever one decides upon, whether good or bad (*Nic. Eth.* 1142b16–22).

87. See also *De anima* 414b1–6.

88. *De anima* II.3 413b21–24, 414b1–6; III.7 431a8–14, 431b8–12; see also III.10 433a28.

89. Trans. Hett (1936).

90. *De anima* III.8 431b20–432a3.

91. As I discussed in chapter 2 earlier, the natural relation of the parts of the soul is such that the part that is lower in the hierarchy is present *potentially* in the higher one, but the case of the relation between the perceptive part and intellectual part does not easily conform to this relation.

92. When I speak of perception in this section, I refer to the perceptual part of the soul and its activity when apprehending a current particular object. As we saw in the first chapter, this is the perception of incidental objects of perception (which includes perceiving special and common objects), as influenced by memory and *phantasia*. The problem

that the akratic suffers from is that this part of the soul operates independently of the intellectual—the akratic perceives objects just as nonrational animals do. This is a problem because, unlike nonrational animals, the apparent and true good are not naturally aligned for humans. The perceptual part of the soul apprehends the apparent good, and if this is to align with the true good, this part of the soul must be harmonized with the intellectual part.

93. Destrée (2007) and Moss (2012) adopt similar strategies. Destrée justifies this move with Aristotle's invocation of the *phusikos* explanation at 1147a24 (148, 151).

94. Moss (2009) and Destrée (2007) use the former term, Charles (2007) the latter.

95. For example, Robinson (1977) and Grgić (2002).

96. For example, Dahl (1984).

97. In this camp, see Destrée (2007), Charles (2007), and Moss (2009).

98. Moss (2009, revised and reprinted as chapter 5 in her 2012) argues persuasively for the compatibility of these two characterizations. Destrée (2007) similarly argues for the compatibility of the explanation of *akrasia* in terms of a conflict of desire and the explanation from ignorance.

99. Though, as Moss (2009) points out, it is also clearly present in the *Nicomachean Ethics*. Moss cites I.13 1102b13–25.

100. Moss (2012) argues, similarly, that all desire—rational or nonrational—depends upon an evaluative cognition, that is, finding something good. See chapter 1 for the argument that desire depends upon evaluative cognition, and chapter 2 for the distinction between rational and nonrational desires. So, similarly, does Destrée (2007), 150.

101. Moss (2012), 18, similarly reads this as distinguishing between the good, which is grasped by intellect, and the apparent good, which is grasped by some other faculty.

102. Moss (2012), 6, citing Irwin (1990), makes a similar point. To apprehend something as good requires the operations of the intellectual capacity, and for creatures without such a capacity, the good is simply the pleasant, that is, what appears good.

103. See Wiggins (1980) for an argument that the meaning of "choice" (*prohairesis*) is the same in both *Nic. Eth.* III and VII.

104. With Rorty (1980), 270, I take this *not* to describe the epistemic state of the akratic in particular, but only to show one ordinary case in which a person can be said to act contrary to his knowledge. I take it that this is not the akratic's epistemic state, first, because this describes a case of acting out of ignorance of the particular, which Aristotle characterizes as an involuntary act and therefore deserving of pity instead of blame (*Nic. Eth.* III.1 1111a2–21). But *akrasia* is blameworthy, and therefore voluntary. Moreover, in Aristotle's account of *akrasia*, he remarks specifically that the minor premise is active, that is, the knowledge of the particular—"this is sweet"—is active. Second, Aristotle marks a shift in account when he begins to describe the state of the akratic (1147a17–18: "It is clear, then, that those lacking self-restraint must be said to be in a state similar to such people"), saying, "Further, another way of having science, different from those just now mentioned . . ." (1147a10–11).

105. Contra Burnyeat (1980), who sees no answer in *Nic. Eth.* VII.3 to why the better knowledge is overcome: "The treatment of knowledge pinpoints what is to be explained. It is not itself the explanation" (85). Burnyeat instead finds an answer in the overeager spirited part of the soul that Aristotle discusses in *Nic. Eth.* VII.6. But it seems that Aristotle himself thinks that he has found a solution in *Nic. Eth.* III.3.

106. Rorty (1980) suggests that the abstract way in which the akratic "knows" what is good is a result of forgetting oneself: "To forget what sort of man one is can be to forget

how one's character embeds one's ends. This is compatible with remembering those ends, but remembering them abstractly" (273).

107. Moss (2009), 132; see also Lorenz (2006), 197.

108. That the two accounts are complementary is indicated by the way Aristotle introduces the second account. Aristotle introduces the second account by saying, "Further, someone might also look at the cause of the lack of self-restraint in terms of nature [*phusikōs*], as follows" (*Nic. Eth.* 1147a24–25). The *phusikōs* here indicates that Aristotle will articulate the cause of *akrasia* from a new perspective, not that he will provide an alternative and competing explanation. (See also *De anima* I.1 403a24–b16. Here he offers two compatible explanations of anger, one of which is the explanation that the natural scientist gives; the other is that which the dialectician will give, and one who studies the soul must take both into account. A multiplicity of perspectives produces a multiplicity of complementary explanations.)

109. In this sense, the akratic behaves like a child or a nonrational animal. See MacIntyre (1999), 70–71.

110. Cooper (1975) offers a quite different interpretation of these passages. He argues that appetite prevents the avoidance of the sweet because it prevents the recognition "this is chocolate" (49–50). This seems to render the akratic *too* ignorant of his own action—how can a person *not* know that what he is eating is chocolate? Anyone who has experienced an akratic moment will attest that she *knew* that she was eating chocolate. What she is ignorant of is, rather, her own investment in not eating chocolate.

111. See McDowell (1998), 46–48, and Burnyeat (1980), 83, for similar points. See Wiggins (1980b) on the difference between the akratic and the enkratic's knowledge and perception.

112. As Moss (2012), 39, points out, Aristotle considers the vicious person's pleasure in base things "as a kind of malfunctioning of the pleasure-taking apparatus, akin to ordinary perceptual error," citing *Nic. Eth.* 1173b20–25. The vicious person's perceptual soul is in a bad state; similarly, although less extremely, so is the akratic's, for taking pleasure in the wrong things. See also Lorenz (2006), 198–201.

113. See Moss (2009), who argues that *akrasia* is parallel to perceptual illusion: that when the akratic behaves akratically, her intellect is "covered over" and is unable to apprehend the difference between the perceived good and the true good. Intellect is compromised such that *choosing*, that is, deliberately desiring, is no longer available to the akratic agent.

114. This dual aspect of *akrasia* also explains why the akratic's lack of knowledge of the particular does not render the act involuntary. The akratic is responsible for the ignorance of the particular because he is responsible for being the sort of person who is easily overcome by passion. The parallel case is the person who acts in ignorance while drunk: he is responsible for his action because he is responsible for his drunken condition (*Nic. Eth.* III.5 1113b30–1114a3). Similarly, the akratic is ultimately responsible for the state of passion that overcomes him because he has made himself the sort of character who is vulnerable to such fits (as I will argue below).

115. Moss (2009) emphasizes the physiological underpinnings of *akrasia*.

116. See Kosman (1980) for an account of the habituation of passion. Burnyeat (1980) offers an account of moral development generally. He views *akrasia* as a stage in the development of virtue, before one's habits have made internal what one has learned is good (84–86).

117. Aristotle does not consider our bodily conditions to be merely natural. We are responsible for the "vices of the body" (*Nic. Eth.* 1114a21–23) that arise due to our behavior. Correlatively, it would seem, we are responsible for the good condition of our bodies, and also molding them to *be* good conditions for virtuous action.

Chapter 4

1. I limit myself to discuss the *orthos logos*, and not the *horos* (boundary, standard) to which the person with reason looks. The *horos* in this introductory passage seems to name the boundary of the range of actions that, in one situation or another, constitute the middle action or passion of virtue. I am interested here in the specific middle action/passion that the *phronimos* determines. For an account of the *horos*, see Peterson (1988) and Goméz-Lobo (1992).

2. Specifically, the action (and passion) that hits the middle course is undertaken "when one ought and at the things one ought, in relation to those people whom one ought, for the sake of what and as one ought" (*Nic. Eth.* 1106b21–23).

3. The comments here at the opening of *Nicomachean Ethics* II pick up on earlier comments in I about method (1094b11–1095a3, 1098a26–b2), and there is a distinction to be drawn between arguments concerning ethics as a matter of study and arguments about what one ought to do or what the middle course is that one is aiming at. The distinction, however, is not a very sharp one; after all, we are studying ethics not for the sake of knowledge but for the sake of becoming good (1095a4–6, 1103b26–30). More importantly for my purposes here, Aristotle moves in this passage at the opening of II from referring to the imprecision of arguments about ethics as a matter of study to arguments about what a person ought to do. He begins the passage by referring back to the earlier methodological remarks ("just as we said at the beginning" [1104a2–3]), but adds a further imprecision due to the particularity of action ("And since such is the character of the general argument, still less precise is the argument concerned with particulars" [1104a5–6]), and as a result "those who act ought themselves always to examine what pertains to the opportune moment" (1104a7–8). The imprecision of ethics as a study rests in the imprecision of action generally and specifically the inability to provide an accurate *logos* for virtuous action.

4. Modrak (1991a) recognizes this problem in identifying the *orthos logos* (186). Her solution is that the *logos* is "the application of the correct general principle to the concrete situation . . . The special skill of the *phronimos* is the ability to recognize when the prescriptive principle should be put into play and when it should not." However, the problem runs deeper than this solution suggests: in order even to decide whether a principle applies to a concrete situation, one must first of all see the situation in a certain way, as, for example, an occasion for courage (whether courage in this situation means standing one's ground or running away). See Nussbaum (1990), chap. 2.

5. This is consistent with the general character of virtue as what "brings that of which it is the virtue into good condition and causes the work belonging to that thing to be done well" (*Nic. Eth.* 1106a15–17). *Phronēsis*, as an intellectual virtue, is what causes the work of practical thinking to be done well. See Lorenz (2009) for a similar point based on the analysis of adjectives ending in *–ikos* and with reference to *phronēsis* as a *hexis praktikē*.

6. Contrary to Broadie (1991), 203, I do not see Aristotle identifying *phronēsis* with good deliberation. Broadie cites *Nic. Eth.* 1140a25–26, but there, as elsewhere, what Aristotle says is that it belongs to the *phronimos* to be able to deliberate well (*dokei dē phronimou einai to dunasthai kalōs bouleusasthai*), not that deliberating well *is phronēsis*. Broadie

recognizes that deliberating well cannot be all there is to *phronēsis*, because good practical thinking also requires the ability to decide when deliberation is necessary (211), although she does not find this in Aristotle's account. We do find it, however, if we do not identify *phronēsis* with good deliberation, but with the condition or power for good deliberation. See Bostock (2000), 84–85, who draws a similar distinction between the deliberative aspect of *phronēsis* and the true apprehension of the end; and Schollmeier (1989), who distinguishes between an intuitive and a discursive function of *phronēsis*.

7. Perceiving particulars *as* ethically significant is, I take it, the same as what McDowell (1998) calls perceiving "action-inviting" features, and Nussbaum (1990) calls the discernment of perception, what Wiggins (1980a) calls situational appreciation, and what Louden (1986) calls practical perception. It is similar but not identical to Moss's (2012) notion of evaluative perception. Moss considers evaluative perception to be the perception of pleasure and pain as such, whether or not there is intellectual input, and that this is the basis of ethical cognition. But this is the limit to what perception can do, on Moss's account. Perception, understood as the faculty sensitive to the present particular, must be the faculty receptive to the ethical significance of a particular, but it does this by virtue of operating within an intellectual context. See Louden (1986) for a similar view of perception (especially 170).

8. David Wiggins helpfully expresses this gap between intention, preparation, and successful action in Aristotelian terms of having a *disposition*. One may have a disposition to do something, and that means that ordinarily one will accomplish it, but it does not guarantee that one will be successful. Wiggins (1980b), 244.

9. Purshouse (2006) explains Neoptolemus's circumstance as a conflict between a *phantasia* developed in the course of a foregone moral education, and a new conceptual scheme or worldview that has not yet altered the basic impression that Philoctetes makes upon him (213–16), parallel to the feelings a lapsed Catholic might have at the prospect of premarital sex (215). "If Neoptolemus acts on the basis of this emotion, he acts 'for the sake of the noble'; at least, for the sake of what he once thought was noble and what still has, for him, a phantasia of nobility, as opposed to disgrace. We might also say his emotion is, in some sense, obedient to his reason, in that it follows a past element of his reasoning, albeit not the reasoned judgement he entertains at the time of action . . . Hence, his passion is linked not only with reason, but with right reason: an element of his rational mind that had judged correctly" (215). One reason to think that Neoptolemus's case is rather to be explained in terms of flexible sensitivity, as opposed to slipping back into a prior way of thinking, comes from Aristotle's remarks immediately preceding the invocation of Neoptolemus. In these remarks, Aristotle distinguishes the stubborn from the self-controlled (enkratic) on the basis that the former, but not the latter, are hard to persuade otherwise (*Nic. Eth.* 1151b4–10). Conversely, Neoptolemus, although he departs from his reasoned opinion on the basis of a passion, is not akratic for the reason that it is his passion, and not his opinion, that is good and true. This suggests that what is at stake here is sensitivity to the good—the stubborn person is not enkratic because she is insensitive to truth, and Neoptolemus is not akratic because he *is* sensitive to truth.

10. Cooper (1975) takes *kath' hekasta* to refer not to concrete particulars but to determinate kinds or species (28–32). But see Engberg-Pedersen (1983), 199n; and Louden (1991), 164–67, for refutations of this view.

11. Engberg-Pedersen (1983) raises a similar question (202–4). His answer is that perception *becomes* rational by being used in a rational context, namely, deliberation, and

thereby being formulated universally. I answer this question differently because I adopt a broader notion of rationality than he does (see his chapter 5).

12. I take this proposal to be similar to Louden's (1986) proposal that practical perception (*aisthēsis*) (perception of ethically relevant particulars) is *phronēsis* applied to the level of particular situations of choice (169). I find, however, that Louden leaves obscure the precise relationship between intellect (*nous*) and perception (*aisthēsis*) as distinct psychological faculties. For example, he interprets Aristotle's comment at *Nic. Eth.* VI.8 1143b5 that *aisthēsis* is *nous* to mean that *nous* is a noninferential grasp of the particulars of action (173), which seems to elide the distinction between *aisthēsis* and *nous* entirely. I am indebted to Olmsted (1948) for drawing the close connection between the mean of perception and the mean of virtue, although the connection I draw is rather different than his.

13. Because of how cursory the discussions of the other intellectual virtues (scientific knowledge [*epistēmē*], art [*technē*], wisdom [*sophia*], and intellect [*nous*]) are relative to the discussions of *phronēsis*, I take Aristotle to introduce them for the sake of enumerating the virtues completely, but also for the sake of comparing and contrasting them with *phronēsis* (as he does many times in *Nic. Eth.* VI).

14. Engberg-Pederson (1983) points out that Aristotle uses *hupolēpsis* as a generic term to cover all rational states (144–45).

15. Trans. Sachs (1999).

16. Fortenbaugh (1964), 78, for example, argues that perceiving particulars correctly is the accomplishment of virtue of character (moral virtue), giving *phronēsis* an instrumental role in completing the process of deliberation (80). Fortenbaugh rightly emphasizes Aristotle's view that "what sort of character a man has determines what appears good to him" (81) and that only the virtuous person truly apprehends the practical good in its particularity.

17. Fortenbaugh recognizes these challenges, meeting the first by interpreting the passage at *Nic. Eth.* 1142a23–30 as identifying the commonsense power as necessary *for* practical reasoning, but not the work of *phronēsis* itself (85). This interpretation is problematic because it rests on identifying the mathematical perception of a triangle *as* the ultimate figure with the ordinary perception of a triangle. He meets the second challenge by claiming that Aristotle is not describing *phronēsis* accurately at 1144a29–30, but instead is making reference to a passage in Plato's *Republic* 533d (86). This, too, is a problematic response, both because it does not explain why Aristotle would make such a misleading reference, and also because it does not take into account the second instance of the characterization of *phronēsis* as the vision of moral virtue implicit in the passage at 1144b8–12.

18. McDowell (1998), 39, makes a similar point.

19. I return at the conclusion of the chapter to consider why *phronēsis* is insufficient without virtue in considering the much-discussed issue of whether virtue or *phronēsis* provides the end of action and choice.

20. I am not distinguishing between natural virtue and virtue of character. (See, for example, Bostock [2000], 87, for such a distinction.) The point I ultimately wish to make—that it is *phronēsis* that enables one to identify the middle course in any particular circumstance—holds whether or not natural virtue is distinct from virtue of character. Neither of these latter types of virtue is fully virtue, and both suffer from imprecision.

21. Nussbaum (1990), 71–72.

22. See also *Nic. Eth.* 1141a25–26: "they would assert that that which observes [*theōrein*] the good condition [*to eu*] for each thing is *phronimos*, and they would entrust such con-

cerns to this"; 1142b32–33: "good deliberation would be a correctness that accords with what is advantageous in relation to the end, about which end *phronēsis* is a true conviction."

23. This passage also illustrates why virtue is necessary for *phronēsis*. Recall that *phronēsis* and virtue mutually require one another—virtue is only natural virtue in the absence of *phronēsis*, and *phronēsis* is not possible without virtue (*Nic. Eth.* 1144b30–32). *Phronēsis* provides the guiding sight of the particular to virtue, and virtue is a condition for such a sight because it removes the corrupting influence of pleasure and pain. See also Woods (1986).

24. Broadie (1991) refutes this idea (198–202); see Bostock (2000), 82–93, for a rebuttal.

25. See Nussbaum (1990), 70, and Wiggins (1980), 231 for similar discussions of the Lesbian rule passage.

26. I say "at least" because I am sympathetic to McDowell's (1998) stronger conclusion that "practical wisdom *is* the properly molded state of the motivational propensities [provided by the virtues of character] in a reflectively adjusted form; the sense in which it is a state of the intellect does not interfere with its also being a state of the desiderative element" (40). This conclusion has the advantage of explaining why Aristotle considers virtue of character and *phronēsis* to be mutually dependent upon one another, and why Aristotle claims that if one has *phronēsis*, one has all the rest of virtue, too.

27. *Republic* 331c.

28. See Woods (1986), 146.

29. Although some scholars (e.g., Moss [2012], 41) take Aristotle to be using *aisthēsis* loosely when he likens *phronēsis* to it, there are also a number of scholars who take this claim literally. Among those who take Aristotle at his word when he likens *phronēsis* to perception are John Cooper (1975), John McDowell (1998), Martha Nussbaum (1990), Richard Sorabji (1980), Deborah Modrak (1991a), Troels Engberg-Pedersen (1983), and Robert Louden (1986). While these discussions are enlightening, I find that either they are mostly reticent with regard to how to understand this unusual power of perception (McDowell, Nussbaum, Louden), or they treat it as a perception that is subsumed under a universal (Sorabji, Modrak, Cooper). Nussbaum persuasively argues that this latter way of understanding the nature of practical thinking fails to accommodate the variability and unpredictability of concrete ethical situations (66–75). The task I aim to accomplish is to show the nature of phronetic perception and to explain how it may be *influenced* by intellect without thereby understanding it to be subsumed under a universal. Louden moves in this direction (172–74), but the relationship between intellect and perception remains unclear. My position is closest to McDowell's, who argues that *phronēsis* is perception that is informed by one's conception of the end (30).

30. Aristotle identifies shape as one of the objects of perception, a common sensible, and some commentators (as, for example, Modrak [1991a] and Engberg-Pederson [1983], 206) have identified this as the kind of perception invoked here. However, I think it is mistaken to identify the kind of perception spoken of here as perception of the common sensible, shape, because Aristotle does not liken *phronēsis* to the perception of a *triangle*, a perception available to nonrational animals, but of a triangle *as* the ultimate figure in mathematics.

31. Cooper (1975) and Louden (1986), 169 understand the triangle to be ultimate in the sense of being the first term in the construction of geometrical proofs, and, analogously, the ultimate object of *phronēsis* to be the conclusion of deliberation, which is the first step one must take in accomplishing one's aim. Engberg-Pedersen (1983), 206 adds

that it is the last object of analysis in looking for a simple figure to serve as the basis for other geometrical constructions. (Compare Wiggins [1980], 235–36.) It does not seem to me to be necessary to interpret the analogy in this way, and, moreover, to interpret the analogy this way seems to obscure the point of the passage, which is to distinguish *phronēsis* from *epistēmē*. *Epistēmē* is knowledge that is the conclusion of a demonstration; on Cooper's reading, this passage makes *phronēsis* the conclusion of deliberation. On this interpretation, then, it seems that *phronēsis* is rather like *epistēmē*, not distinct from it. In a similar vein, Cooper does not address the seemingly nondiscursive nature of *phronēsis*, brought out in the comparison to *nous*'s grasp of those things that have no *logos*. See Bostock (2000), 101 for other objections.

32. McDowell (1998), 27–30, argues similarly that *phronēsis* is "the perceptual capacity that determines which feature of a situation should engage a standing concern" (30). Engberg-Pedersen argues that it is "contextual perception" in the sense that it is the perception of a particular *as* relevant to a rational argument (207). This seems to be the other side of McDowell's coin: to perceive a particular as engaging one's concern may mean to perceive it as relevant to one's reasoning about what to do, or it may mean that it is the salient feature upon which to act.

33. Mostly in agreement with Cooper, this explains why mathematical perception is *more* perception than *phronēsis* is: *phronēsis* perceives something in light of some aim to be achieved, and this aim is not yet present to be perceived. The mathematician, presumably, actually *sees* triangles.

34. I say "perceptual awareness" to mark a distinction between the analysis of perception in abstraction from the life of the animal of which it is a part and the discussion of perception in its capacity of being of service to the living being. It is only in abstraction that we get perception of the proper perceptible as such, but in the broader awareness by which an animal lives, such things are always perceived as organized by the animal's aims and desires.

35. Lorenz (2006) argues that being able to comprehend for-the-sake-of relations distinguishes human practical thinking from the nonrational animal equivalent (174–85). This does not preclude that the perception of nonrational animals is informed by their goals, even if they are not aware of their goals *as* goals for the sake of which they act.

36. Owens (1991), 144.

37. Ibid., 147.

38. Nussbaum (1990), 67.

39. By contrast, intellect is nothing before it thinks (*De anima* 429a24).

40. See Russon (1995).

41. The decisive remark occurs at *Nic. Eth.* 1113a32–b1: "the serious person is distinguished perhaps most of all by his seeing what is true in each case, just as if he were a rule and measure of them. But in the case of most people, a deception appears to occur on account of the pleasure involved, for what is not good appears to them as good."

42. The whole passage reads: "Further, pleasure has been a part of the upbringing of us all from infancy; it is difficult to remove this experience, since our life has been so ingrained with it. We also take pleasure and pain as the rule of our actions, some of us to a greater degree, some to a lesser. It is on account of this that one's entire concern necessarily pertains to pleasure and pain, for taking delight and feeling pain make no small contribution to our actions' being well or badly done" (*Nic. Eth.* 1105a1–7). See also 1104b11–13 and X.1 1172a19–26.

43. "Thus one must be brought up in a certain way straight from childhood, as Plato asserts, so as to enjoy as well as to be pained by what one ought, for this is correct education" (*Nic. Eth.* 1104b11–13).

44. See the distinction between the unqualifiedly good and the good for some particular person drawn in the discussion of pleasure in *Nic. Eth.* VII.12.

45. Similar, perhaps, to reaching the right conclusion on the basis of a faulty middle premise (*Nic. Eth.* VI.9).

46. For animals, of course, "ethical" experience in the sense of distinguishing between good and bad *is* preprogrammed in the soul in the mean of perception.

47. Much has been written on the topic of the relationship between *phronēsis* and virtue of character with regard to means-ends. It is well documented in Moss (2011).

Conclusion

1. Trans. Simpson (1997).
2. Trans. Sachs (2009).
3. Trans. Benardete and Davis (2002).

BIBLIOGRAPHY

Works by Aristotle

Ars Rhetorica. 1959. Edited by David Ross. Oxford: Oxford University Press.
De Anima. 1956. Edited by David Ross. Oxford: Oxford University Press.
De Arte Poetica Liber. 1993. Edited by R. Kassel. Oxford: Oxford University Press.
De Motu Animalium. 1978. Edited by Martha Nussbaum. Princeton, N.J.: Princeton University Press.
Ethica Eudemia. 1991. Edited by R. R. Walzer and J. M. Mingray. Oxford: Oxford University Press, 1991.
Ethica Nicomachea. 1993. Edited by I. Bywater. Oxford: Oxford University Press.
Metaphysica. 1957. Edited by W. Jaeger. Oxford: Oxford University Press.
Organon Volume 1: Categories, On Interpretation, Prior Analytics. 1938. Translated by Hugh Tredennick and Harold Cooke. Loeb Classical Library. Cambridge, Mass.: Harvard University Press.
Organon Volume 2: Posterior Analytics, Topics. 1960. Translated by Hugh Tredennick and E. S. Forster. Loeb Classical Library. Cambridge, Mass.: Harvard University Press.
Physica. 1951. Edited by David Ross. Oxford: Oxford University Press.
Politika. 1957. Edited by David Ross. Oxford: Oxford University Press.

Other Sources

Ackrill, J. L. 1972–73. "Aristotle's Definitions of *Psuchē*." *Proceedings of the Aristotelian Society* 73: 119–33.
Annas, J. 1993. *The Morality of Happiness*. Oxford: Oxford University Press.
Anton, J. P., and A. Preus, eds. 1991. *Essays in Ancient Greek Philosophy IV: Aristotle's Ethics*. Albany: SUNY Press.
———. 1992. *Essays in Ancient Greek Philosophy V: Aristotle's Ontology*. Albany: SUNY Press.
Apostle, H. G. 1981. *Aristotle's "On the Soul."* Grinnell, Iowa: Peripatetic.
Barnes, J. 1971–72. "Aristotle's Concept of Mind." *Proceedings of the Aristotelian Society* 72: 101–14.
———. 1993. *Aristotle Posterior Analytics, Translation and Commentary*. 2nd ed. Oxford: Oxford University Press.
———, ed. 1984. *The Complete Works of Aristotle*: *The Revised Oxford Translation*, vol. 1. Princeton, N.J.: Princeton University Press.
———, ed. 1984. *The Complete Works of Aristotle*: *The Revised Oxford Translation*, vol. 2. Princeton, N.J.: Princeton University Press.
Barnes, J., M. Schofield, and R. Sorabji, eds. 1977. *Articles on Aristotle. 2: Ethics and Politics*. London: Duckworth.

———. 1978. *Articles on Aristotle. 4: Psychology and Aesthetics*. London: Duckworth.

Bartlett, R. C., and S. D. Collins. 2011. *Aristotle's Nicomachean Ethics*. Chicago: University of Chicago Press.

Baumrin, B. H. 1967–68. "Aristotle's Ethical Intuitionism." *New Scholasticism* 42: 1–17.

Benardete, S., and M. Davis, trans. 2002. *Aristotle, On Poetics*. South Bend, Ind.: St. Augustine's.

Block, I. 1961. "The Order of Aristotle's Psychological Writings." *The American Journal of Philology* 82, no. 1: 50–77.

Blum, L. 1994. *Moral Perception and Particularity*. Cambridge: Cambridge University Press.

Bobonich, C., and P. Destrée, eds. 2007. *Akrasia in Greek Philosophy: From Socrates to Plotinus*. Leiden: Brill.

Bolton, R. 1978. "Aristotle's Definitions of Soul: *De Anima* II, 1–3." *Phronesis* 23: 258–78.

Bos, A. 2010. "Aristotle on the Differences between Plants, Animals, and Human Beings and on the Elements as Instruments of the Soul (*De Anima* II.4 415b18)." *Review of Metaphysics* 63: 821–41.

Bostock, D. 2000. *Aristotle's Ethics*. Oxford: Oxford University Press.

Bradshaw, D. 1997. "Aristotle on Perception: The Dual-Logos Theory." *Apeiron* 30: 143–61.

Brentano, F. (1867) 1977. *The Psychology of Aristotle*. Translated by G. Rolf. Berkeley: University of California Press.

Broadie, S. 1991. *Ethics with Aristotle*. Oxford: Oxford University Press.

———. 1997. "*Nous* and Nature in Aristotle's *De Anima* III." *Proceedings of the Boston Area Colloquium in Ancient Philosophy* 12: 163–76.

Broadie, S., and C. Rowe. 2002. *Aristotle, Nicomachean Ethics: Translation, Introduction, and Commentary*. Oxford: Oxford University Press.

Bronstein, D. 2012. "The Origin and Aim of *Posterior Analytics* II.19." *Phronesis* 57: 29–62.

Burnyeat, M. 1980. "Aristotle on Learning to Be Good." In *Essays on Aristotle's Ethics*, edited by Rorty, 69–92. Berkeley: University of California Press.

———. 1992. "Is an Aristotelian Philosophy of Mind Still Credible? A Draft." In *Essays on Aristotle's De Anima*, edited by Nussbaum and Rorty, 15–26. Oxford: Oxford University Press.

Cashdollar, S. 1973. "Aristotle's Account of Incidental Perception." *Phronēsis* 18: 156–75.

Caston, V. 1996. "Why Aristotle Needs Imagination." *Phronesis* 51: 20–55.

———. 1999. "Aristotle's Two Intellects: A Modest Proposal." *Phronesis* 44, no. 3: 199–227.

———. 2004. "More on Aristotle on Consciousness: A Reply to Sisko." *Mind*, n.s. 113, no. 451: 523–33.

———. 2005. "The Spirit and the Letter: Aristotle on Perception." In *Metaphysics, Soul, and Ethics in Ancient Thought: Themes from the Work of Richard Sorabji*, edited by Salles, 245–320. Oxford: Oxford University Press.

Charles, D. 2007. "Aristotle's Weak *Akrates*: What Does Her Ignorance Consist in?" In *Akrasia in Greek Philosophy*, edited by Bobonich and Destrée, 193–214. Leiden: Brill.

Charlton, W. 1980. "Aristotle's Definition of Soul." *Phronesis* 25, no. 2: 170–86.

Code, A., and J. Moravcsik. 1980. "Explaining Various Forms of Living." In *Essays on Aristotle's De Anima*, edited by Nussbaum and Rorty, 129–46. Oxford: Oxford University Press.

Cooper, J. 1975. *Reason and Human Good in Aristotle*. Cambridge: Cambridge University Press.

———. 1999. *Reason and Emotion*. Princeton, N.J.: Princeton University Press.

Corcilius, K., and P. Gregoric. 2010. "Separability vs. Difference: Parts and Capacities of the Soul in Aristotle." *Oxford Studies in Ancient Philosophy* 39: 81–120.

Dahl, N. O. 1984. *Practical Reason, Aristotle, and Weakness of the Will*. Minneapolis: University of Minnesota Press.

Destrée, P. 2007. "Aristotle on the Causes of *Akrasia*." In *Akrasia in Greek Philosophy*, edited by Bobonich and Destrée, 139–66. Leiden: Brill.

Engberg-Pedersen, T. 1983. *Aristotle's Theory of Moral Insight*. Oxford: Oxford University Press.

Engstrom, S., and J. Whiting, eds. 1996. *Aristotle, Kant, and the Stoics: Rethinking Happiness and Duty*. Cambridge: Cambridge University Press.

Everson, S. 1997. *Aristotle on Perception*. Oxford: Oxford University Press.

Fortenbaugh, W. W. 1964. "Aristotle's Conception of Moral Virtue and Its Perceptive Role." *Transactions and Proceedings of the American Philological Association* 95: 77–87.

———. 1991. "Aristotle's Distinction between Moral Virtue and Practical Wisdom." In *Essays in Ancient Greek Philosophy IV: Aristotle's Ethics*, edited by Anton and Preus, 97–106. Albany: SUNY Press.

Frede, D. 1992. "The Cognitive Role of *Phantasia* in Aristotle." In *Essays on Aristotle's De Anima*, edited by Nussbaum and Rorty, 279–96. Oxford: Oxford University Press.

Frede, M. 1992. "On Aristotle's Conception of Soul." In *Essays on Aristotle's De Anima*, edited by Nussbaum and Rorty, 93–108. Oxford: Oxford University Press.

Freeland, C. A. 1994. "Aristotle on Perception, Appetition, and Self-Motion." In *Self-Motion: Aristotle to Newton*, edited by Gill and Lennox, 35–64. Princeton, N.J.: Princeton University Press.

———, ed. 1998. *Feminist Interpretations of Aristotle*. University Park: Pennsylvania State University Press.

Gendler, T. S. 2008. "Alief and Belief." *Journal of Philosophy* 105: 634–63.

Gerson, L. 2004. "The Unity of Aristotle's Intellect in *De Anima*." *Phronesis* 49, no. 4: 348–73.

Gill, M. L., and J. G. Lennox, eds. 1994. *Self-Motion: Aristotle to Newton*. Princeton, N.J.: Princeton University Press.

Gómez-Lobo, A. 1992. "Aristotle's 'Right Reason.'" *Apeiron* 25, no. 4: 15–34.

Gotthelf, A. 1987. "Aristotle's Conception of Final Causality." In *Philosophical Issues in Aristotle's Biology*, edited by Gotthelf and Lennox, 204–42. Cambridge: Cambridge University Press.

Gotthelf, A., and J. G. Lennox, eds. 1987. *Philosophical Issues in Aristotle's Biology*. Cambridge: Cambridge University Press.

Greenwood, L. H. G. 1909. *Aristotle, Nicomachean Ethics Book VI*. Cambridge: Cambridge University Press.

Gregoric, P. 2007. *Aristotle on the Common Sense*. Oxford: Oxford University Press.

Gregoric, P., and F. Grgić. 2006. "Aristotle's Notion of Experience." *Archiv für Geschichte der Philosophie* 88, no. 1: 1–30.

Grgić, F. 2002. "Aristotle on the Akratic's Knowledge." *Phronesis* 47, no. 4: 336–58.

Groenhout, R. 1998. "The Virtue of Care: Aristotelian Ethics and Contemporary Ethics of Care." In *Feminist Interpretations of Aristotle*, edited by Freeland, 171–200. University Park: Pennsylvania State University Press.

Hamlyn, D. W. 1968. *De Anima Books II and III*, translation and commentary. Oxford: Oxford University Press.

———. 1968. "*Koinē Aisthēsis*." *The Monist* 52, no. 2: 195–209.

Hardie, W. F. R. 1968. *Aristotle's Ethical Theory*. Oxford: Oxford University Press.

Heinaman, R. 1990. "Aristotle and the Mind-Body Problem." *Phronesis* 35, no. 1: 83–102.

Hett, W. S. 1936. *Aristotle, On the Soul, Parva Naturalia, On Breath*. Loeb Classical Library. Cambridge, Mass.: Harvard University Press.

Hursthouse, R. 2006. "Practical Wisdom: A Mundane Account." *Proceedings of the Aristotelian Society New Series* 106: 285–389.

Irwin, T. H. 1975. "Aristotle on Reason, Desire and Virtue." *Journal of Philosophy* 73: 567–78.

———. 1980. "The Metaphysical and Psychological Basis of Aristotle's Ethics." In *Essays on Aristotle's De Anima*, edited by Rorty, 35–54. Oxford: Oxford University Press.

———. 1988. *Aristotle's First Principles*. Oxford: Oxford University Press.

Joachim, H. H. 1951. *Aristotle: The Nicomachean Ethics*. Oxford: Oxford University Press.

Johansen, T. K. 2005. "In Defense of Inner Sense: Aristotle on Perceiving That One Sees." In *Proceedings of the Boston Area Colloquium in Ancient Philosophy XXI*, edited by Cleary and Gurtler, 235–76. Leiden: Brill.

———. 2012. *The Powers of Aristotle's Soul*. Oxford: Oxford University Press.

Jost, L. J. 1976. "Is Aristotle an Ethical Intuitionist?" *Apeiron* 10, no. 1: 15–19.

Kahn, C. 1966. "Sensation and Consciousness in Aristotle's Psychology." *Archiv für Geschichte der Philosophie* 48: 43–81.

———. 1992. "Aristotle on Thinking." In *Essays on Aristotle's De Anima*, edited by Nussbaum and Rorty, 359–80. Oxford: Oxford University Press.

Korsgaard, C. 1996. "From Duty and for the Sake of the Noble: Kant and Aristotle on Morally Good Action." In *Aristotle, Kant, and the Stoics: Rethinking Happiness and Duty*, edited by Engstrom and Whiting, 203–36. Cambridge: Cambridge University Press.

Kosman, L. A. 1975. "Perceiving That We Perceive: *On the Soul* III.2." *Philosophical Review* 84: 499–519.

———. 1980. "Being Properly Affected: Virtues and Feelings in Aristotle's Ethics." In *Essays on Aristotle's Ethics*, edited by Rorty, 103–16. Berkeley: University of California Press.

———. 1987. "Animals and Other Beings in Aristotle." In *Philosophical Issues in Aristotle's Biology*, edited by Gotthelf and Lennox, 360–91. Cambridge: Cambridge University Press.

———. 1992. "What Does Maker Mind Make?" In *Essays on Aristotle's De Anima*, edited by Nussbaum and Rorty, 343–58. Oxford: Oxford University Press.

———. 2005. "Commentary on Johansen." In *Proceedings of the Boston Area Colloquium in Ancient Philosophy XXI*, edited by Cleary and Gurtler, 277–83. Leiden: Brill.

Lear, J. 1988. *The Desire to Understand*. Cambridge: Cambridge University Press.

Lloyd, G. E. R., and G. E. L. Owen, eds. 1978. *Aristotle on Mind and the Senses*. Cambridge: Cambridge University Press.

Lorenz, H. 2006. *The Brute Within: Appetitive Desire in Plato and Aristotle*. Oxford: Oxford University Press.

———. 2009. "Virtue of Character in Aristotle's *Nicomachean Ethics*." *Oxford Studies in Ancient Philosophy* 37: 177–212.

Louden, R. 1986. "Aristotle's Practical Particularism." *Ancient Philosophy* 6: 123–38.

MacIntyre, A. 1998. *Dependent Rational Animals: Why Human Beings Need the Virtues*. Peru, Ill.: Carus.

Madigan, A. 1986. "Dimensions of Voluntariness in *EN* iii.12 1119a21–33." *Ancient Philosophy* 6: 139–52.

Matthews, G. 1992. "*De Anima* 2.2–4 and the Meaning of Life." In *Essays on Aristotle's De Anima*, edited by Nussbaum and Rorty, 185–94. Oxford: Oxford University Press.

McCoy, M. 2005. "Philosophy, Elenchus, and Charmides's Definitions of Sophrosune." *Arethusa* 38: 133–59.

———. 2008. *Plato on the Rhetoric of Philosophers and Sophists*. Cambridge: Cambridge University Press.

McDowell, J. 1998. *Mind, Value, and Reality*. Cambridge, Mass.: Harvard University Press.

Menn, S. 2002. "Aristotle's Definition of Soul and the Programme of the *De Anima*." *Oxford Studies in Ancient Philosophy* 22: 83–139.

Merleau-Ponty, M. 1962. *Phenomenology of Perception*. Translated by Colin Smith. New York: Routledge.

Miller, M. 1999. "Figure, Ratio, Form: Plato's Five Mathematical Studies." *Apeiron* 32, no. 4: 73–88.

Modrak, D. 1987. *Aristotle: The Power of Perception*. Chicago: University of Chicago Press.

———. 1991a. "Aristotle on Reason, Practical Reason, and Living Well." In *Essays in Ancient Greek Philosophy IV: Aristotle's Ethics*, edited by Anton and Preus, 179–92. Albany: SUNY Press.

———. 1991b. "The Nous-Body Problem in Aristotle." *The Review of Metaphysics* 44, no. 4: 755–74.

Morrison, D. 1985. "*Chōristos* in Aristotle." *Harvard Studies in Classical Philology* 89: 89–105.

Moss, J. 2007. "*Akrasia* and Perceptual Illusion." *Archiv für Geschichte der Philosophie* 91: 119–56.

———. 2011. "'Virtue Makes the Goal Right': Virtue and *Phronēsis* in Aristotle's Ethics." *Phronesis* 56: 204–61.

———. 2012. *Aristotle on the Apparent Good*. Oxford: Oxford University Press.

Murdoch, I. 1970. *The Sovereignty of Good*. London: Routledge.

Nussbaum, M. C. 1978. *Aristotle's De Motu Animalium*. Princeton, N.J.: Princeton University Press.

———. 1990. *Love's Knowledge*. Oxford: Oxford University Press.

———. 1998. "Aristotle, Feminism, and Needs for Functioning." In *Feminist Interpretations of Aristotle*, edited by Freeland, 248–59. University Park: Pennsylvania State University Press.

Nussbaum, M. C., and H. Putnam. 1992. "Changing Aristotle's Mind." In *Essays on Aristotle's De Anima*, edited by Nussbaum and Rorty, 27–56. Oxford: Oxford University Press.

Nussbaum, M. C., and A. O. Rorty, eds. 1992. *Essays on Aristotle's De Anima*. Oxford: Oxford University Press.

Olmsted, E. H. 1948. "The 'Moral Sense' Aspect of Aristotle's Ethical Theory." *The American Journal of Philology*, 69, no. 1: 42–61.

Osborne, C. 1983. "*De Anima* 3.2: How Do We Perceive That We See and Hear?" *The Classical Quarterly* 33, no. 2: 401–11.

Owens, J. 1991. "Value and Practical Knowledge in Aristotle." In *Essays in Ancient Greek Philosophy IV: Aristotle's Ethics*, edited by Anton and Preus, 143–58. Albany: SUNY Press.

Peterson, S. 1988. "*Horos* (Limit) in Aristotle's *Nicomachean Ethics*." *Phronesis* 33, no. 3: 233–50.

Pickavé, M., and J. Whiting. 2008. "*Nicomachean Ethics* 7.3 on Akratic Ignorance." *Oxford Studies in Ancient Philosophy* 34: 323–72.

Polansky, R. 2007. *Aristotle's De Anima*. Cambridge: Cambridge University Press.

Politis, V. 2001. "Aristotle's Account of Intellect as Pure Capacity." *Ancient Philosophy* 21: 375–408.

Purshouse, L. 2006. "Neoptolemus' Soul and the Taxonomy of Ethical Characters in Aristotle's *Nicomachean Ethics*." *British Journal for the History of Philosophy* 14, no. 2: 205–23.

Rabinoff, E. 2015a. "Aristotle on the Intelligibility of Perception." *Review of Metaphysics* 68, no. 3: 521–44.

———. 2015b. "Rational and Non-Rational Perception in Aristotle's *De Anima*." *Epoché* 19, no. 2: 279–309.

Reeve, C. D. C. 1992. *Practices of Reason: Aristotle's Nicomachean Ethics*. Oxford: Oxford University Press.

Richardson, H. S. 1992. "Desire and the Good in *De Anima*." In *Essays on Aristotle's De Anima*, edited by Nussbaum and Rorty, 381–400. Oxford: Oxford University Press.

Robinson, H. M. 1978. "Mind and Body in Aristotle." *The Classical Quarterly* 28, no. 1: 105–24.

Robinson, R. 1977. "Aristotle on *Akrasia*." In *Articles on Aristotle. 2: Ethics and Politics*, edited by Barnes, Schofield, and Sorabji, 79–91. London: Duckworth.

Rorty, A. O., ed. 1980. *Essays on Aristotle's Ethics*. Berkeley: University of California Press.

———. 1980a. "*Akrasia* and Pleasure: *Nicomachean Ethics* Book 7." In *Essays on Aristotle's Ethics*, edited by Rorty, 267–84. Berkeley: University of California Press.

Ross, W. D. 1949. *Aristotle*. 5th ed. London: Methuen.

Russon, J. 1995. "Aristotle's Animative Epistemology." *Idealistic Studies* 25: 241–53.

———. 1996. "Self-Consciousness and the Tradition in Aristotle's Psychology." *Laval Théologique et Philosophique* 52: 777–803.

Sachs, J. 1999. *Aristotle's Metaphysics*. Santa Fe, N.M.: Green Lion.

———. 2001. *Aristotle's On the Soul and On Memory and Recollection*. Santa Fe, N.M.: Green Lion.

———. 2002. *Aristotle's Nicomachean Ethics*. Newburyport, Mass.: Focus.

———. 2009. *Plato, Gorgias and Aristotle, Rhetoric*. Newburyport, Mass.: Focus.

Salles, R., ed. 2005. *Metaphysics, Soul, and Ethics in Ancient Thought: Themes from the Work of Richard Sorabji*. Oxford: Oxford University Press.

Schofield, M. 1978. "Aristotle on Imagination." In *Aristotle on Mind and the Senses*, edited by G. E. R. Lloyd and G. E. L. Owen, 40–70. Cambridge: Cambridge University Press.

Schollmeier, P. 1989. "Aristotle on Practical Wisdom." *Zeitschrift für philosophische Forschung* 43, no. 1: 124–32.

Shields, C. 1988. "Soul as Subject in Aristotle's *De Anima*." *The Classical Quarterly* 38, no. 1: 140–49.

Shiffman, M. 2011. *Aristotle, De Anima*. Newburyport, Mass.: Focus.

Shiner, Roger A. 1979. "Ethical Perception in Aristotle." *Apeiron* 13, no. 2: 79–85.

Silverman, A. 1989. "Color and Color-Perception in Aristotle's *De Anima*." *Ancient Philosophy* 9: 271–92.

Simpson, P. L. P. 1997. *The Politics of Aristotle*. Chapel Hill: University of North Carolina Press.

Sisko, J. 1999. "On Separating Intellect from the Body: Aristotle's *De Anima* III.4, 429a10–b5." *Archiv für Geschichte der Philosophie* 81: 249–67.

———. 2004. "Reflexive Awareness Does Belong to the Main Function of Perception: Reply to Victor Caston." *Mind*, n.s. 113, no. 451: 513–21.

Slakey, T. J. 1961. "Aristotle on Sense Perception." *The Philosophical Review* 70: 470–84.

Smith, A. 2010. *The Theory of Moral Sentiments*. Edited by Ryan Patrick Hanley. New York: Penguin. First published 1759.

Sorabji, R. 1972. *Aristotle on Memory, Translation and Commentary*. 2nd ed. Chicago: University of Chicago Press.

———. 1974. "Body and Soul in Aristotle." *Philosophy* 49: 63–89.

———. 1980. "Aristotle on the Role of Intellect in Virtue." In *Essays on Aristotle's Ethics*, edited by Rorty, 201–20. Berkeley: University of California Press.

———. 1992. "Intentionality and Physiological Processes: Aristotle's Theory of Sense-Perception." In *Essays on Aristotle's De Anima*, edited by Nussbaum and Rorty, 195–226. Oxford: Oxford University Press.

Tuozzo, T. 1994. "Conceptualized and Unconceptualized Desire in Aristotle." *Journal of the History of Philosophy* 32: 525–49.

———. 1996. "The Function of Human Beings and the Rationality of the Whole: Aristotle and Zeno on Parts and Wholes." *Phoenix* 50: 146–61.

Urmson, J. O. 1980. "Aristotle's Doctrine of the Mean." In *Essays on Aristotle's Ethics*, edited by Rorty, 157–70. Berkeley: University of California Press.

Vasiliou, I. 1996. "The Role of Good Upbringing in Aristotle's Ethics." *Philosophy and Phenomenological Research* 56, no. 4: 771–97.

Ward, J. K. 1988. "Perception and *Logos* in *De anima* II.12." *Ancient Philosophy* 16: 113–28.

———. 1996. "Souls and Figures: Defining the Soul in *De Anima* ii.3." *Ancient Philosophy* 16: 113–28.

Wedin, M. 1988. *Mind and Imagination in Aristotle*. New Haven, Conn.: Yale University Press.

Whiting, J. 1992. "Living Bodies." In *Essays on Aristotle's De Anima*, edited by Nussbaum and Rorty, 75–92. Oxford: Oxford University Press.

———. 2002. "Locomotive Soul: The Parts of the Soul in Aristotle's Scientific Works." *Oxford Studies in Ancient Philosophy* 22: 141–200.

Wians, W. 1992. "Saving Aristotle from Nussbaum's *Phainomena*." In *Essays in Ancient Greek Philosophy, Vol. V*, edited by Preus and Anton, 133–50. Albany: SUNY Press.

———. 2006. "The Philosopher's Knowledge of Non-Contradiction." *Ancient Philosophy* 26: 1–21.

———. 2008. "Aristotle and the Problem of Human Knowledge." *The International Journal of the Platonic Tradition* 2: 41–64.

Wiggins, D. 1980a. "Deliberation and Practical Reason." In *Essays on Aristotle's Ethics*, edited by Rorty, 221–40. Berkeley: University of California Press.

———. 1980b. "Weakness of Will, Commensurability, and the Objects of Deliberation and Desire." In *Essays on Aristotle's Ethics*, edited by Rorty, 241–66. Berkeley: University of California Press.

Woods, M. 1986. "Intuition and Perception in Aristotle's Ethics." *Oxford Studies in Ancient Philosophy* 4: 145–66.

GENERAL INDEX

INDEX LOCORUM